LIVERPOOL FROM THE INSIDE

LIVERPOOL
FROM THE INSIDE

STAN LIVERSEDGE

RICHARD "TRICKY" WEIL
MUSEUM

MAINSTREAM
PUBLISHING

EDINBURGH AND LONDON

First published in Great Britain in 1995 by
MAINSTREAM PUBLISHING COMPANY (EDINBURGH) LTD
7 Albany Street
Edinburgh EH1 3UG

ISBN 1 85158 758 6

Photographs by courtesy of John Cocks and Popperfoto

A catalogue record for this book is available from the British Library

Typeset in Times by Litho Link Ltd, Welshpool, Powys, Wales
Printed and bound in Great Britain by Butler & Tanner Ltd, Frome, Somerset

CONTENTS

INTRODUCTION
Little Sir Echo? Not Me!

*If you'd been standing here, in front of me,
I'd have clobbered you.*
FORMER EVERTON CHAIRMAN, GEORGE WATTS

ON FA Cup-final day in 1938, as I kicked a ball around in the yard
behind my dad's shop, I listened to the radio commentary on the
Preston North End – Huddersfield Town duel at Wembley. The match
was won by an extra-time penalty scored by Preston's George Mutch,
whose team-mates included a fellow named Andy Beattie and another
called Bill Shankly. Remarkably, *Daily Express* sportswriter Henry
Rose turned out to be prophetic – he had stuck out his neck and made
the prediction that this final would be settled only after extra time.

That forecast did nothing to diminish Henry's reputation as a
showman, or his fame. Little did I realise then that almost two decades
later Henry, as sports editor of the *Express* in Manchester, would be
inviting me to join his staff. Neither did I know that I would ghost a
series of articles for Andy Beattie when I was deputy northern sports
editor of *The People* and he was the manager of Huddersfield Town.

He it was who pointed out to me a spindly-legged lad who (said
Andy) was destined to become a soccer star – 'but don't mention him,
because we want to get him signed up as a professional before the big
clubs step in'. The kid's name was Denis Law. Years later, when he was
a star with Manchester United, he and I had a fall-out in the foyer of an
hotel in Belgrade; and we became friends again at United's
championship dinner in the banqueting suite of the Midland Hotel in
Manchester.

I travelled around Europe with Matt Busby and United, with John
Moores and Everton, with Bill Shankly, Bob Paisley and Liverpool;

but, of course, on Cup-final day in 1938 I never envisaged this – or that I would be writing the programme notes for Howard Kendall when he managed Blackburn Rovers, or for Bill Shankly, Bob Paisley, Joe Fagan and Kenny Dalglish during their time as managers at Liverpool. But *not* for Graeme Souness.

To the best of my knowledge, I was the only sportswriter able to visit John Moores regularly at his office in Cases Street, Liverpool (where his secretary, Miss Mitchell, used to appear with the tea service), and he became a valuable source of information for me. So much so that his manager, Harry Catterick (who had often been my guest at a 3s 6d lunch when he managed Rochdale), finally lost patience, and Moores summoned me to a summit meeting to clear the air with his manager. Not that we got anywhere . . .

For the most part, Moores presented a bland face, but he showed me he could be ruthless and unforgiving, while I also fell foul of George Watts when he was Everton's chairman – 'If you'd been standing here, in front of me,' he told me over the telephone, 'I'd have clobbered you.' In fact, I'd dared to answer back when Watts had informed me that 'the *Liverpool Echo* needs Everton'. My retort was 'Yes, that's true – and Everton need the *Liverpool Echo*!'

John Moores had shown his ruthless streak when he fired a manager during a taxi ride across London, and when I crossed 'Little John', that was the end of our relationship. He became Sir John Moores and reached the age of 97, and despite our parting of the ways I always liked him. I'm certain Harry Catterick never knew that, after he had steered Everton to the League title, his chairman had asked me: 'How much do you think we should give Harry as a bonus?' Taken aback, I thought quickly, then said: 'Well . . . I should think £1,000 . . .' And while my brain was still clicking, I added: 'Tax-free, of course.' Remember that £1,000 was a fair bit of money at the start of the 1960s.

Though Moores's first love was Everton, he did have a foot in the Liverpool camp as well – the appointment of Littlewoods chief executive Eric Sawyer to the Anfield board stemmed from John Moores. Sawyer became one of the most influential directors at Liverpool after having joined the board in the early 1960s, and when he died, in 1979, the tributes to him were many and genuine. He headed the finance committee, played an important role in the development of Liverpool Football Club as it reached a position of real eminence, and on his death he was described by the club's chairman at the time, John Smith (who had not then been knighted for his services to sport), as 'a financial genius whose contribution to the club helped us to our leading position in the world of football today'. Indeed, John Smith termed Eric Sawyer's death 'the greatest loss to the club since the death of Mr T.V. Williams, our late chairman and, subsequently, president. Off the field, Mr Sawyer and T.V. Williams between them created the great club of the 1960s. Mr Sawyer, who ran the financial side, made sure the money was there to buy players, and he masterminded the fundraising needed to rebuild Anfield into the modern stadium it is today.' Eric Sawyer would have enjoyed seeing the stadium in its even greater, present-day glory.

As for John Moores, he played another role in the affairs of Liverpool Football Club, because he gave Bob Paisley a helping hand in the days when Bob was looking to the future, once his playing days had become numbered. Bob took up the study of physiotherapy, via a correspondence course, and it was Moores who arranged for him to visit local hospitals so that he could see for himself the kind of equipment being used, and the way in which it worked, in enabling people to regain fitness.

At one stage of my own career, I moved to Merseyside to take charge of the sports department at the *Liverpool Echo*, and I gained first-hand experience of the rivalry between Liverpool and Everton, as Liverpool directors complained about the publicity Everton received – and then Everton complained about the space Liverpool were getting.

I had a bust-up with Bill Shankly about one transfer story and an argument with Harry Catterick about another story which was splashed across the back page. And it was a story in *The People* which, two decades later, brought me into contact with John Moores's nephew, David, who had become chairman of Liverpool.

By that time I had relinquished my job as Liverpool's programme editor after close on 20 years, during which I did pieces with virtually all the big-name players who graced the Anfield stage. There were times when a player disagreed with a team-mate – I recall the Anfield Iron, Tommy Smith, accusing Steve Heighway of having cost his team-mates money – and there were occasions when players didn't see eye to eye with the managers.

When I decided to bow out I gave notice to Liverpool's chief executive, Peter Robinson, in good time for him to find a successor, and he indicated that I would receive some financial reward for the service I had given. I remember how Peter told me that before I got the job in the first place, Bill Shankly was consulted as to whether or not he felt he could work with me. When I learned that I could expect a farewell pay-off, the thought flashed through my mind that another Liverpool employee had told me the club was 'mean as muck'.

Friends had predicted that I would receive a handsome sum, but I knew differently. Over the years, I had become well aware of Liverpool's determination not to spend a penny more than necessary. And I didn't blame them. During the club's golden glory years, I had enjoyed various forms of hospitality – trips abroad and to finals at Wembley, a Christmas turkey, a bottle of whisky and a bottle of gin. Then with the recession, the purse strings had been tightened. So I was not surprised when I found I would receive a lot less than some of my friends had forecast. I wasn't in a mood to grumble, though; I had done a job and been paid for it, and the fact that two people were now going to do the same job (and, I was given to understand, get more money for it overall) didn't weigh heavily with me, either. I was satisfied.

I didn't get a letter of thanks, however – that kind of thing was left to people such as Cliff Butler at Manchester United, and others at Tottenham Hotspur and Southampton. From Liverpool, not a word. I wondered if some of the directors even knew I was going at the end of the season – at one stage while I was working for the club, one director had mistaken me for a travel agent who organised trips abroad for Liverpool.

I did receive a copy of an article which appeared in the Liverpool fanzine. It came from a supporter, and it extolled my virtues as editor of the programme. 'Well,' I thought, 'at least somebody noticed.' And it was nice to remember that during my time as editor, I'd received letters from hundreds of fans – most of them complimentary.

CHAPTER 1

THE HOT SEAT
The Stress of Management

There's always pressure . . . and, yes, I did have sleepless
nights – more than a few.
FORMER LIVERPOOL MANAGER, JOE FAGAN

BILLY LIDDELL, the flying Scot, became a Liverpool legend in his own lifetime. During his playing days, he and I used to go down to the old Kardomah café for a cup of coffee after he had finished training, and we would talk football. By the mid 1990s Billy was well into his 70s, but he still went down to Anfield on match days to give the current team his support.

I often used to wonder why he had never become a manager; possibly, even, the manager of Liverpool. I never did ask him; but I got the answer when I was talking to Billy's wife one day, not long after Roy Evans had been promoted to take charge of team affairs at the club. She explained, in very few words, why Bill hadn't followed in the footsteps of former team-mates such as Phil Taylor and Bob Paisley, and the late Sir Matt Busby (another one-time Liverpool star), who had played a part in taking the young Liddell from Scotland to Anfield.

'Billy looked up to Matt Busby and regarded him as a father-figure. And in the course of a conversation they had [about going into management] Matt Busby told Billy, "I have made my bed, and it turned out to be a good one . . . but not many managers can say the same as me".' So Billy Liddell never tested the temperature; he never occupied the hot seat at Anfield or anywhere else. Billy was always quiet and reserved by nature; and maybe he didn't feel he would be suited to endure the kind of hassle which comes with the managerial territory.

Graeme Souness, a fellow-Scot, was heard to declare that he thrived on that kind of situation; he was also ready to admit that in taking charge at Liverpool he was tackling 'a monstrous job'. On day one, he could surely never have envisaged that inside three years he would be giving up the unequal struggle and walking away, as the pressure finally proved too much.

When Souness made his decision to depart, my mind went back to the time shortly after his arrival at Anfield, the second time around. He had been a star player for Liverpool – their captain, indeed – and now he had become their manager. It's natural for players to ponder upon the significance of a managerial change, and to wonder what effect it will have on them personally.

Ian Rush seemingly had no doubts about the appointment of Graeme Souness, because a few months later he was saying he believed he had been the right man for the job. At that time, Rush reckoned that after the shock departure of Kenny Dalglish, the arrival of Souness had acted as a tonic. According to the Welsh international, the job required someone who knew how things were done at Liverpool, someone who wouldn't set out to make sweeping changes to the routine. At the same time, Rush reckoned the club needed a man capable of being tough, even ruthless. For him, Souness was that man: hard, but also fair.

There came a time when Rush was not quite so much on the side of Graeme Souness, after the manager had axed him from the team; there came a time, also, when Rush spoke out in defence of Liverpool's manager; and there came a time when Rush – not a man noted for becoming involved in the politics of football – was offering some advice to Liverpool Football Club, as he declared that they should come straight out with it and put an end to the guessing game about their beleaguered manager. Rush took the view that Liverpool should say if Souness was staying – or going.

After the resignation of Dalglish, Rush came to Kenny's defence. Some people had criticised Dalglish for having quit at such a critical stage of the season, but the man who had been Kenny's partner on the playing field refused to offer any complaints. He preferred to regard the Dalglish decision as something which had called for the qualities of guts and common sense, considering that the manager had been under strain, and he suggested that if Dalglish had soldiered on, he might even have wound up having a heart attack. As Rush asked: What would people have said then?

When Alan Hansen, then the captain of Liverpool, was about to bow out as a player, I suggested to him that he might well consider going into management. He was quite firm about it when he answered: 'No.' And when I asked him what alternative he had in mind, he said: 'Well, I think I could end up going into radio or television.' And he is now a TV pundit. He had been tipped as a possible Liverpool manager, in succession to Kenny Dalglish, and he is both intelligent and articulate, not to mention steeped in virtually all aspects of football. But he opted out of becoming a team boss, at Liverpool or anywhere else.

The stress of management? Of course, it does exist; although whether or not it is a killer must be open to debate. Former Everton manager Harry Catterick once drove himself to hospital after a match – a heart attack was suspected, after he had suffered chest pains; Jock Stein died after having collapsed on the touchline; Don Revie became a victim of motor-neurone disease; Bob Paisley bowed out through ill-health at a time when he was a director of Liverpool; Graeme Souness had heart-bypass surgery not long after he had become Liverpool's manager. Don Howe was another who needed a bypass operation.

This is not to suggest that all or any of them became the victims of a stressful job; but while people may talk glibly of sacked managers laughing all the way to the bank, often there is a price to pay. Alan Murray, a close friend of Souness since their playing days at Middlesbrough (and, for a spell, a manager himself at Hartlepool United), had this to say about Souness striving to succeed at Anfield: 'There was a big danger of Graeme ending up as the fall-guy when he took the job. Even after more than 25 years of success, there can never be a guarantee that a club will keep on winning.' Ultimately, Liverpool – and Souness – lost out.

Kenny Dalglish stunned Liverpool's then chairman, Noel White, and chief executive Peter Robinson when he dropped his 'I want to go' bolt from the blue on the morning after an FA Cup replay with Everton. Dalglish had bottled things up for months; his health suffered; it was said he had come out in a rash and that match day had become something almost unbearable. Maybe, at the back of his mind when he came to his decision to quit, was the memory of what had happened to his mentor at Celtic, Jock Stein. 'The big man', as Stein was known, suffered one suspected heart attack which put him in a coronary ward and made a comeback after having been seriously injured in a car crash to take up the reins at Parkhead again. But fate had something further in store.

Stein took on the task of trying to steer Scotland to the World Cup finals in Mexico, and no one could have undertaken a more demanding job. The Scots went to Ninian Park, Cardiff, for a make-or-break match against Wales (shades of Ally McLeod and the Scots in their duel with Wales in an Anfield World Cup qualifier in 1977). Ninian Park was packed with 40,000 vociferous fans, and with no more than ten minutes to go it was the Welsh who seemed set for victory, with the Scots doomed never to see Mexico. Then Scotland struck from the penalty spot – the equaliser put them through to a final eliminator with Australia. However, Jock Stein was destined never to see the outcome of those two games. Unknown to the majority of the Ninian Park crowd, he had collapsed by the touchline and been carried to the quiet of the dressing-room. Once again, it seemed, he had suffered a heart attack – only this time, sadly, there was no recovery. Within minutes, Jock Stein was dead.

As it happened, Kenny Dalglish wasn't at Cardiff, but there can be little doubt that he would have retained a vivid memory of Stein's demise; not least, the manner of it. Did Dalglish, one wonders, fear that something similar might happen to him if he carried on with his job at Liverpool? It was a job which has been described as one of the most difficult in the country, one in which the expectations are always of the highest. And, as Joe Fagan confirmed to me, once you have achieved what seems to be the pinnacle of success, you are left to wonder where you go from there. As one expert on stress observed, the decision in the final analysis becomes: 'I want out.' There comes a requirement for you to put your life in perspective and, in the case of Kenny Dalglish, he had spent five years and more of his life striving to bring Liverpool Football Club ever more success.

Jack Charlton once said that a manager shouldn't stay at a club for more than four or five years, because players become familiar with just about everything he has to offer when it comes to training, tactics and motivation. George Graham, who had collected half a dozen trophies in eight years at Highbury, reckoned that 'there is a bit of sense in what Jack said' – although, when it came to himself, 'I love being manager of Arsenal. They have always let me get on with doing the job, with no interference.' (This was before he was sacked.)

Peter Robinson declared that at Liverpool, the manager was allowed to get on with the job and given full support from the boardroom, and I never heard any of the men who managed the club express the view that he was being restricted by the directors in his efforts to do the job in the way he thought best. I did get some interesting reactions, however, when I talked to people who had had a close insight into the trials and tribulations of being a manager, notably at Liverpool.

I spoke to Bob Paisley's wife, Jessie; to Joe Fagan; to a former Liverpool captain, Phil Neal, as well as canvassing views elsewhere. When I asked Jessie Paisley about the problems and the stress which Bob faced when he managed Liverpool, she told me: 'There were times when he had sleepless nights – but that was after a game, and when he was a player. He didn't have sleepless nights when he was a manager – but there were times when he would get a bit "ratty", as he did occasionally with the players, and times when he would turn round and say, "That's it. I'm packing it in." But the next morning he wasn't 'packing it in'. He would make his way down to Anfield, as usual.

'No, I cannot say that I ever really saw him bothered by the pressure of the job; it was something he seemed to be able to take in his stride. He never appeared to get frantic about anything, even after a bad result or if things hadn't gone as he thought they should have done.' Well, no one could claim to know Bob Paisley better than his wife, and certainly from my own knowledge of him he rarely gave the impression of being a man on edge. Yet I also know that there were times when he was under pressure, after a run of two or three bad results.

Phil Neal is a former Liverpool captain who might well have nourished ambitions of becoming manager when Joe Fagan bowed out; that didn't come about, but he can speak with the experience of having managed at Bolton Wanderers and Coventry City. There were times when he had a rough ride at Bolton, as he battled to get results on a relatively tight budget, and when he went to Coventry he took on a Premiership-survival job.

Neal, who claimed 50 England caps as a player, also served under Graham Taylor for a while during England's ill-fated bid to qualify for the finals of the World Cup in the United States in 1994, and he was able to see at first-hand just how the pressures of being the England team boss got to Taylor – as, indeed, did the whole nation via the award-winning documentary screened on television.

Phil told me: 'I learned a lot from Bob [he was Paisley's first signing] and from Joe and Graham. When I was at Liverpool, playing first for Bob and then for Joe, there was total common sense about everything they did. I was never really coached, told to "Do this, do that". Basically, I was asked to play to the best of my ability, and with enthusiasm. Yes, we played with passion: we wanted to win every game.

'In so many ways, things have changed in the game, these days. For instance, players come up to you and ask, "What do I do now, boss?". It would seem the modern professional wants to be instructed. And then there's the transfer market – managers are now dealing in a market where fees have escalated so much, and that makes it hard work.

'Yes, you do feel the pressures. You might show what I call a soft coating on the outside – but inwardly, you can be seething. And dealing with the media presents another problem for managers – in fact, this can become almost a full-time job. There was all the publicity over the transfer of Phil Babb, for instance – and once he had gone to Liverpool, that wasn't the end of it, because I was kept in the office phoning other managers as I tried to line up a replacement.

'There are other aspects; you see stories leaked, dirty washing regularly aired in the press. At one time, Liverpool did their transfer business, *then* they invited the press in to tell them about the signing. But there's been a total transformation in the way that so many things are done, these days, and it all adds to the pressure. You cannot do business quietly any more.

'I wouldn't say that being the manager of Liverpool is necessarily the toughest or most stressful job in football – managers are all under severe pressure, and the media can make you or break you. If you manage to achieve success early on, you can carry on for a longer period of time; but all managers face the prospect of the sack sooner or later. I was at one match where it was frightening, the way the fans turned on the manager of the home team . . . there seemed to be total hatred. [A few weeks later, that manager got the sack.]

'A lot of managers think they're strong enough to leave the worries of the job behind when they go home, but they cannot really do that. I spoke about common sense, but I don't know if it prevails in football now. When it comes to cash, I don't begrudge players the money they get today, but some of them earn more in one week than I got when we won the Championship.' Neal himself parted company with Coventry City early in 1995.

Neal's son, Ashley, became an apprentice professional at Anfield, and Phil acknowledged: 'I'm still a Liverpool fan. I want Liverpool to get back to playing in Europe. The experience I gained from those games certainly made me a better international player.'

Liverpool boss Roy Evans wanted his club to get back into Europe, too – he said that 'Anfield without European football is like a banquet without wine' – and when Phil Neal spoke about the man who had taken over the hot seat from Graeme Souness, he reckoned that Evans was cast in a similar mould to Bob Paisley and Joe Fagan. 'You might get the odd flash of temper from Bob or Joe, but that was it. I remember one occasion when Joe pulled us all in and told us, "I've had a gutful of this. Come on now, pull up your socks." We went on to win the League title.'

Roy Evans said of Fagan, who led Liverpool to a treble: 'I often wonder if his achievement was fully appreciated outside Liverpool.' And when I asked Joe about his time as manager, he admitted candidly: 'There's always pressure – it's a combination of things. And yes, I did have sleepless nights . . . more than a few.'

Joe, who had joined Liverpool in 1958 and retired in 1985, was 62 when he became manager and, as he told me at the time: 'Yes, I did want a crack at the job.' By the time Roy Evans was in charge, Joe was looking back on his own days as manager and, when I asked if it had been harder than he thought, he was telling me: 'No. I don't think it seems as hard – until you've been in it for a few months!'

That was an echo of what Roy Evans said when he admitted that 'when I took the job, I tended to think I knew all the aspects of it; but there were far more than I thought'.

Joe Fagan's memory was of the way that things 'started to pile up on you. Then you find it's rather a difficult job. And that's putting it mildly. How managers stick it for so many years goodness only knows – I don't. I was the wrong age for being a manager, but I was fresh to the job, and the time I spent in the job was enough, at my age.

'I always thought I would last for two or three years, and during my time I was fortunate to have had two men – Peter Robinson and Sir

John Smith – backing me all the way. They were of immense help. Even so, I did become tired, and it started to tell. There was no such thing as going to bed at night, getting your head down and sleeping through. You went to sleep, then you awoke and began pondering upon team problems.

'One of the worst things was having to drop a player – I preferred to talk about leaving him out. That's something you never want to do. [Bob Paisley told me that during his first season as manager, he tried to please everyone, then realised it just couldn't be done.]

'Bill Shankly didn't seem to show the stress he was under, but I think he sometimes put on a bit of an act when it came to telling a player he was dropped. A player used to come out of Bill's office wondering why he'd been axed when he'd just been made to feel he was the greatest player in the world! Managers do have feelings, and they don't want to drop players. But it's a job that has to be done, at times. And that's when you don't want to get up in a morning and go into the club.

'From my own experience, I would say that for Bill Shankly, Bob Paisley and Kenny Dalglish, the stress must have been great, on occasion. And that's it – full stop. You wonder how they stuck it, once you've been in the job yourself. When the manager retires, everyone wants to know why. The answer must be that he's had a fair whack at it.

'I reckon, too, that success must be more stressful than failure. It's harder to live up to, once you've achieved something. With failure, yes – you get the sack and that's stressful; but you can go home and sleep at night without thinking about this problem or that problem. With success, once you've done something you have to set your sights even higher, and yet the problems, of one kind or another, are still there.'

Like Joe Fagan, Joe Mercer never played for Liverpool; he gave sterling service to their great rivals, Everton, and to Arsenal, before managing Sheffield United, Aston Villa and Manchester City (plus, for a brief term, England). Like Fagan, also, Mercer knew the stresses of being a soccer boss, and he suffered for his pains. He was one of two men whom I have known to be pushed to the edge, the other being Kenny Dalglish.

'Uncle Joe', as they called Mercer, had a genial smile and, with Manchester City, he enjoyed success, while with England he was acknowledged to have done a good job. But Sheffield United and Aston

Villa were different kettles of fish, because each club suffered relegation. Joe used to tell a story against himself . . . that as he was sitting in his office at Villa Park one day, holding his head in his hands, he was handed a telegram. He thought it was from someone sending a message of sympathy, but when he opened the telegram (from Dick Wragg, who had been chairman of Sheffield United, as well as of the England-international committee) it read: 'Congratulations . . . you've done it again!'

Like Kenny Dalglish, Joe Mercer had a spell when his health deteriorated, through the stresses of the game. Football – 'my very life-blood', as he called it – had driven him to a state of nervous exhaustion, and when he returned to the game in July 1965, as Manchester City's manager, he had spent a year out of football. Indeed he admitted to me: 'I felt I had learned a great lesson. In retrospect, maybe that illness wasn't such a bad thing. I learned patience.'

When he started his job at Maine Road, patience was a virtue he was counselling to others, and his motto was 'Make haste slowly'. In tandem with Malcolm Allison, Mercer steered City to honours at home and in Europe, as he succeeded in what, at the time he took it on, was termed 'the toughest job in football'. One newspaper referred to 'The Mountain at Maine Road', and a similar description could have been applied to the task Kenny Dalglish undertook at Anfield, when he took over from Joe Fagan.

Dalglish was to succeed beyond probably even his wildest dreams – and this despite the traumas of Heysel and Hillsborough. Yet at the end, he was pictured as a man – and a manager – who had come to the end of his tether, as he walked into a meeting with his chairman and chief executive. I was told, from within the club, that there was 'nothing sinister' about what had happened; Dalglish had simply informed Noel White and Peter Robinson that he could no longer cope. They were shocked, they were astonished – after all, he had signed a new contract only six months previously; a contract designed to keep him at Anfield for three more years; a contract which carried with it a substantial signing-on fee. Now he was telling them he had been thinking about quitting for months. No, he hadn't had another offer; no, he hadn't any quarrel with the club. Everyone had been good to him, but the job had got on top of him. He wasn't seeing enough of his family – they were growing up more or less without him – and while he could cope with the job during the week, on match days his head felt as if it were going to explode. He simply couldn't go on any longer. His health had suffered, he had come out in a rash, and finally he had come to a decision. This was the end of his reign as Liverpool's manager.

Apart from the memory of Jock Stein's tragic end, Kenny Dalglish had gone though the personal traumas engendered by the disasters of the Heysel Stadium in Brussels and the short-lived FA Cup semi-final contest with Nottingham Forest at Hillsborough. When he walked out of Liverpool in February 1991, he was also walking out on a job which carried with it a salary reputed to be in the region of £200,000 a year – and that's a great deal of money.

There's an old saying that 'money isn't everything', and I can vouch for this from my own experience – I once threw up a job which had become impossible, telling my wife that 'I would rather sweep the streets than carry on like this.' In the case of Kenny Dalglish, there was clearly no question of his having to sweep the streets of Liverpool or anywhere else, once he had told his chairman he wanted to leave. In fact, he made a point of answering all the speculation by saying bluntly that 'I've told the truth, and if people don't believe me, that's up to them.'

Perhaps Joe Fagan, better than most, would be able to understand the way that Kenny's mind was working, because Joe himself left Anfield under tragic circumstances which caused him to shed tears. The last thing he would have wanted as he took his final bow at a European Cup final was the disaster which struck and ended people's lives in the Heysel Stadium in Brussels.

Joe had been going, anyway – his decision had been made months previously; Dalglish had been thinking about going, months before he dropped his bombshell upon Liverpool Football Club, and while so many people claimed they could not understand just why he had walked away so suddenly, in retrospect his decision can be seen as sensible – brave, even. If Kenny Dalglish really had been reduced to such a low point, if the strain of the job was getting to him to such an extent, then *before* the crunch came, there was only one thing to do . . . turn his back upon football and give himself time to reflect, time to put life itself into perspective.

I cannot help but think that there was a parallel between the cases of Kenny Dalglish and Joe Mercer. Tension, tiredness, nervous exhaustion; Joe took a year out of football, while Dalglish took several months, during which time he was able to recharge his batteries; and by the time Jack Walker had persuaded him to occupy the hot seat of management once more, with Blackburn Rovers, he appeared to have learned a lesson, one which helped him to be more relaxed in his job, even when the going got a little bit rough. As it did, on occasion – such as Blackburn Rovers losing a UEFA Cup-tie. From what I have seen of Kenny Dalglish in recent seasons, also, I believe he has benefited from having the experienced Ray Harford as his right-hand man. For my money, Kenny chose wisely when he appointed Harford, who became team boss when Dalglish moved 'upstairs'.

Between the departure of Dalglish and the arrival of another abrasive character, Graeme Souness, long-serving Ronnie Moran was given a fleeting taste of what the job was like – and he had certainly seen them come and go, during his time at the club. For instance, Moran could remember how a one-time Liverpool captain, Phil Taylor, had chucked up the reins of management at Anfield because his health had suffered. As a player, Taylor had clocked up 345 appearances before taking on coaching duties; then, in 1956, he was named manager in succession to Don Welsh, and it seemed success was within his grasp almost at once. But at the end of his first season Liverpool finished third . . . then they came fourth (missing promotion by two points) and fourth again. It was at this stage that Taylor, on 17 November 1959, gave up, saying sadly: 'I'm tired. The strain of trying to win promotion has proved too much.'

Pressure? I read a quote attributed to Michael Parkinson that this was 'something nurses know about, or people who grind out a living in a factory, or men who dig coal a mile underground. Pressure is being poor or unemployed, homeless or hopeless.' Yes, it most certainly is. But the business of managing a football club, at an astronomical salary, brings its own brand of pressure, because the quest for success is relentless.

In quick succession towards the end of 1994, Tottenham Hotspur dispensed with the services of Ossie Ardiles, Everton fired Mike Walker (ten months after having snapped him up from Norwich City) and Aston Villa parted company with Ron Atkinson (who the previous season had steered Villa into Europe). Atkinson admitted he was 'stunned'; Ardiles walked away from White Hart Lane being praised for the dignified manner in which he had taken dismissal; and Walker was said to be the likely recipient of a £450,000 pay-off. But no matter what golden handshake each man could expect, there was no doubt about one thing: pride had been badly dented, and before the axe fell there had been weeks of unrelenting pressure as results failed to materialise.

One man who didn't want to be a manager was former England striker Gary Lineker. He declared: 'I cannot see myself out on the training ground every day, snarling at players to get them going and having all the moodies. No one likes you when you are a manager. The crowd are against you most of the time and not many managers, I suspect, are happy. It's a job that doesn't appeal to me.'

Manchester United boss Alex Ferguson had something to say about the job of being manager, too. Like this: 'If anything brings discredit to football, it's the way managers are sacked and the way they are treated in such pressurised jobs.'

Mike Walker, it was true, had seen his Everton team win no more than half a dozen games out of 35 during his spell in charge – but his dismissal came after Everton had picked up five points out of nine. No wonder Liverpool manager Roy Evans was moved to express his sympathy for his closest rival. Maybe Evans himself was also moved to ponder upon his own situation at Liverpool, where he, like Walker, had been handed a three-year contract. Fortunately for him, at that stage of season 1994–95, Liverpool were challenging the leaders at the top of the Premiership and, in the Coca-Cola Cup, were on their way to success at Wembley.

Even so, like Ronnie Moran, Evans had seen how the pressures of the Liverpool job had reduced Kenny Dalglish to a man almost in torment; how Graeme Souness had been affected and, finally, had felt forced to quit. And as for Joe Fagan, former players had described how he appeared to have changed during the later stages of his managerial career – and that was before the tragedy at Heysel. When I talked to Joe, he made no secret of the fact that he had felt the stressful side of the job.

Souness, too, had something to say about the pressures of management. After having joined Liverpool, he talked about his earlier days as a team boss – 'when I was new to this job, I took it home with me. It ruined one relationship . . . I'm not going to allow it to happen again.' His marriage to Danielle had broken up because, she claimed, he had given too much of himself to Glasgow Rangers. Nine months after having had open-heart surgery, and during his time at Liverpool, Souness was saying: 'I try not to let it [the job] get through to the people close to me.'

Later still, several months after he had turned his back on Liverpool and, it seemed (at least, temporarily), upon football, Souness was making more points about the way the job at Anfield had gone – and about his reaction to being on the sidelines after so many years of close involvement in the game.

Souness pointed a finger at some of the players he had left behind as he said he had struggled to make them feel 'as passionate about the game as I was', adding: 'I felt as though I had been let down by some people. There were people at Liverpool who could have looked after themselves better during the week. I felt I was not getting the professionalism needed.'

Right through his career at Liverpool, Souness had shown that he was intensely professional – some might have argued that there were times when he became too intense in his involvement – but it was interesting to see how he felt after having been out of the game for the best part of a year. In between leaving Liverpool after the FA Cup defeat in the January, and coming into the final month of 1994, Graeme Souness had married again, seen his name linked with several jobs which were going, and told the world something which might well have surprised people, even those who knew him well: 'I'm not missing football much.' He added: 'I don't follow it in a big way. When you have the chance to stand back and have a look, you see things totally differently. I now realise the kind of pressure I was under and what it did to me. I now feel I'm a better person to be with than when I was involved in football. I'm enjoying my life like I never did before. I have no rush to throw myself back into the pressures I've had before.' However, in the summer of 1995 the pull of football proved strong enough to take him to Turkey, and Galatasaray.

The pressures of the job? There is the memory of Graeme Souness at Wembley for the FA Cup final, shortly after his heart-bypass surgery, when the club doctor was on hand to touch his shoulder and offer a cautionary reminder not to get too excited. And I can recall an occasion when Liverpool played a European tie in Germany and, as they were under the cosh and looking likely to miss out on the trophy at stake, I heard a colleague muttering: 'If Liverpool lose this one, I'm not flying back on the same plane as Shanks!' Fortunately, Liverpool didn't miss out; but I can still see Shankly now, soon after he had emerged from the bath. His face looked white and drawn.

As for Ronnie Moran, one wonders how he felt, having seen Dalglish, Souness and Evans in turn handed the top job at Liverpool. It has to be said that he gave not the slightest indication of having coveted the manager's post when it was passed on after Fagan had stepped down, and while, logically, many people may have assumed that Moran would be the next in line, I was assured by someone who knows him that he didn't really want to be 'the boss' at Anfield.

In the interim between the departure of Dalglish and the arrival of Souness, Moran did occupy the managerial chair, albeit briefly. After Dalglish had gone, leaving Liverpool top of the League and still in the FA Cup, Moran's attitude was this: 'My main concern is to keep the League title here. That's more important than me or anybody else getting the job. I'm not looking further than that.'

In the event, the League title eluded Liverpool, the manager's job eluded Ronnie Moran. And who can say? Maybe he had a lucky escape as well. He was still around at Anfield, however, when the baton was passed on to Roy Evans who, like Moran himself, had stood on the Kop as a kid. By the time the Kop was being dismantled in favour of an all-seater stand, Ronnie Moran had been in Liverpool's employ for no fewer than 44 years while Evans was recalling *his* first-ever visit to Anfield. He could remember it with absolute clarity.

He was wearing red (of course), and he carried in his hands a heavy, wooden rattle – the old-fashioned type which, as he observed, in the year of grace 1994 would have been classed as a dangerous object! Like Moran, Evans remembered the arrival of Bill Shankly; and that, in Evans's own words, was when 'the greatest of all manager-supporter relationships began'. Evans admitted that 'it will never be equalled'.

There came a time when Shankly himself, having retired from the job of managing Liverpool, went and stood on the Kop; and after he had died, his ashes were taken to his beloved Anfield, the place where he had been idolised by the faithful who flocked to the ground on match days. Bob Paisley, on taking over from Shankly, told me: 'I know I can never have the same rapport with the fans that Bill had . . . I just hope that I can let the team do the talking for me.' As, indeed, it did so eloquently.

And so, when season 1994–95 got under way, we saw Roy Evans squaring up to the challenge and knowing also that his team would have to 'do the talking' for him, in the main . . . even though, as a Scouser born and bred, he still remained one of the ordinary (or should it be extraordinary?) fans. He did claim: 'I feel more on top of every part of the job now than I did at the end of last season.'

He was also able to draw upon his knowledge of three previous generations of management at the club as he offered the firm opinion that 'nothing is beyond the bounds of possibility in this game – especially at Liverpool'. And yet, and yet . . . the bottom line to it all had been provided by chief executive Peter Robinson when he stressed: 'The longer you go without success, the bigger the chance of losing a generation of people who support the club.' And speaking with the benefit of 29 years' experience behind him at Anfield, he delivered the punchline: 'We have to be successful on the pitch. That's the top and bottom of it.'

For Roy Evans the message could not have been spelled out more clearly, no matter how pleased his bosses were with the start he had made to this most demanding of jobs. He had not been too proud to take it, after having been passed over twice; he had seen for himself what had happened to people like Joe Fagan, Kenny Dalglish, Graeme Souness. Now it was his turn to grasp the nettle.

He soon found that the job of managing Liverpool could be a frustrating one, as he sought to bring in new players. He talked of 'four long months of negative telephone inquiries' during his first attempt at summer shopping 'in football's supermarket: a baptism I will never forget'. All his efforts over those four months came to nothing; then he landed Phil Babb and John Scales, described as 'the most expensive defenders in the country'.

If football had been Roy Evans's life before, it became his reason for existing even more, once he had taken on the job of managing Liverpool. It embraced not only himself, but his wife, Mary, and his children, Stephen and Stacey. Suddenly, he found himself being asked to do interviews, to offer opinions, and his job was more time-consuming than ever before. There were so many phone calls, more hours of travelling, more meetings to attend at Anfield. He had to step up a gear – and then some.

His wife admitted she had been 'amazed' at the way he had been able to handle the greater responsibilities, and that she had had some fears for him, at the start. 'We all feel more nervous before games now,' she said, 'it would be strange if we didn't.' But the man himself hadn't changed. And this became evident as Liverpool came towards the turn of the year in 1994 and won four matches on the trot, to put some pressure on Manchester United and Blackburn Rovers in the title race. After a victory at Leeds, marksman Robbie Fowler was moved to say: 'Maybe now people will recognise us as genuine contenders.' Evans permitted himself a couple of phlegmatic observations: 'We've done ourselves no harm at all over the Christmas period. We've got ourselves into a position where, if the leaders do slip up, we could take advantage.' Then he added: 'But we've got to keep on trying to pick up three points whenever we can. It's heads down, and keep on going.'

He must have wondered, soon afterwards, if Liverpool would manage to 'keep on going' in the League, because lowly Ipswich Town, seemingly candidates for relegation, went to Anfield in January 1995, and inflicted a shock 1–0 defeat upon Evans's team. Forty-eight hours later, however, Evans went from a low to a high, as he learned that his efforts were indeed appreciated. There were just a couple of weeks to go to the anniversary of his appointment as manager when he was offered a two-year extension to his contract, and chief executive Peter Robinson was saying: 'The board are delighted with the way Roy has faced up to the job. He still has 18 months remaining on his present contract, so effectively this means he would have a three-and-a-half year contract. I'm certain it will be concluded in the next couple of weeks.'

Evans's reaction was to admit his pleasure that the board felt things were going 'in the right direction' – but he tempered his delight with the reminder that 'we are not getting carried away. We have still got nothing on the table. We've won nothing yet.' Like every other manager, he knew that the job was all about getting results.

And on the first Saturday of February, in 1995, as he watched his team battle to salvage a point from Nottingham Forest at the City Ground, a few miles up the road the father of one of his players, Jamie Redknapp, was enduring all the tensions of a man almost in torment, as he watched his players striving to extract points from a side in even more trouble than his own. Harry Redknapp, manager of West Ham, saw the Hammers score two goals to Leicester City's one at Filbert Street – and afterwards, when discussing the pressures of the job in an interview which was seen by millions of television viewers, he delivered his verdict. When it was suggested that after this precious victory he might be able to enjoy a round of golf on the Sunday, he rejected the idea, with a sentence which consisted of six telling words. 'No . . . I just can't switch off.'

CHAPTER 2

THE LAIRD OF ANFIELD
Bill Shankly

*Gentlemen, I can assure you that we will win a match at Anfield
this season.*
BILL SHANKLY, AFTER HAVING SEEN CARDIFF CITY BEAT
LIVERPOOL 4–0 AT ANFIELD, ON HIS FIRST DAY IN CHARGE OF
TEAM AFFAIRS

MY FIRST meeting with Bill Shankly took place in the dungeon-like atmosphere of what seemed to be little more than a shed under the main stand at Huddersfield Town's Leeds Road ground, and at that time, when I introduced myself, it was as a sportswriter with *The People* newspaper. Bill had been assistant manager to Andy Beattie, after spells as team boss at Carlisle, Grimsby Town and Workington, and when Beattie retired in November 1956, Bill took over the reins.

On 1 December 1959 he was named as Liverpool's new manager, although he had agreed to stay with Huddersfield (where he wasn't on contract) for a further month. Shankly said he regarded the Liverpool job as a challenge 'similar to that confronting Joe Mercer when he left Sheffield United for Aston Villa and when Alan Brown left Burnley for Sunderland'.

Oddly enough, Bill had been an interested spectator as Huddersfield beat Liverpool, and his reaction was typical: 'Huddersfield were the better side, but at least Liverpool did fight. Nobody realises more than I do what a tough job getting Liverpool back into the First Division will be.' Several managers – Don Welsh and Phil Taylor among them – had had a go, but without success; and Bill's first game in charge at Anfield didn't bode well: Cardiff thrashed Liverpool 4–0. One of the players on the losing side that day was Ronnie Moran.

Shankly's after-match reaction was terse: 'Save your sympathy; I can look after myself, and I can look after my team.' And while his new employers in the boardroom were possibly pondering what fate held in store for the club, the story goes that Shanks walked in to say: 'Gentlemen, I can assure you that we *will* win a match at Anfield this season.' This assurance came from someone who, for the first time in the club's long history, had been given sole responsibility for picking the team – a job where, previously, the directors had had the final say, as Bob Paisley had good cause to remember (he lost out on a split vote when Liverpool's team for the 1950 FA Cup final was named).

After Shankly arrived, he built up a backroom team which became renowned – his henchmen were Bob Paisley, Joe Fagan and Reuben Bennett – and he made it clear he would tolerate no cliques; it was one for all, all for one, with teamwork the overriding priority. Like Bill, Reuben Bennett was a Scot; a rather dour, down-to-earth man who didn't waste words. He had been a goalkeeper north of the border and had brought with him a reputation as the man who had taken the longest goal kick in football history: he gave the ball such 'welly' that it soared out of the ground, landed on the back of a lorry – and finished up in Carlisle.

The backroom team had no frills about them, as a whole, but they were soon discussing one of the mysteries of life under their new boss, because after a match at Anfield he would pick up a football and a tracksuit, then disappear back to his home in Huddersfield. In the course of time, the staff learned what was going on: Bill was taking tracksuit and ball and putting them to good use in a Sunday-morning kickabout with the locals at Huddersfield.

He was a great fan of the television series *The Untouchables*, thought the sun shone out of his former Preston team-mate, Tom Finney; he had a voice which could grate like gravel, kept his hair close-cropped, and you could almost see your face in the shine on his black shoes, which made his feet appear, if not dainty, then certainly neat. I came to know him well and, I think, to understand him; in fact, there were occasions when, at the after-match press conference, I used to wince inwardly as I heard some unsuspecting reporter go barging in with what I knew Bill would consider to be a stupid or a presumptuous question.

Almost invariably, as he walked down the corridor from the dressing-room to meet the media, Bill would start off by saying:

'Hullo, boys.' Then someone would kick off with an observation or the first question, while Bill looked straight ahead or down at those black shoes. One Saturday, after an Anfield defeat (and there weren't many of those), a reporter was foolhardy enough to inform Bill that Liverpool hadn't played very well that afternoon. Shankly stood there, head down, eyes surveying those shoes of his; then he looked up and stared unblinkingly at the questioner, as he rasped: 'DON'T lean on that wall! It's just been painted!' And that was his answer.

On another occasion when Liverpool had suffered an Anfield reverse, a wit in the press box, imitating Shankly's gravel-like tone, declared: 'The Fitba' League wull nivver accept this result!' And it was said that when Liverpool did lose a game at Anfield, Bill went home and, to get the taste of defeat out of his system, got down grimly to cleaning the cooker.

I used to go and see him when I worked on *The People*, though I rarely expected to be given a story. Bill kept his business strictly to himself, but at least he would do you the courtesy of giving you the time of day. On one occasion we were discussing a teenage player who was being 'beefed up' on a diet of steak, eggs and sherry, and I learned that the lad, who was courting, now had to face up to another problem, because his young lady was expecting a baby. As Bill mused upon this turn of events, he said: 'By Christ, it seems we've bred a stallion!'

Then there was the time Liverpool played the Dutch aces of Ajax in a European tie, and after the first leg they finished up on the wrong end of a 5–1 scoreline. During that match, played in Holland, a youngster by the name of Johan Cruyff scored twice. Shortly before the Anfield return, I was with Bill in his office and, as we discussed the second leg, I felt on reasonably safe ground as I offered the opinion that this would be a tough test for Liverpool. Whereupon Shankly ground out: 'Ajax? They're a bunch of bluidy peasants!' He would never concede that his team (who drew the second leg 2–2) were inferior.

There was also the time I was writing a series of articles about great players, past and present, who had worn the Liverpool jersey and – not surprisingly – Bill was fulsome in his praise of his compatriot, Billy Liddell, among others. When I addressed Bill Shankly about John Toshack, who formed such an effective striking partnership with Kevin Keegan, there was a pause, then Bill observed about the Welsh international who had cost Liverpool more than £100,000: 'He's an essential in modern-day fitba'.' And that was the beginning and the end of the conversation.

It certainly wasn't always all sweetness and light between Bill Shankly and his players, much as he thought of them and much as they respected him. For instance, the 1974 FA Cup final was notable not only for Liverpool's 3–0 victory over Newcastle United, but for a pre-match incident which involved Phil Boersma, who was a great pal of team-mate Steve Heighway, and who later joined Graeme Souness not only at Glasgow Rangers, but at Liverpool when Souness returned as manager. Like Souness, Boersma also had a spell as a player with Middlesbrough.

'Boey', as he was known, was a Liverpool lad, and although he never commanded a regular first-team spot, he could always be relied upon to do a job during the seven seasons that he spent at Anfield. He made almost a century of full appearances, with around a score of games as substitute thrown in, and it was because of the role he was handed – or, rather, not handed – at Wembley in 1974 that he blew his top.

At that time, only one substitute was allowed, and there was considerable speculation as to which player would be on the bench for Liverpool. Many people expected that Boersma would get the nod from Shankly, but in the event it was Chris Lawler who was made substitute. Not surprisingly, Boersma was very upset to find that he was the odd man out – upset enough, indeed, to shake the dust of Wembley Stadium from his feet.

According to one of the players to whom I talked, Liverpool's manager had a penchant for leaving team selection almost to the last minute, and while I cannot say if Boersma discovered his omission from the side at the last minute, there was no doubt that Shankly's method did create problems on occasion. In fact, left-back Alec Lindsay was to suffer from this late-selection business.

Shankly never tired of telling people what a lethal left foot Lindsay had, and Alec totted up close on 250 first-team appearances for Liverpool in his eight seasons with them. But there was one time he didn't make it. In fact, he had already taken off his jacket and his tie, and was unbuttoning his shirt when he discovered that this time out, he wouldn't be playing. He didn't utter a word; he put his things back on, then made his exit from the dressing-room.

Shankly was something of a psychologist, too – hence the *This Is Anfield* notice above the tunnel where the teams go out. The notice was calculated to put the fear of death into the opposition, as they took in the message on their way to do battle. Bill wasn't malicious, though, and he could certainly be generous, as Liverpool supporters could testify – there were occasions when, before a game, he would slip tickets into the hands of fans who had gone along living in hope, but not really expecting to be able to see the action.

When I started to edit Liverpool's match-day programme, I used to phone Bill at home to discuss what he wanted to say in his notes. Then I would do the writing, send him a copy of the article for his approval or otherwise, and ring him to check. I don't recall him ever changing anything – but there was one time when he and I clashed over a piece I had done for him. In my view, it was such a good article that it deserved a wider audience, so I had a word with Alan Hughes, then the editor of *Goal* magazine, and explained what it was about. He was enthusiastic about using the piece, even though I made the condition that it must appear in the programme first. I felt sure that Shankly would agree to my proposition, so when I met him I started to explain what I would like to do. To my surprise, however, he came down on me like a ton of bricks. 'That article is for the programme – and nowhere else!' he snapped. And that was that.

Before I became the club's programme editor, I worked briefly for the local evening paper, the *Liverpool Echo*, where I had been asked to take charge of the sports department. Right at the outset, I determined there was only one way to do the job – fairly, but firmly, when it came to the big two Merseyside clubs. On my first trip abroad with Liverpool, as I chatted with the directors, they made it clear pretty quickly that they felt Everton were getting the lion's share of publicity in the *Echo*.

I told them there and then: 'So far as I'm concerned, the best story gets the best show, whether it's about Liverpool or Everton.' Within a few months, Everton manager Harry Catterick was complaining to me that the *Echo* had become 'a Liverpool bonanza', while George Watts, the Everton chairman at that time, was complaining vociferously to me on the telephone and, when I dared to stand up for myself, he told me that had we been face to face, he would have 'clobbered' me for the way I was talking to him.

Immediately, I arranged to go and see him, along with the reporter who covered Everton affairs for the paper. But when we did come face to face in his office, we got nowhere – though I wasn't 'clobbered'. A good job, too – Watts was bigger than me.

On taking charge at the *Echo*, I had spoken with Bill Shankly and promised him: 'If I ever get a story about Liverpool, I'll let you know and give you the chance to have your say.' He knew, and I knew, that I was referring specifically to stories involving transfers in and out at Anfield.

Oddly enough, I had just arranged to go and see him one Monday morning to discuss some articles I wanted him to do for the paper when I was presented with a very real problem, because that weekend I learned Liverpool had made an offer of around £200,000 for a Stoke City player named Terry Conroy, whom I knew well. He was a Republic of Ireland international, and had plenty of skill.

True to my promise, and not wishing to wait until my 11 o'clock date with Bill at Anfield, when I walked into the office that Monday morning, I rang him about 9.30, and started to remind him of the undertaking I had given him. Then I told him about Terry Conroy. For a few seconds, there was total silence at the other end of the phone; then came the explosion. 'I know where you got this from! You've got it from your bluidy pal at Stoke!' Shankly yelled at me. My 'pal', I assumed, being the chairman, Albert Henshall, with whom I had close and regular contact.

Nothing was said about the 11 o'clock meeting, as Shankly and I parted company on the phone, but I determined I was still going up to Anfield to beard him in his den. I had no idea how he would react – he might throw me off the premises, refuse to do the articles – who could tell? When I got there and we came face to face, I wasted no time on preliminaries. 'Before we go any further, Bill,' I told him, 'I've left instructions with my deputy that the Conroy story goes in the first edition, across the back page.' Shankly gave a kind of grunt, acknowledging what I'd just said . . . and the subject was never referred to again. So we got down to talking about the articles, and he answered all the questions I had prepared beforehand.

After more than an hour we had just about finished, so I got up from my chair, shook Bill's hand, thanked him for his co-operation and departed, heaving a sigh of relief once I had gone through his office door. We ran the Conroy story, we ran the series of articles – and Bill never even asked for a penny.

Bill never held a grudge; at least not so far as I was concerned. And that was one of the things I liked about him. But there were occasions when I wondered if he was being deadly serious, or if he was kidding me a bit. Like the time I met him at a Tranmere Rovers game at Prenton Park, and he buttonholed me, to talk about an article I had recently had published concerning Liverpool's success story. 'Hello, Stan. That was a guid article ye wrote,' was how he greeted me. And just as I was almost glowing with such praise, he delivered the punchline: 'But ye forgot one thing – we won the Charity Shield as well!'

He once confided to me that he had thought his great side of the 1960s, with players like Yeats, St John, Hunt, Callaghan and company, would have lasted longer than it did, before he needed to dismantle it; but once he decided the break-up had to come, he didn't shirk the decision, though it grieved him to wield the axe on men who had given the club such stalwart service. He went out and paid £100,000 – at the time, a record fee for a teenager – to sign Alun Evans from Wolves. This blond-haired forward, whose distinctive mop earned him the nickname 'Rag Doll' among the pressmen who covered Liverpool, once struck a hat-trick against Bayern Munich in a European match.

When it came to the parting of the ways it was a sad occasion for players as well. Ian St John told me about his feelings, as he began to realise what was happening. When he found himself being substituted or sitting on the bench at the start of a game, he told himself he was still worth a place in the side over the full 90 minutes. But in the end, honesty prevailed as Ian told me: 'Once I faced up to it, I had to admit that while my brain was still telling me where to go and what to do, my legs wouldn't take me any more.' Ian showed team-mate Steve Heighway just what a good professional he was when both were playing in Liverpool's reserve side. As Steve told me, Ian found it difficult to accept that he no longer rated an automatic place in the first team – 'but he was still giving it all he'd got, and he was ready to help any other of his team-mates. That, to me, seemed the mark of the real professional'.

There was one amusing incident which concerned Ian St John, and it became a talking point among the other players, even after the Scot had departed from Anfield. At Christmas time, as I can confirm from personal experience, Liverpool used to provide a turkey apiece for the players and for various other people at the club. I used to be the recipient of such a gift for several years (until the recession brought about yet another economy), and during St John's time at Anfield the practice of the Christmas-turkey gift was well established.

On this particular occasion, however, the bird which had been earmarked for Ian St John was not quite as plumptious (to use a Ken Dodd phrase) as the turkeys which were destined for some of the other players, and Ian was heard to mutter: 'When you're out, you're out. They've given me a bloody sparrow!'

After the Ajax episode, I never felt quite sure how much (or how little) Bill Shankly respected Liverpool's Continental opponents, although he did take the precaution of sending Tom Saunders on spying missions. And whether or not he held the club's European rivals in high regard, there was no doubt that one of his counterparts thought a great deal of him. This was Miljan Miljanic, the coach of Red Star Belgrade, one of the few clubs to triumph over Liverpool home and away.

I travelled with Liverpool to Belgrade and talked to Miljanic about Shankly. What did he have to say? 'There is no one for whom I have a higher regard in football. What impressed me, the first time I met him, in 1965, when I went to Liverpool, was his deep knowledge and love of the game. And he has this wonderful ability to bring the best out of his players. He has bought players, of course, but he has also found and groomed young footballers who have won success.'

As for Liverpool, they were 'the best British side I have seen recently. They are so hard to beat. They play the game hard, but correctly; they are a team that plays its football honestly.' Miljanic himself had become a hero in his own country, and he had become the target for overtures from Real Madrid and Barcelona. He smiled, as he asked me: 'Can you imagine Bill Shankly leaving Liverpool?' It would have been difficult, if not impossible, to think of Bill going anywhere else.

There were one or two occasions, though, when Liverpool travelled abroad and I feared the worst for their manager – not least because each time we had ventured behind what was then known as the Iron Curtain. One incident took place at the airport where we were waiting to board our plane for home. We were shepherded into the lounge which served for arrivals and departures to find, to our surprise, that there were three sections, each roped off. A red carpet covered the centre section, but we had to stand and wait in one or other of the outer sections. We waited and waited, with no sign of a signal to board our plane. Meanwhile, Bill Shankly was becoming visibly irritated, and more and more vociferous in his complaints about the delay and in his condemnation of 'bluidy foreigners'.

The word filtered through that everyone was waiting for an incoming aircraft to land, and then we would be on our way. Then we heard that aboard the approaching plane were some very important people – indeed, they were Russian military top brass who were on their way to the funeral of Egypt's President Nasser. Finally, the aircraft touched down, and when the lounge doors opened it was to admit these be-medalled characters as they marched, unsmilingly, along the red-carpeted section between the ropes, while we stood and scanned them with some curiosity.

Once they had disappeared, we were allowed to go through the lounge doors ourselves and make our way to the plane bound for England. And silently I gave thanks that no one had either heard or understood what Mr Shankly had been saying so emotionally, when we had been forced to hang around. Otherwise, we might all have been arrested.

Stories about Bill abounded, of course; including the one where he goes to the barber, who asks him: 'Anything off the top?' To which Shankly was alleged to have replied: 'Only the other-r-r team!' – meaning Everton.

I recall another occasion when Bill gave vent to his feelings as Liverpool clinched the League Championship. At the end of season 1972–73, they had beaten Leeds United at Anfield, and this meant that they needed only a point from their final home match, against Leicester City, to claim the title. They got their point (it was a 0–0 draw), and shortly afterwards I was in Peter Robinson's office when in marched Bill Shankly. He didn't say a word as he went straight to a telephone, dialled a number, then said: 'Hullo, Nessie [his wife]. We've done it. There's nae one can catch us now!'

In 1974, as we celebrated Liverpool's FA Cup triumph over Newcastle United with a banquet at a plush London hotel, none of us realised that this was Bill's swan-song as manager. Having become the first and only man to steer Liverpool to FA Cup success not once, but twice, he had decided to bow out, and his decision came as a real shock to many people – although, I learned later, there were those close to him who suspected that as time went by he came to regret his decision to quit.

On occasion he helped other clubs out, giving them advice and lending moral support, but somehow, after his departure from Anfield, he seemed to be a man on his own, almost as if he had lost his sense of direction. Which wouldn't have been totally surprising, considering that the Anfield club had been his whole existence for some 15 years.

People used to ask the secret of Liverpool's success, and Steve Heighway – who succeeded Tom Saunders as the club's youth-development officer – told me how Bill Shankly instructed his players to 'pass the ball to the nearest red shirt'. He believed in keeping the game simple; and he also believed in fighting to the final whistle, which was why Liverpool used to win so many of their games in the last ten minutes or so. They never gave up.

I have one memory of Bill Shankly which remains vivid above all others, and it concerns an occasion when he was 200 miles away from his beloved Anfield, the place where he had such a tremendous rapport with the fans (he even went to stand on the Kop on at least one occasion). Bill never received a knighthood, although he was awarded an OBE for his services to soccer, the game he rated as being more important than life and death. My mind goes back to the time the Laird of Anfield travelled to London for the annual Manager-of-the-Year luncheon at the Savoy Hotel. He knew what it was all about, of course, because he had been named Manager of the Year himself, during his days in command at Liverpool; but on this occasion everyone present was paying homage to that canny Geordie, Bob Paisley, who had become Bill's even more successful successor. Liverpool, under Bob, had just won the League Championship and the European Cup, so it was entirely fitting that he should be acclaimed and presented with the major managerial award. Who better, then, than Bill Shankly to do the honours?

This was the second year in succession that Paisley had been named as the country's top manager, and as Bill Shankly rose to his feet and started to speak, the ghost of a smile flitted across his craggy features. At that moment I guessed that he was thinking to himself about his own years of triumph at Anfield, years in which he had taken Liverpool to Championships, to the FA Cup twice, and to European honours –

although he had missed out by such a narrow margin on the supreme trophy of them all, the European Champions Cup.

As Shankly spoke in fulsome praise of his successor, he ventured to suggest to those present that they might just be wondering how he was feeling. That ghost of a smile remained in place when he told his attentive audience: 'If ye're thinking I'm feeling a wee bit jealous . . . by Christ, ye're bluidy right!'

CHAPTER 3

A 'FAMILY' AFFAIR
Bob Paisley and Joe Fagan

I know I can never have the same rapport with the fans that Bill
Shankly had, I just hope that the team will do the talking for me.
BOB PAISLEY, ON TAKING OVER AS LIVERPOOL MANAGER

NEVER WAS there a more reluctant hero than Bob Paisley. For three
weeks, after the shock news that Bill Shankly had decided to throw in
the towel as manager, Bob tried to persuade his boss to change his
mind. When that proved impossible, and the job (in a sense) was thrust
upon him, Bob told me: 'I know I can never have the same rapport with
the fans that Bill had. I just hope the team will do the talking for me.'
And it did.

As we were discussing Bill and what he had achieved for Liverpool,
I ventured the opinion that perhaps Bob had been a restraining
influence on Shanks, at times; maybe, even, that he had persuaded Bill
not to pursue a certain line of action which could have caused some
complications. Bob said not a word; he just smiled that quiet smile of
his, and the matter was closed.

He did tell me that at one stage of his career it seemed likely that he
would be going back to his old job as a bricklayer. But he stuck with
Liverpool, and in his days at Anfield Bob was a player, trainer, physio,
assistant to the manager and manager. Not a bad record, quite apart
from the honours he brought to the club.

Having joined Liverpool on 8 May 1939, Bob had already served the
club for 35 years when Shankly retired, and he went on to make it a
half-century as he vacated the managerial chair for a seat on the board.
Not until February 1992 did he finally bow out, because of ill-health;
and when I spoke to Bob at his home then, he told me that one of the
first to call him had been Kenny Dalglish. That was a nice gesture from

the man Bob had signed as the big-name successor to Kevin Keegan, and if there were times when (as Bob's wife, Jessie, had told me) he became 'a bit ratty', for the most part there were very few people ready to quarrel with Bob Paisley. And even before he had returned to soccer's sidelines for good, there were plenty of people who had good things to say about him.

Brian Clough may have aroused the ire of the Liverpool faithful with his comments about Hillsborough and the Liverpool fans, but when he succeeded Bob Paisley as Manager of the Year, he had this to say about his predecessor: 'He's broken this silly myth that nice guys don't win anything. He's one of the nicest guys you could meet in any industry or any walk of life – and he is a winner.' My sentiments exactly.

When Tony Book was manager of Manchester City, he revealed: 'The highest compliment I can pay to Bob Paisley is that whenever I am trying to set my own stall out, I'm always looking at Liverpool. When a manager like Bob can help his players to obtain such consistent results, he has to have something special. Not only is Bob Paisley a fine manager, he's a gentleman as well. He's had a tremendous amount of success, but still has his feet firmly planted on the ground.'

Jimmy Armfield, then the manager of Leeds United – one of Liverpool's greatest rivals – had this to say about Paisley: 'Bob is one of the old school, with a wealth of knowledge. He, Joe Fagan and Ronnie Moran give the club that homely appearance, but beneath what might seem a soft exterior there is a hard centre. Bob has always got the best out of players.'

And two of Paisley's former players, Gordon Milne and Ian Callaghan, talked to me about the man who had been their boss. 'I knew Bob when he was a No. 2,' said Milne, 'and, having experienced management myself [he was then at Coventry City] I'm delighted at the success he has had since he took over what was a difficult job. The club had had so much success, it seemed impossible to do better, but Bob has improved even on what had gone before – and done it while being his own man.' And Cally, a veteran of more than 850 games who had known Paisley longer and better than most, told me: 'I think the feeling within the club was that he was the only one who could take over as manager in 1974 – I certainly wanted him to get the job. His success hasn't surprised me. His knowledge of the game is unquestioned and virtually unrivalled, and he has proved himself a great manager.

Everyone has the utmost respect for him. He is a player's man, simplifies everything, has no side to him. He knows what makes players tick.' Indeed he did.

When Paisley finally bowed out, Brian Clough was among the first to salute him again for all he had achieved, and for the manner in which he had conducted himself, and it can fairly be said that as a player, as a backroom man and as 'the boss', Bob was the epitome of loyalty. He once told me he regarded himself as 'part of the furniture' at Anfield, and while football was his life, he was also a family man.

Some memories stick in your mind – like the train journey back after Liverpool had lost the 1977 FA Cup final against Manchester United, and as we sat in the diner Bob walked past. He didn't appear to see anyone, and was clearly deep in thought – probably pondering on how he was going to gee up his players for the European Cup final in Rome the following Wednesday. He knew the 'impossible dream' had vanished – Liverpool had claimed the title, lost the FA Cup – but that evening, on the way back to Merseyside, he wasn't to know that in a matter of days he would be savouring his greatest triumph to date.

The first time I ever met Bob Paisley was when I worked on the *Liverpool Echo*, and I decided that a fellow who had been so long at Anfield must have something worth saying, without dishing the dirt, as they say. I contacted Bob, and he agreed to do a series of articles for the paper. He received a munificent sum, by way of payment – £80. In later years I ghosted his programme notes, as well as a book which bore his name, and never once did we have an argument or even a disagreement. Bob was as good as gold, and a pleasure to work with. Of course, not all the players who served under him would say the same . . .

In his first term as Liverpool's manager, the club finished second to Brian Clough's League champions, Derby County, and it was after that that Bob confided to me: 'I tried to please everyone, but I've come to realise that it just can't be done.' So there were times when players were axed from the side, and they didn't regard Bob in the greatest light – as one player admitted to me later: 'When I was out, I thought he was a rotten so-and-so. When I got back in, I realised just what a good judge he was!'

I can recall a derby game against Everton at Goodison Park when Bob really was coming under pressure. Liverpool had lost at Ipswich and at home to Arsenal, so a third defeat on the trot, and against the old

enemy, would really have put the cat among the pigeons. For that
Goodison derby game, Bob pitched his first signing, Phil Neal, into the
fray, so he took a gamble there. The game ended as a scoreless draw,
and so Liverpool stopped the threatened rot. But it was a long time
before Bob emerged to face the press. When he did so, he apologised
for the delay and made it clear he hadn't kept the reporters waiting
deliberately. Although, as he told me later, he knew that some of them
had been waiting for him to fall flat on his face. He wasn't daft.

When we talked about his Liverpool career, Bob recalled how he
was dropped from the FA Cup-final team in 1950, by a split vote in the
boardroom. The directors decided, by five to four, that Bill Jones
should be in the side. Bob felt it was ironic that Jimmy Logie, the man
he would have marked, laid on both of Arsenal's goals for Reg Lewis.
'I'd played against Logie before and kept a tight hold on him. I was
sure I could have handled him at Wembley,' Bob told me. Bob also said
that after having learned his Cup-final fate from the evening paper, he
was so upset that he came very close to asking Liverpool for a transfer,
while his father was so incensed by Bob's omission that he refused to
go to the game.

While he was still a player, Bob spent hours studying the science of
physiotherapy, by means of a correspondence course; and he was also
grateful to John Moores of Everton for giving him a helping hand.
Moores it was who arranged for Bob to visit hospitals in order to learn
first-hand about the various items of equipment used in the treatment
of sports injuries. Years of experience later on enabled Bob Paisley to
spot straight away just what kind of an injury a player had suffered, and
how serious it might be – the moment the player went down, indeed,
Bob could detect what the problem was.

When Bill Shankly signed Ray Clemence, Kevin Keegan and Steve
Heighway, it was Bob Paisley who had played a decisive role in the
arrival of these football stars in the making – although, as he admitted
to me later, he turned out to have been wrong in his assessment of one
of the trio.

Bob related how it was after a shock FA Cup defeat at Watford
during season 1969–70 that Shankly came to the conclusion that the
changes would have to be rung; and Clemence – after his two-and-a-
half-year wait to claim his place as the successor to Tommy Lawrence
– became one of the newcomers in Liverpool's side. Even so, and

despite good first impressions, Bob Paisley still remained to be convinced that Clem could measure up to the demands. Ultimately, it was in a match against West Bromwich Albion that the keeper passed the Paisley test. Bob told me: 'He kept Liverpool in the game with three superb saves in the first quarter of an hour, and after that I was able to relax. I knew then that Ray had arrived.' Bob knew, too, when he watched Kevin Keegan in action at Scunthorpe (Clemence's former club) that he had spotted another winner.

Liverpool had paid Scunthorpe United something like £20,000 for Clemence, and he went on to establish himself as the first-team choice and total more than 650 appearances before moving on to Tottenham Hotspur. In landing Keegan for all of £35,000, Liverpool pulled off another masterstroke, because after the player had given them sterling service and helped to take the European Cup to Anfield for the first time, they received no less than half a million pounds when Kevin was transferred to SportVerein Hamburg. Not only that, they still had some change left after they had secured the signature of Kenny Dalglish from Celtic as Keegan's big-name replacement.

Liverpool were not the only club weighing up Keegan's all-action style at Scunthorpe but, as usual, all the onlookers were asking themselves if he really could measure up to the demands of the game at top level. Bill Shankly sent Bob Paisley to look, and to deliver his verdict. So one evening Bob and Joe Fagan travelled across-country to Scunthorpe.

That canny Scot, Andy Beattie, had been pushing Keegan's claims but, as Bob said, 'We had to see for ourselves.' That night, Keegan skippered Scunthorpe, and after 20 minutes of close scrutiny, the Liverpool deputation had seen enough – sufficient, indeed, to set off for home. When Shanks asked, 'Well, what about it?', the verdict was succinct. Bob Paisley simply said: 'Take him.' And Liverpool did.

Bob always gave the credit for the discovery of Steve Heighway to his sons, Graham and Robert, because, as he told me, they were the first to tell him about this high-stepping winger who was playing as an amateur for Skelmersdale in the Cheshire League, while combining soccer with his studies for a BA degree at Warwick University.

Bob took his sons' advice and went to watch Steve, and he told Tony Waiters, who was coaching at Liverpool, 'This is the best amateur footballer I've seen.' And Bob knew what he was talking about, since he had won a medal with those famed Amateur Cup fighters, Bishop Auckland, before becoming a professional with Liverpool. In fact, his transfer to Anfield was delayed so that he could play in the Bishops side which won the Amateur Cup final at Wembley.

Bob saw Steve torment the South Liverpool defence, and when Tony Waiters checked the winger out, he was equally impressed. So Bill Shankly went down to Warwick and persuaded Steve to sign on the dotted line . . . at £40 a week. Then Bob began to have reservations about Steve's ability to make the grade at First Division level. Steve had come into professional football at the age of 23, and he seemed to Bob to have some self-doubts. Steve later admitted to me that there were times when his head went down and he wondered, also, if he would spend more time on the treatment table than on the pitch. His high-stepping style made him vulnerable to injury, and there was at least one occasion when Bob Paisley treated him with scant sympathy when he was on the treatment table, while in terms of experience he was an utter novice, compared with the likes of players who had been at the club since they were teenagers. Tommy Smith, for instance – who, during a train journey back from London one day accused Steve of having 'cost us money today'. Steve had tried a shot at goal and missed, when he might have passed to a team-mate better placed to score.

There was also the time when Steve was about to make his first-team bow in a League game, at Burnley, and the team stayed in an hotel on the Friday night. Not realising it was the custom for the players to gather for tea and toast around 9.45 that evening, Steve decided to retire to his room (he was the odd man out in the squad of 13, so he had a room to himself) and watch television, while having a bite of supper. He called room service and ordered some chicken sandwiches and a Coke. It was Tommy Smith, that arch-professional, who spotted the waiter bearing a tray, and Peter Thompson who tracked the waiter to Steve's door. Peter put Steve wise as to the routine for future occasions. Then there was the time Steve made his Anfield debut – it was in a testimonial match for Gerry Byrne, a veteran of Merseyside derby games – and during the kickabout Steve turned to a team-mate to ask: 'Which end is the Kop?' The team-mate, Everton full-back Alex Parker, blinked at that one.

When it came to derby games, Steve had a couple of enduring memories. At times, he used to suffer from severe migraine, and before one game against Everton he seemed likely to be a non-starter, as the migraine struck. Bill Shankly immediately ordered him to bed in the team's hotel, and after a few hours had passed Steve had recovered sufficiently to play. He also told me how it was brought home to him just what it meant to win a derby game after Liverpool (thanks to Chris Lawler) had staged a comeback to triumph 3–2. 'It was only then, when we'd won, that I realised just how much it meant to the local-born players, and to the fans.'

Since Steve and Kevin Keegan arrived on the Anfield scene more or less at the same time, it was natural that they should feel an affinity, even if their backgrounds had been different – when Steve held out for £40 a week, he was thinking of giving football a year and, if things didn't go well, switching to the teaching profession. Once at Anfield, he became firm friends with Keegan – and an admirer, as well. Steve once told me, with a smile and a shake of the head, 'I just don't know how Kev manages to cope with all the demands on his time. Whether it's in training or in a match, he'll cover every blade of grass – then he'll be off to Yorkshire or to a charity function or some other event. Talk about stamina – the man's a human dynamo. I'd be shattered, if I tried to do what he does.'

In fact, Steve Heighway was 'shattered' by the demands of his new career on more than one occasion, but he showed that he could stay the course; and, for once, Bob Paisley made a forecast which turned out to be wide of the mark. He offered the opinion to me that another university graduate, Brian Hall, would clock up more first-team appearances than Steve Heighway. Brian had a BSc degree, and the team-mates were known in the club as Big Bamber (Steve) and Little Bamber, after Bamber Gascoigne, of television's *University Challenge* fame. In the event, Brian totalled around 200 appearances while Steve clocked up some 460 (and scored 76 goals).

By the early 1990s, both men were back at Anfield; Steve after having played soccer in the United States, where it seemed he might well be ready to stay for the rest of his working life (after having hung up his boots, he had landed a good job). When his Liverpool career was drawing to a close, he told me he never wanted to play for another club in this country and, indeed, he confessed that he regarded himself as 'a Liverpool snob'. When he did come back to Anfield, it was as the successor to Tom Saunders, the club's youth-development officer.

Meanwhile, Brian Hall's role was as community-care officer. And both men seemed well suited for their new roles at Liverpool. As for Kevin Keegan, he had been persuaded to return from exile and become a manager – like Kenny Dalglish.

When Liverpool agreed to part company with Keegan in 1977, Bob Paisley knew the fans would not be happy about losing their idol. Then he came up with Kenny Dalglish. And though it was SV Hamburg who landed Keegan, Bob revealed that the first club to make an approach was Real Madrid – Real's general manager even met Liverpool officials in London. But Hamburg won the race, and Keegan went on to become European Footballer of the Year (after some early difficulties at his new club) twice, in 1978 and 1979.

So why did Bob Paisley go for Kenny Dalglish? It wasn't simply because he was losing Kevin Keegan. 'Kenny seemed to me to be what I call a Liverpool-type player: he did the simple things, and he was so consistent. He scored goals in clinical fashion, and made goals for team-mates, too.' And, as it turned out, he was as much a success at Liverpool as Keegan had been before him.

As I had done with Bill Shankly, so I followed the same pattern with Bob Paisley when it came to compiling his programme notes. I would phone Bob at home, discuss what he wanted to say, and send him a copy for his approval. Like Shanks, he never made any alterations, so I must have achieved some success in interpreting just what Bob was getting at, as he spoke in that Geordie accent of his.

There were times when Bob could present an inscrutable expression and you wondered just what he was thinking, but I liked him, as well as respecting him. It wasn't often he was caught out, but there was such an occasion when he boarded the team coach for home, after a game against Queen's Park Rangers in London. At least, Bob – who hadn't been too happy with life, considering that Liverpool had just been beaten – thought they were heading for home . . . until he was confronted by a familiar figure. As he sat in his seat, Eammon Andrews appeared and leaned over his shoulder to tell him: 'Bob Paisley, *This Is Your Life!*' And so, instead of heading north up the motorway for Merseyside, Bob found himself being steered towards the television studio. The evening turned out to be a success, as did Bob's ventures into the transfer market – Phil Neal, for instance, was just as shrewd a signing as Kenny Dalglish, though the fees were vastly different. One deal which didn't materialise, however, concerned 'Super-sub' David Fairclough, and Manchester City's England winger, Peter Barnes.

Oddly enough, I can recall a couple of games when Fairclough turned out to be a real tormentor against opposition from Manchester. The first match was played on Easter Monday 1976, against Manchester City at Maine Road, and Liverpool were bidding for the League title, so victory was imperative. With the scoreline reading 0–0, Bob Paisley sent on Fairclough as a substitute, and he ran City ragged – he scored twice, laid on a goal for Steve Heighway, and Liverpool won 3–0. At that time the lad from Cantril Farm had played only five full games and eight as substitute, and his unorthodox style soon earned him the nickname of Charlie Chaplin from his team-mates. But when Fairclough set off on one of his gangling runs, the opposition found it was no laughing matter.

After City, it was Manchester United who felt the impact of David Fairclough's shooting when, on Boxing Day 1978, more than 54,000 fans saw Liverpool beat United and Fairclough strike a magnificent third goal – all this, at Old Trafford. He took the ball down on the right, tricked one opponent, turned and tricked another, bored his way through towards goal despite the attentions of other United players – then stabbed the ball home. As the Liverpool supporters roared, Fairclough himself was lying prone on the turf.

This former Liverpool schoolboy player who also became a Sunday league footballer could count on scoring between 60 and 80 goals most seasons. Naturally left-footed, he practised shooting with his right until he could use that equally effectively. He served his apprenticeship with Liverpool, signed professional in January 1974, and harboured ambitions to nail down a first-team spot. But his fans still called him 'Super-sub', a title he came to dislike, and it was during a conversation with Bob Paisley one day that I began to wonder if David would ever become a regular first choice. The way Bob talked, I got the impression that he felt David was likely to remain on the bench, a player who could go on and turn a game.

Bob told me how, for a while, he considered offering his Super-sub to Manchester City in exchange for their England winger, Peter Barnes, but it was a notion which never got off the starting blocks, and while both players made headline news with transfers abroad, neither man could be said to have reached the pinnacle for which, at the start, he had seemed destined.

During the early part of the 1990s I met David Fairclough fairly regularly, because by that time he had embarked upon another career, while still involved in football. He was doing a stint as a match reporter for a national Sunday newspaper and, by all accounts, making a very fair job of it. As a striker who could claim to have averaged about one goal every three games, he could certainly weigh up the abilities of the latest crop of marksmen, while also sizing up the defensive qualities of those whose job it was to stop them.

By then, of course, things had changed greatly at Liverpool: Bob Paisley had vacated the managerial chair for a seat in the boardroom, and after him came Joe Fagan, as Liverpool once again kept the job 'in the family'. Joe, in turn, kept the club on course for even more success, even though he was no chicken when he stepped up from being the No. 2 to take charge of team affairs. 'Yes,' he told me at the time, 'I did want a crack at being the manager.'

There was a difference in style between Joe, Bob and Bill Shankly. Shanks could be abrasive, Bob presented that avuncular image, and while Bill always came straight out with it, sometimes in Bob's case – as I found when it came to doing his notes for the match-day programme – you needed to interpret just what he meant because, apart from understanding his Geordie accent, he would sometimes trot out a phrase which made you ponder for a moment. However, anyone who took Bob Paisley for a fool would have spent his money badly – he wasn't inarticulate, by any means, and he was possessed of a dry wit. He was a canny fellow, all right – and don't let that woolly-cardigan image fool you.

Joe Fagan was different again, but while his reign lasted only from 1983 to 1985, the record books show that he achieved a success which, even by Liverpool standards, was unique. Bill Shankly had become the first Liverpool manager to lift the FA Cup (he did it twice) and steer the club to the League title and a European trophy (the UEFA Cup) in the same season; Bob Paisley had been the first to add the European Cup to the club's list of honours (and he did that three times). As for Joe Fagan, he delivered a remarkable treble in his first season as manager – League Championship, European Cup and League Cup.

As I had done with Bill Shankly and then Bob Paisley, I started to get down to work with Joe Fagan. I would pick up the phone and ring him at home, then between us we would come up with something which could be fitted into the programme notes under Joe's name. Through close on 20 years, I always tried to bother each of the managers with whom I worked as little as possible; hence the phone calls, rather than a constant knocking on the office door at Anfield. The manager's job was not to produce the match-day programme, but to produce a team which would win trophies, and so 'the boss' wanted as few distractions as possible.

During his days as manager of Grimsby Town, Bill Shankly had tried to sign Joe Fagan from Manchester City, so he knew all about Joe when he joined the backroom staff at Anfield. By then, Joe had done a stint as player-manager at Nelson and trainer at Rochdale and, like Shankly and Paisley, he wasn't given to putting on airs and graces. but he was steeped in soccer, and he had a lively wit.

Joe wasn't an aggressive sort of man, but he wanted his team to win; I remember a European tie which was played at Anfield, when Liverpool failed to score against Athletic Bilbao. That 0–0 result left more than a few people looking a bit down in the mouth, with the return game still to come in Spain. But when Joe walked into the press room, he was smiling and he chided us: 'Hey – we can still win this one, you know. Don't forget, they haven't scored a goal against us. And we're quite capable of getting one in Bilbao.' Liverpool turned out to be every bit as good as Joe's forecast, too, because they won the second leg with a goal from Ian Rush; and seven months later, they were claiming the European Champions Cup after having won a penalty shoot-out in Rome.

As with Bob Paisley, Joe Fagan and I never had a cross word when I was compiling his notes for the match-day programme, but one thing about him did surprise me a little. I had been on nodding terms with Joe for years, but without having got close to him; yet, when we got down to doing those programme notes, I discovered that my job was more or less a sinecure, because as Joe talked and I made notes, I could almost write down the conversation word for word, and that was it. He knew what he wanted to say, and it didn't need much polishing by me.

It was nothing less than a tragedy that Joe Fagan's reign as manager of Liverpool should come to an end in the manner that it did, with the shadow of the Heysel disaster hanging over his departure. He deserved a much more fitting finale than that. But if it was a bitter ending for Joe, he could console himself with the knowledge that he had achieved a unique treble in his first season as team boss, and taken Liverpool to the final of the European Cup the second time around.

After that, of course, the task of following in Joe's footsteps was going to be far from easy, no matter who might land the Liverpool job. And immediately the word got out that Joe Fagan was stepping down, the guessing game began, with various names being touted as his successor. Three names in the frame were John Toshack, Phil Neal and Kenny Dalglish.

CHAPTER 4

CANNY KING KENNY
Kenny Dalglish

Och, well – the worst thing they can do is sack me.
KENNY DALGLISH, ON TAKING OVER AS LIVERPOOL MANAGER

I DON'T know how John Toshack felt when Liverpool named Kenny Dalglish as the man to succeed Joe Fagan, but Phil Neal was said to be a very disappointed loser and, maybe, so was Ronnie Moran, who had packed many years of service into his career both as player and backroom man at Anfield. While Liverpool once again kept the job in the family, it hadn't been passed on to the next man in the chain of command – Moran – nor had Neal's hopes been realised.

It was said that Phil had had good reason to anticipate that he would land a job on the backroom side when his playing days had ended, and if he were not to become the manager, then perhaps there would be another role for him to play. In the event, Kenny Dalglish was named, and he had the unusual title of player-team manager, which led me to wonder if there were some who doubted his ability to be 'the boss'.

If Phil Neal was unhappy with the way things had turned out, Kenny Dalglish was his usual, inscrutable self. True, he had shown often enough as a player that he could smile, especially when he scored a goal or when his side won, but all of a sudden he had to have a foot in both camps. He remained a player, yet he was the man responsible for picking the team and dictating the tactics. It was not surprising, therefore, that there should be questions asked and doubts expressed as to how he would perform in his dual capacity. And while nobody behind the scenes ever voiced such doubts to me, Kenny had to be an unknown quantity as team boss.

When Dalglish, priced at £440,000, became Liverpool's costliest signing and the replacement for the departed Kevin Keegan, another

Scotland international and former Celtic star, Lou Macari, offered the view that Liverpool had made a good investment. Dalglish, said Macari, was not just a gifted marksman: he was a team player in every sense of the word. And so it proved. Macari told me, with something of a wistful tone in his voice, 'He would have been great for Manchester United,' and it was a reminder that he and Dalglish had formed a fine partnership during their days together at Parkhead. 'I never thought he would be allowed to move,' said Lou.

Manchester City's manager at the time, Tony Book, had caused something of a stir when he signed Mick Channon for £300,000, and he admitted: 'When we signed him, I believed he had tipped the scales in our favour. But now [with Dalglish having arrived at Anfield] things have balanced out again.' Kevin Keegan rated Dalglish 'the best Scottish player for the last four years . . . he is such a good player he would fit in anywhere'.

Keegan declared: 'Liverpool have come up with a ready-made replacement. The Liverpool fans will like him. We are completely different, with different qualities and strengths. What we have in common is a desire to see the ball in the back of the net, whether we put it there or help one of our team-mates to do the job.' Keegan also said: 'It's a lot of money, but I think it's money well spent. Liverpool have done well by their fans, using the money they got for me. I think it's unfair to compare us, for many different reasons. I went to Liverpool for just over £30,000 – a pittance – and they sold me for close on half a million. I went to Liverpool as a youngster who still had to prove himself . . . Liverpool spent the money they got for me on Kenny, who had already proved himself with Celtic and Scotland.'

Keegan rated Dalglish, like himself, to be 'fortunate to be a key player in a tremendous team' and added, 'Each of us happens to occupy a vital position where our strengths could be seen to play a part in the success of the team. When Kenny Dalglish is on song, so are Liverpool; and I was the same. Each of us takes more than his share of responsibility, because of the position in which we play – but that's a privilege, both for me and for Kenny. I need not to be restricted, and I respond by doing my utmost; I think Kenny is exactly the same. He is the complete team player.' This was a view echoed by Dalglish himself, when I talked to him after his arrival at Anfield. Never mind all the goals he had scored – and was going to score – he told me he didn't regard himself simply as a marksman; he rated himself a team player. And, indeed, he was.

Keegan made another telling point about his Anfield successor. 'Look at our respective records over the years, and you'll realise that neither of us has missed many matches through injury – yet that's not because we have been afraid to go in where it hurts.' Keegan recalled that his most memorable game for Liverpool had been the 1977 European Cup-final triumph in Rome, 'a fairytale ending to what had been a fairytale career with Liverpool'.

It was a fairytale start for Dalglish, too – he scored for Liverpool only seven minutes into his debut, against Middlesbrough at Ayresome Park. And team-mate Emlyn Hughes, who knew what it was like to play for England against Kenny Dalglish, reckoned that 'possibly he and Trevor Francis are the only two who could have come here and replaced Kevin Keegan. Kenny seems to 'get lost' – you think you've held on to him, and the next minute he's free and sticking the ball into the net. He can lose markers very easily – I can see him getting a lot of goals, maybe more than Kevin did.' Well, Keegan scored 100 goals for Liverpool, and Dalglish eclipsed even that considerable tally.

Dalglish told me: 'I'm not trying to take over from Kevin – I'll just try to be my own man. At Celtic I got into the habit of collecting silverware, and it's one I want to continue.' He said the size of the fee didn't worry him. 'I don't have to carry a price tag on my back – just play to the best of my ability.' And by the beginning of May 1978 he was looking forward to a European Cup-final appearance against FC Bruges.

During that season, he had lived up to his reputation as a marksman and was confirming what his manager, Bob Paisley, had said about him several months earlier: 'By signing him, we've got one of the best players – if not the best player – in Britain. He has so much ability, and he can play in any position, as all good players can.' Kenny's Liverpool team-mate and England rival, Ray Clemence, who had had the Scot in his sights more than once as an international opponent, admitted: 'He has never failed to impress me by his work-rate. The goals he scored against me [a winner at Hampden, Scotland's second at Wembley] might not have been spectacular, but they all count, and he consistently scored 20-odd goals a season in Scotland. His strongest asset,' Clemence went on, 'is that he can go late from midfield and finish up with a tremendously accurate shot – something a lot of forwards don't do, these days. When Kenny gets into a shooting position, almost always he forces the keeper to make a save.'

At that stage of his career, Kenny Dalglish had been on the winning side twice against England – and on the wrong end of a 5–1 scoreline as well. By the time he was coming to the close of his first season in English football, he was telling me: 'Things have gone well, and I'd like to thank everyone at the club – and the fans – for helping me to settle in.'

He also said that he hadn't seen himself as Keegan's replacement when he arrived, 'I didn't look at things that way, although I'll admit I was a bit nervous at the start. But not overawed. Liverpool signed me because they wanted me to play for them. It's as simple as that. I got away to a flier when I scored at Middlesbrough, and the goals have kept going in since. But the main thing that gives you confidence is if the manager keeps picking you week after week.'

Dalglish recalled having watched the 1967 European Cup final between Celtic and Inter Milan on television, while in 1970 he was there to see Celtic tackle Feyenoord. 'Now I'm hoping to play in a European Cup final – and, frankly, when I joined Liverpool, I felt it was possible for anything to happen. I've found that at Anfield it's a case of taking each game as it comes, and everyone plays for each other. No one plays just for himself. So that makes Liverpool a difficult side to beat, and that's the team's biggest strength, I feel. We've all worked together to achieve something this season, and at the end of it we're going to Wembley for the European Cup. We've had our disappointments, but the big prize is still there for us to take, and my hope is that I'll finish off the season by collecting a winners' medal – although, if I do, it will still have been the team effort that made it possible.'

As he looked forward to that Wembley date against FC Bruges, Kenny Dalglish was not to know that he would emerge as Liverpool's match-winner. The game itself wasn't such a great one – certainly not as thrilling as the 1977 final against Borussia Moenchengladbach had been in Rome. But, pragmatic as ever, Dalglish and Liverpool were setting out their stall to win against Bruges at Wembley and thus retain the trophy they had captured twelve months previously. They succeeded, too.

One telling pass from Graeme Souness found Dalglish out in space, on the right, and canny Kenny looked goalwards, spotted how the keeper was reacting, and clipped the ball firmly – and to deadly effect – towards the target. It was a perfect example of what Bob Paisley had described as the Dalglish art of finishing a move in clinical fashion. And that goal, the only one of the game, ensured that Liverpool carried the European Cup back to Anfield once more.

The Dalglish career with Liverpool as a player went from strength to strength; the goals flowed from his feet, and he made goals for team-mates as well. And as the goals piled up and the results were achieved, in competition at home and abroad, so the medals were handed round, with Kenny Dalglish claiming his share. By the mid-1980s he was regarded as a hero by the Liverpool supporters, and it seemed that he could do no wrong. Then came the tragedy of Heysel, as Liverpool awaited their European Cup final with Juventus . . . and Dalglish found himself being handed another role; that of team boss, in succession to Joe Fagan.

One of the points made, when Kenny's name was announced, was that Bob Paisley, who had been the most successful team boss in the club's long and illustrious history, would still be available to pass on his advice, if needed; in effect, although he had relinquished the managerial reins at Anfield, his vast experience could be utilised on a consultancy basis. Bob had signed Kenny; he knew him inside-out as a player and as a person; and there could be nobody better equipped to lend a helping hand, should this be required by the newcomer to football management. Kenny himself was certainly a canny fellow, as he had demonstrated many, many times when playing for Liverpool. Now, he had the added responsibility of trying to steer the team to even greater success. Treading in the footsteps of people like Shankly, Paisley and Fagan was a difficult act to follow – indeed, it seemed as if it might well be an impossible task. However, Bob Paisley would be there, if wanted. As time went by, of course, it became increasingly clear that Kenny Dalglish was very much his own man as team boss, notably when he played what people called 'the numbers game'. By then, he was naming a squad, rather than a team, and he played his cards very close to his chest.

There came a day when he and Bob Paisley were making headline news; headline news which, I am certain, neither man would have sought. Bob had been interviewed by a reporter from a national newspaper, and one of the points which emerged from the interview and ended up in print was the suggestion that the Paisley – Dalglish relationship was no longer as close as people might have imagined. The inference was that the lines of communication were weakened, that Kenny no longer confided in his former manager, and the story caused genuine embarrassment all round, not least to Bob Paisley.

Not having been present at the interview, I don't know what was said, or how it was said; but from personal experience I know that sometimes what Bob said didn't come out quite as he had intended it. In this particular case, he felt compelled to make his peace with Kenny, and so the matter was concluded; but it was clearly an incident which both men must have regretted and could well have done without – not least, because Kenny and Bob were normally very cautious in their dealings with the media.

My first close encounter with Kenny had come about while he was still very much a player, and the management of Liverpool Football Club was not even on the agenda. I made an approach to him about doing a book, and we agreed to meet after he had finished training. So I arrived at Anfield around lunch-time, and when we met Kenny unhesitatingly led me into one of the private rooms upstairs. It struck me then that this was a measure of his standing at the club.

When we got down to talking, I put my proposition to him and, in fairly quick time, I got down to the bottom line – the amount of money he would be paid as an advance. He didn't take more than a few seconds to turn me down, and when I pointed out to him that he would be receiving considerably more than I would be getting, even though I would be doing the donkey work as it were, he didn't budge. Kenny simply said he wasn't interested in my proposition – for the sort of money being offered, it wasn't worth his while. It didn't matter to him that I was prepared to do the job for my particular slice of the financial cake, he didn't even want to know what kind of money I would be receiving. 'I'm nae interested in that; it's your business. But I won't do it for what I'm being offered,' he told me.

It was a decision which I had no option but to accept, and as we shook hands we parted company without any hard feelings. I was philosophical about the whole business, because I had learned long ago that you win some and you lose some; and this one I had most certainly lost. Frankly, in one way, I left Anfield feeling somewhat relieved, because given Kenny's reputation for playing things close to his chest I felt that trying to get sufficient material out of him to make a book might well have proved a chore and a half.

I once asked a team-mate what Kenny was like, because he came across as someone who gave nothing away (and I don't mean money). The team-mate laughed and said: 'Kenny's all right. But I don't think he trusts anyone, not even himself!' When he was named as player-team manager, I felt the occasion called for a face-to-face chat, so I arranged to see him at Anfield. As we sat in his office, the telephone rang, and when he answered it soon became clear that whoever was on the other end of the line knew him well enough – for a start, he'd got the number.

I heard Kenny respond to what were obvious congratulations by saying: 'Och, well, the worst thing they can do is sack me.' Then, the conversation over, I made it clear to Kenny that while I was a newspaperman, when it came to Liverpool Football Club, he and I were both on the same side. 'I'm working for the club, just like you, so there's no way I'm going to do anything to embarrass Liverpool.' He accepted what I said, but when I asked him for his home telephone number, he refused to give it to me. I did have the home number he had used when he was purely a player, because occasionally I had needed to ring him for a piece for the programme, but I felt sure that, given his new role, he would be changing his phone number and, of course, it would be ex-directory again. Kenny told me that I could always get in touch with him during working hours at the ground or, if he were not available, I could leave a message for him to ring me.

It was an arrangement I had no option but to accept, and I could understand his reasoning. In fact, as time passed, we established a pretty good working relationship. Only once did I receive a call to ring Kenny away from Anfield, and on that occasion I was given the number of his car phone. I think he was on his way back from a match which had been played in Glasgow the previous night.

For the most part, when I checked with him about his programme notes, he would say: 'Nae problem.' But on the odd occasion he would ring me or get Sheila Walsh, his secretary, to phone with a message that something should be amended or deleted. Now and again, I must admit, I felt Kenny was being over-cautious; but, since the notes were going in under his name, he was entitled to have the final say.

He wasn't always flavour of the month with the journalists whose job it was to record the affairs of the club, and at one stage there was some concern behind the scenes about what was considered to be a deteriorating relationship between Kenny and the press. He gave nothing away about team selection, for example, never mind his dealings in the transfer market. Indeed, after he had taken on the job of steering Blackburn Rovers into the Premier League I saw some journalists, in press rooms at other clubs, smirk with satisfaction and I heard their derisive comments as the Rovers seemed to be stumbling towards their goal. I wasn't one of Kenny's critics, however.

I will confess that I started out not expecting to like Kenny Dalglish all that much (though I doubt if this would have bothered him, anyway), just as I had felt at the start that Bill Shankly was a bit overbearing at times. But I ended up having great respect for both men; I came to realise they were concerned only with doing their job for the club that employed them, to the best of their ability. And if anyone else didn't like it, then that was just too bad.

One Anfield insider told me he found it 'difficult' to get a decision from Dalglish; another member of the staff who worked closely with him said he was 'smashing – he lets you get on with your job and expects you to let him get on with his'. He was certainly decisive enough when it came to dropping the bombshell that he was quitting as Liverpool's manager, and when I inquired discreetly what it had all been about, I was told, on the best authority: 'There was nothing sinister. He simply came in and said he felt he couldn't cope with the job any more.'

I have always felt that the disasters of Heysel and Hillsborough affected Kenny Dalglish deeply, and I wasn't the only one to think so. Kevin Keegan, for instance, reckoned that it wasn't surprising Dalglish had opted out, given all the pressure he had been under – not least, the tragedy of Hillsborough, which left so many scars. So it would not surprise me if Hillsborough had contributed and in no small way to Kenny's decision to quit, a matter of hours after Liverpool and Everton had drawn 4–4, in an FA Cup-tie at Goodison Park. Yes, even though Liverpool were at the time sitting on top of the First Division.

A few years later, when Dalglish was asked about his memories of the Kop, as the face of that revered institution was about to be changed for all time, he recalled a Friday night when, with son Paul and daughter Kelly, he had walked through the Kop. Most people had left Anfield that Friday evening, but the memory remained imprinted indelibly upon Kenny Dalglish. It was shortly after Hillsborough, and he and his children stood and looked at the hundreds of floral tributes which had been left at Anfield. That was the one and only time Dalglish had stood on the Kop, and he probably never imagined, then, that his Liverpool career would come to an end, in a sense, with an FA Cup-tie against Everton.

That Cup-tie at Goodison Park was described as 'one of the greatest Merseyside – if not football – has ever seen'. The man who pronounced this verdict was the then Everton manager, Howard Kendall – and he had every reason to be happy, since he had seen his side come from behind no fewer than four times.

It was a match in which Ian Rush scored his 24th goal in derby-game duels, and it was his 37th in the FA Cup competition, leaving him only four goals short of Denis Law's all-time record. Rush said afterwards: 'When you score four away from home, you expect to win . . . but you have to give Everton credit.'

The game had been going just over half an hour when Peter Beardsley pounced to give Liverpool the lead. It was centre-back Kevin Ratcliffe who gifted the ball to his Welsh-international team-mate and Liverpool rival, Ian Rush, and as Andy Hinchcliffe moved to kick the ball away, Rush headed it down and Beardsley drove in a shot which skimmed Hinchcliffe's legs and finished in the net.

Two minutes into the second half, and Everton had drawn level, as Graeme Sharp struck for his first goal in nine matches. From the left flank, Hinchcliffe delivered a cross which Sharp met with his head, and Bruce Grobbelaar was a beaten man.

In the 71st minute, Beardsley was on target again. This time he was played in by David Burrows, and he shrugged aside a challenge from Pat Nevin to carry on, then curl a left-footer out of Neville Southall's reach. Liverpool were heading for the quarter-finals – or so it seemed.

Only two more minutes had gone by, however, when there was more excitement. Just as Grobbelaar seemed to have the ball safely covered, Steve Nicol took a hand – or, rather, a foot – in the proceedings, as he more or less kicked the ball from the goalkeeper's grasp. Sharp was there once more, to snap up this chance and stab the ball into the net. So Everton were on level terms again.

But with 13 minutes left on the referee's watch, it was Rush who –
seemingly – plunged the dagger blow as he twisted and turned, and
found the net from no more than eight yards. Yet still the drama hadn't
finished.

Tony Cottee, Everton's £2 million striker, who had been on the field
fewer than five minutes, after having replaced the leg-weary Nevin, did
the damage this time. An Everton free-kick was helped on by Stuart
McCall, and as defender Gary Ablett appeared to be caught in two
minds, Cottee pounced to drag Everton level yet again and, this time,
take the tie into extra time.

Even then, it seemed as if Liverpool were fated to emerge victorious,
because with just over 100 minutes gone John Barnes got into the
scoring act. Up to then he had not really made much of an impact on
the game, but when he did strike, it was with a goal which probably
only he, of all the players on the park, would have had the sheer nerve
to attempt in the first place.

Barnes first collected the ball on the left-hand side of the pitch; then
he began to move inside, while keeper Southall was on the alert,
leaving scarcely a gap between himself and the post. But Barnes tried
his luck, and his effort curled across, clipped the inside of the far
upright, then finished in the back of the net. Now it was Liverpool 4,
Everton 3.

The minutes ticked away, and there were no more than half a dozen
left to go. By then, virtually all the spectators had decided that it was
going to be Liverpool's night after all. But then Ratcliffe began to
desert his defensive role, and as he moved forward, Cottee sped
towards goal as well. His turn of speed left Jan Molby stranded, and
when he gained possession he didn't hesitate – he was in like a flash to
drill the ball between the legs of Grobbelaar and send the Everton
supporters into ecstasies of delight.

Cottee said: 'It's been a high for me, tonight.' Sharp agreed: 'That's
the greatest game I've ever played in.' Molby echoed that Sharp
verdict, while Ablett admitted: 'I haven't played in a game like that
since I was at school. When you score four, you expect to win, but we
were sloppy at the back and got punished for it. We were told that in
the dressing-room afterwards.'

Kenny Dalglish summed up: 'We've had three great examples of
how to score goals and three bad examples of how to defend. That's

what makes a good Cup-tie. I've certainly never been involved in a derby game like that.' Not a soul realised, as he was speaking, that he was on the verge of making headlines which would be even more sensational, as he announced that he was leaving Liverpool.

Not surprisingly, the club directors were shocked when they learned that their manager was about to depart. He had brought honours to Liverpool since his appointment, and so far as they were concerned if he had asked for a contract which would have kept him in the job until he reached the age of 100, they would have been glad to say: 'Sign here . . .'

As a player, Dalglish had served the club magnificently, having totalled no fewer than 160 goals in 470 appearances since his arrival at Anfield in the summer of 1977. By season 1985–86, he was preparing to hang up his boots and become a permanent backroom man, but he still commanded tremendous respect, not least for the way he behaved after the tragedy of Hillsborough. While Anfield became a kind of shrine for the thousands who queued up to lay wreaths and bunches of flowers, as well as scarves and other items showing their loyalty to Liverpool, Dalglish and his players – and their wives – did everything humanly possible to alleviate the grief of the bereaved. They gave help and counselling, they attended the funerals of the victims; and they conducted themselves not only with dignity, but with deep understanding and sympathy.

The behaviour of Kenny Dalglish was impeccable, and it reflected great credit not only upon himself, but upon Liverpool Football Club. Like Kevin Keegan, I don't believe you can go through a traumatic experience such as that without it affecting you deeply. So the shock decision to call it a day was not a sudden one – it had been coming for a considerable time.

When he broke the news to chairman Noel White and chief executive Peter Robinson, he was offered the chance to go away and forget about football for a spell, then to come back when he had recharged the batteries. But he was adamant; he had made up his mind to go, and he could not be deflected. So they had to respect his decision, even if they were staggered by the timing of it. After all, Liverpool topped the table, and they had a Cup replay coming up.

The fateful meeting with chairman and chief executive, it was said, had been going for the best part of half an hour before the crunch came. The 4–4 draw in the Cup-tie against Everton had cropped up, but there were no recriminations about that – simply a rather rueful acceptance that Liverpool had to try to complete the job in a second replay, after having seemingly won the first one four times over.

When Kenny Dalglish dropped his bombshell, there was a moment's utter silence. Then came the explanation that the pressure of the job had got to him – and the admission, also, that he had pondered on whether or not to resign at the end of the previous season. The most stunning aspect of the news was that Liverpool's manager wanted to go virtually there and then. And it became clear that this was no case of a manager looking for pastures new or having had an offer elsewhere which he simply couldn't refuse.

When the full board met and digested the shock news, there was an air of consternation all round. True, there had been the odd problem in the past – for instance, Kenny's relationship with the media – and at least one member of the board, to my knowledge, had had differences of opinion with the manager. Yet never, ever, had anyone suggested that the time had come (or was coming) for Dalglish to make his exit from Anfield.

When he was questioned again about his decision to quit, it soon became clear that he could not be persuaded to change his mind, and so it was agreed that an emergency press conference should be called, so that the news could be given out. At the back of people's minds, even then, was the sneaking thought that maybe Kenny Dalglish would have second thoughts and decide, after all, that he would stay.

But it didn't happen; and so the news was announced, and that was that. For the players and even the backroom staff, it came as a total surprise, just as it had done to the chief executive, the chairman and the directors. For once, Kenny Dalglish the team man had decided to put himself and his family first, and football had been consigned very much to the back seat.

For me, the departure of Kenny Dalglish meant that I had to move swiftly when it came to producing the next match programme – Kenny's column would have to be replaced, and his resignation could not be ignored. So I spoke to Peter Robinson and chairman Noel White, and the programme contained a statement from the chairman of Liverpool Football Club, headed by a note which said that the message 'is addressed primarily to all Liverpool supporters, and it conveys the feelings of everyone at the club'.

Noel White's statement was contained in half a dozen paragraphs, and it read as follows:

'It was with very real regret that we learned of the decision by Kenny Dalglish to resign as team manager, and let me say straight away that I know all our supporters will share this regret with us. I would like to assure our supporters that we did everything in our power to try to persuade him to change his mind, and to continue to do the job which he had done with such conspicuous success during the last five years or so.

'However, he has made it clear – and I know he would tell you this himself – that he was determined to give up active participation in professional football, and he has also assured us that we could do nothing to alter his decision to resign.

'I cannot emphasise too strongly to our supporters that we had no wish to see Kenny Dalglish leave the club he has served so long and so loyally – in fact, I rate myself as one of his greatest fans. But, at the end of the day, there was only one thing that we could do, and that was to respect his wishes and accept his decision as being irrevocable.

'This being so, it remains only for us at Liverpool to wish him every success in the future, and I know that in saying this I am speaking for every Liverpool fan. Liverpool Football Club and Kenny Dalglish have parted on the most amicable terms, and I can say without hesitation that there will always be a warm welcome for him here at Anfield.

'As a player, he gave this club outstanding service, and as team manager his contribution has been no less noteworthy. As I said when announcing the news of his departure, Ronnie Moran has taken over as acting manager, and there are few people who know more about the workings of this club.

'Ronnie has served Liverpool in one capacity or another for close on 40 years, and he has been first-team coach for the past eight years. As he undertakes his new responsibility, I know that you will wish him well.'

Naturally, once Kenny had made public his decision to quit, there was a surge of public opinion begging him to change his mind. The Liverpool fans, as well as those inside the club, felt stunned; and some people found it difficult to accept that Dalglish was indeed walking out. But he went.

There had been those who had expressed the view, previously, that Kenny Dalglish didn't need the kind of money generated by his testimonial match against Real Sociedad at Anfield – some folk even felt it was a bit of a liberty for him to have such a game when so many on Merseyside were the victims of unemployment. But the critics had most certainly been in the minority, as was proved on the night, when more than 30,000 people turned up at Anfield; and that, surely, was an emphatic gesture of support for a player who had given countless thousands so much pleasure.

I know more than a few people in football who hold Dalglish in high regard. Joe Royle, a devout Evertonian, for one; and Gordon Strachan, who gave Aberdeen, Manchester United and Leeds United great service, for another. When a Sunday-afternoon charity match was staged at Oldham Athletic's Boundary Park, Kenny Dalglish was one of those who gave his services, though no one then had the slightest notion that before long he would be leaving Liverpool. As for Gordon Strachan, he recalled that when he and Dalglish were together on international duty, Kenny's behaviour on and off the field prompted him not only to take note, but to follow the Dalglish example and, in doing this, he had been able to prolong his own playing career at the top level.

Briefly, after the departure of Dalglish from Anfield, that old soldier, Ronnie Moran, took charge; but I was given an inkling of what would happen when I rang Bob Paisley one day, about another matter altogether, and during the course of the conversation I happened to ask what he thought Liverpool would do. Graeme Souness had already been tipped as a possible, in some quarters, but then, according to reports, he had expressed his intention of staying at Ibrox. So when Bob offered the opinion that 'this fellow', meaning Souness, would arrive at Anfield after all, I was surprised – but I took some notice.

Bob turned out to be right; Souness did indeed arrive, in April 1991; and immediately that posed more problems for the programme, since Liverpool were due to play a home game, and time was suddenly extremely pressing. I thought back to one of the rare times I had spoken to Graeme Souness, during his days as a Liverpool player, when – as I had done with Dalglish – I approached him about doing a book. Souness had declined, but I respected his answer and his honesty, as he told me: 'I've already promised Bob Harris [another journalist] that if I do a book, I'll do it with him.' That was fair enough.

Now Graeme Souness was back at Anfield, and as Liverpool's manager; so I needed to get a couple of pages done for the programme

Some of the men who occupied the chair in the boardroom at Anfield: Liverpool achieved a hat-trick of title successes during Sir John Smith's 17-year reign (top left). In contrast, Noel White (top right) lasted only 15 months as chairman. Present chairman David Moores is pictured below left, next to Liverpool's 'elder statesman' in the boardroom, Tom Saunders. During his career at Anfield, he was talent-spotter, confidant of the various managers, assessor of the opposition at home and abroad, and youth development officer.

The Shankly era marked the start of a tremendous rapport between Bill and the fans. As well as being the first manager to steer Liverpool to success in the FA Cup (and repeating this triumph in 1974, left), his team won the League Championship in 1964, with Shanks greeting skipper Ron Yeats (below).

That winning feeling: Kenny Dalglish (top left) strikes the winner against FC Bruges in 1978 in the final of the European Cup to crown his first season with Liverpool; Phil Neal (bottom right) registers his delight after having opened the scoring against AS Roma in 1984. The glory that was Rome: Tommy Smith and Ian Callaghan (left) – Liverpool's record-breaker in terms of appearances – celebrate victory after the 1977 European Cup Final. Bob Paisley (top right) won many honours for Liverpool, but perhaps the best of all was the European Cup.

The faces may change, but the trophies keep on coming to Anfield. In 1974, Emlyn Hughes was captain when Liverpool lifted the FA Cup for a second time (top right); Kevin Keegan, John Toshack and Steve Heighway (far right) celebrate Liverpool's double of season 1972–73 – League title and UEFA Cup; and Ian Rush, Ronnie Whelan, Alan Hansen and John Barnes share the title trophy (right).

Something to celebrate! For Bob Paisley, this was the start of his managerial career, and it's congratulations from backroom boys Ronnie Moran, Roy Evans and Joe Fagan. Joe and Roy were to follow in Bob's footsteps as manager of Liverpool (below). Joe Fagan (left) and the players who, under his management, won the European Cup in a penalty shoot-out in Rome in 1984 – not to mention the League Championship and the Milk Cup – to make it a unique treble in his first season as team boss.

immediately. I knew that from the moment he arrived, Souness would need 25 hours a day to cope with all the demands made upon him, not least from the media, and so – with a programme deadline to meet – I did what I thought was the best thing. Hurriedly, I typed out a piece which I felt Graeme Souness would agree to, and which would echo his thoughts, and I sent a copy to Anfield for him to read. I explained the situation, pointed out that time was of the essence and that this was why I had done the piece, and said that if he wanted to alter anything, or add anything, he should get in touch with me straight away.

After that, of course, I would contact him to talk about future issues and the way he wanted to do his notes for the programme, in collaboration with me. I didn't really anticipate any problems, so I was surprised when Sheila Walsh rang me to say that Graeme was doing his own notes for the programme. I didn't mind that – he was entitled to say what he wanted – but I asked Sheila to point out to the new manager one or two basic requirements. For instance, the fact that pages were not elastic, and so he would need to write something like 400 words in order to fill the space available. If there were too much, it would have to be cut; if there were too little, we would be left with a hole. Then I contacted the printer, told him to pull out the notes I had done, and to await the results of Mr Souness's efforts. In the event his contribution fell short, so we had to enlarge the type to make sure the notes filled the hole.

I cannot say I was best pleased with what had happened, but if Graeme Souness wanted to carry on writing his own articles for the programme, good luck to him. Just so long as he understood and accepted the requirements of the job. And, since I was about to relinquish the job of editing the programme, after almost 20 years, I knew that the following season the manager's notes would be someone else's headache, in any event.

So I made my exit, Liverpool appointed two journalists to do the job I had done for so long and that, I thought, was the end of the road for me, at least so far as my connection with Liverpool Football Club was concerned. I could not have been more wrong.

CHAPTER 5

A CRERAND WITH BITE
Graeme Souness the Player

*I'm hoping I'll be able to settle in quickly and that things go
well for me. I'm certain about one thing – the competition for
first-team places will keep me on my toes!*
GRAEME SOUNESS, AFTER HAVING SIGNED FOR LIVERPOOL
AS A PLAYER

LONG BEFORE Graeme Souness arrived at Liverpool to grace the
Anfield stage, a compatriot of his, Matt Busby, had gone back to his
native Scotland and spent £56,000 (regarded in those days to be a small
fortune) on one of Celtic's star players. His name was Pat Crerand, and
he was what folk used to call a wing-half. Paddy Crerand was far from
being a greyhound but he could certainly use his brain, which enabled
him to use his feet to telling effect, as he passed the ball with verve and
accuracy.

They said that when Crerand played well, Manchester United played
well; and it could be fairly claimed that when Souness was on song, so
were Liverpool. Each man orchestrated the play from midfield, each
man made a massive contribution to his club's success. Crerand was
one of United's aces when they won the European Cup in 1968;
Souness did the business for Liverpool in the same competition ten
years later, as well as in other finals.

Souness could be described as another Crerand – albeit one with a
dash more arrogance, perhaps, and one with even more bite. Like
Crerand, he could look after himself when the need arose and, again
like Crerand, there were times when he allowed his temper to surface.
He joined Liverpool from Middlesbrough in January 1978 for
£352,000 (then a record deal between British clubs), and inside a few
months he collected a European Cup medal after being hailed as the

man whose astute pass had enabled Kenny Dalglish to clip the ball over the keeper in the 1978 final against FC Bruges at Wembley.

Souness was credited with having made his European bow when he went on as substitute in Dusseldorf; in fact, he had played in European competition previously, for Tottenham Hotspur in the UEFA Cup in Iceland in season 1971–72. He told me: 'I was 18, and making my senior debut. I went on for Martin Peters about 30 minutes before the end.'

It was getting towards the end of season 1977–78 when he admitted that 'this season has been the strangest in my career . . . I've never played so few games in a season, because I've been out through injury or suspension, or because I was ineligible for the League Cup. So I feel as if I'm just starting now – with the European Cup final in sight.

'It's difficult to slot into a side when you're in and out, because it takes a bit of time to settle into the rhythm. But I've got a very firm impression of what makes Liverpool tick. They don't complicate anything; they make everything so simple. Nothing fancy; for me, that's Liverpool's secret. When I signed [on 10 January], I didn't really feel I could be playing in the European Cup final in May. At the time I arrived, such a notion would have been more like a mirage than even a dream. But what seemed a million miles away a few months ago has become a reality, and I hope I get into the action at Wembley on 10 May!'

He did, indeed, and he helped to fashion Liverpool's winner. That European Cup medal was the first of a string of honours he won with the Anfield club – he went on to captain Liverpool – and he stayed with them until 1984 when, after having scored in the penalty shoot-out in Rome to ensure another European triumph, he transferred his undoubted footballing talents to the Italian League, as he joined Sampdoria for a fee of around £650,000.

When Souness left Liverpool, there was no doubt that they missed him. They missed his vision, his passing ability, his intelligent play, his fierce shooting, not to mention his ability to play the game hard, when the occasion demanded. Appropriately, when his autobiography was published in 1985, it was entitled *No Half Measures*.

Born in Edinburgh, Souness had kicked off in football as an apprentice with Tottenham Hotspur at the age of 17, after having arrived at White Hart Lane as a 15-year-old hopeful. He stayed with

Spurs for four years, and he had been with Middlesbrough for five years by the time he joined Liverpool. Indeed, when Boro played at Anfield on the afternoon of Monday, 2 January 1978, his name figured on their team sheet. My programme notes for the match said that Souness was 'a highly-rated player who cost a modest £35,000 when he was signed from Spurs in December 1972. With Scotland through to the World Cup finals, he is eager to regain recognition at international level.' Souness wore the No. 4 jersey that January day, but he couldn't prevent Liverpool from winning 2–0.

By Saturday, 21 January, he was wearing the No. 10 shirt for Liverpool, and talking to me about his career. When he was at Tottenham, for instance, 'I was ambitious, and felt I wasn't getting ahead as quickly as I might be doing.' So when Middlesbrough offered him the chance to play regular first-team football (he had waited in vain for this opportunity with Spurs) he took it. He recalled how he went to the London club in the first place. 'I played for the Scotland Schoolboy side in an international at White Hart Lane, and Dave Mackay – then still a Spurs player – saw the match and recommended me to his club.' But the Spurs – Souness partnership wasn't to last. So it was on to Ayresome Park.

Souness recalled his first match for Boro' at Anfield (he had played against Liverpool around half a dozen times): 'I remember it vividly, because Middlesbrough won a League Cup-tie by the only goal of the game. The fact that my team had won here really meant something, and the atmosphere and the whole place were so impressive.'

He finished up on the winning side with Boro' on two other occasions as they beat Liverpool 2–0 at Anfield and 1–0 at Ayresome Park, and he told me: 'Apart from those results, Anfield and Old Trafford were the two games to which I looked forward every season, because they were something special.' And now he wore Liverpool's colours and had been capped three times by Scotland at full international level, after having won two Under-23 caps.

'If you think Graeme imagines his arrival at Anfield means he's got it made, you are mistaken,' I wrote. Souness looked at the situation, at the competition for places, and took this realistic view: 'I'm not anticipating anything – just because Liverpool have signed me for a big fee doesn't mean that I see myself as an established player in the first team here. I know, without being told, that I've got to do my stuff out there on the park, and so far as I'm concerned, this move means that

I'm starting afresh. I'm hoping that I'll be able to settle in quickly, and that things go well for me. And I'm certain about one thing – the competition for first-team places will keep me on my toes!'

The signing had gone through in a matter of minutes, after Souness had met Liverpool officials at an hotel in Leeds, and he said: 'Liverpool, for me, are the team of the moment . . . in fact, they've been the team for the last ten years and more.'

Souness made his debut in a game against West Brom, swiftly demonstrated his passing ability, and became the focal point of a midfield which boasted Terry McDermott, Ray Kennedy and Jimmy Case. Later, Souness wore the No. 11 jersey with distinction, and it was his incisive pass, allowing Dalglish to score, which paved the way for Liverpool to retain the European Cup in 1978.

He scored a European Cup hat-trick against CSKA Sofia, drilled home the goal which won the Milk Cup for Liverpool in the replayed final against Everton in 1984, and contributed goals and skilled football on many an important occasion – including a game against his first club, Tottenham Hotspur.

That day Souness demonstrated all the characteristics which made him such a fighter on the field of play, as he went on as substitute and showed Spurs what was what. He had been out because of a back injury, and when he plunged into the fray Liverpool were two goals down and looking as if they would wilt even further against the defensive strength of Graham Roberts and his team-mates. By the end of the 90 minutes Souness had helped Liverpool stage a comeback, and the final score was 2–2.

His game, it was recorded, was about 'delicate ball-play and accurate distribution, sprinkled with a touch of arrogance. He wanted to win, and demanded the same, indefatigable approach from his colleagues.' His ambitions to further his international career were well founded, for he finished up with a total of more than 50 caps, and he played more than 350 games and scored 56 goals for Liverpool.

I didn't have a great deal of contact with Souness after he had joined Liverpool, but I knew he was a rather snappy dresser, and one of his team-mates told me they called him Charlie, thus according him something of a 'champagne' image. I was at a testimonial dinner for Steve Heighway one evening, and Souness was there; I remember he was wearing a cream-coloured suit, and he looked very debonair, even handsome.

On the field of play, he sometimes used to bristle when he felt the referee was overdoing it, and as the years passed he fell foul of authority on more than one occasion. He was often controversial during his playing days; on the field, he showed that he could appear smooth as silk or as hard as nails – on his last European appearance at Anfield, in the Champions Cup semi-final, he was accused of having broken the jaw of Dinamo Bucharest's Lica Movila, who was himself reputed to be something of a hard man. He was, according to one report, 'held more in awe than affection by most fans'.

When he left Liverpool, it seemed that little was heard about him during his time with Sampdoria; then he made headline news in Britain once more as he joined Glasgow Rangers and became their player-manager. He soon made an impact there, as he signed players, including a number of big names from English League clubs such as Terry Butcher, Graham Roberts, Chris Woods, Mark Walters, Gary Stevens and Trevor Steven, as well as Trevor Francis, who had been in Italy. He also defied the wrath of those who said a Roman Catholic would never be allowed to play for Rangers – he went out and signed Mo Johnston. And he restored the glory days to Ibrox.

In leaving Italian football to return to Scotland and, in particular, Rangers, Souness was taking up a tremendous challenge, because while he had achieved success as a player, his ability as a manager was still to be proved – and he was being asked to restore the faded fortunes of what most people considered to be the number-one club north of the border.

Just as he had been involved in controversy as a player, so he became involved in controversy as a team boss; but he demonstrated that whatever anyone might think of his methods, he was capable of giving Rangers and their partisan fans what they wanted. It is probably fair to say that he was the strongest manager in Scotland – he had the power to do things his way, and he didn't hesitate to use that power to telling effect. Results showed that he succeeded, too. Indeed, there are those who would claim that Graeme Souness laid the basis for the continued success of the Ibrox club – and, possibly, there are those who would also claim that he felt he needed to display the same kind of authority when he returned to Liverpool as their manager.

In a sense, when Liverpool passed on the managerial post to Graeme Souness, they still kept the job in the family though, in his case, he had been away from Anfield for seven years, while Bob Paisley, Joe Fagan and Kenny Dalglish had all switched straight from their previous roles inside the club. Souness's name had been publicly canvassed for the job, but with his seemingly impregnable position at Ibrox and his shareholding in Rangers, the 'Souness for Liverpool' bandwagon appeared to have stalled, so far as the media were concerned.

However, it seemed as if he had had a change of heart, and so he arrived in April 1991 to take on the task of following in the footsteps of four men – Shankly, Paisley, Fagan and Dalglish – who had all, in their various ways, kept Liverpool Football Club at the top of the pile. And Graeme Souness, in his first signed programme article, had this to say to the Anfield faithful:

'I cannot put into words the feelings that I have had in the last week. I could come out with many clichés, but I just want to say *it's great to be back*. As I am sure you have read, it is not my intention to make big changes. There is a wealth of experience here in Ronnie Moran, Roy Evans and the rest of the staff, which I intend to call upon when required. Why change a formula which has been the most successful in the history of British football?

'My philosophy is very simple. I demand that my players give 100 per cent to Liverpool Football Club every time they cross that white line. We all know it is impossible for us to play well every game, but if I get that 100 per cent commitment I can ask for no more. The players here have got to realise what an honour it is to play for this club – the most famous and the most successful football club in the world. You can never make any promises in football, but what I can say is that every effort will be made to maintain the standards this club has set in the past.

'As a player here I fully understood and accepted the disciplines and responsibilities that go with being a Liverpool player, and I fully expect that those who follow will also be equally committed to the cause. Our immediate aim is to win the League Championship and, whilst matters are not entirely in our own hands, we will strive to achieve our objective.

'In football, anything can happen, and in my book there is no such thing as a lost cause. Liverpool supporters are regarded throughout Europe as the most passionate and knowledgeable spectators in the game. When I played here the support was vital to our performances.

A player never means to make a bad pass or to make what appears to be an obvious mistake. I know it is hard to contain criticism at that particular time, because you, the supporter, sometimes become frustrated; but at the end of the day we all want the same thing – continued success for Liverpool Football Club. I would ask you to please get behind the team, especially in the run-in to the Championship. Your very special kind of support is vital!'

And, of course, Graeme Souness was certainly not understating the case when it came to the fans. The task that he had undertaken was to prove one in which, to a degree, he did succeed, in that under his management, Liverpool carried off the FA Cup. But overall, the Souness years became noted more for the controversy they generated than for trophies on the Anfield sideboard.

CHAPTER 6

THE SOUNESS SAGA
Graeme Souness the Manager

Nobody is ever going to be bigger than Liverpool . . .
unfortunately, it looks as though Graeme Souness is trying.
FORMER LIVERPOOL PLAYER, TOMMY SMITH

ONE QUOTE by Graeme Souness which did *not* appear in any of the
newspapers, tabloid or otherwise, was: 'I daren't play in a five-a-side at
Anfield, because if I collapsed, no one would give me the kiss of life!'
That statement came from him towards the end of season 1992–93,
when his managerial career at Liverpool appeared to be hanging by a
thread – indeed, it was being predicted that at almost any minute you
could expect the axe to fall. One thing you had to say in Souness's
favour, though; despite the unrelenting pressures of the previous weeks,
and the fact that he appeared to be still doing a tight-rope act to retain
his job, he had also managed to retain his sense of humour.

Little more than 12 months previously his very life, never mind his
job, had been hanging by a thread as he was taken into hospital to
undergo open-heart surgery. I knew exactly what it was like because,
ten years earlier, I had undergone the same, traumatic experience, and
I felt that Graeme Souness must be feeling more than a little
apprehensive about his impending operation. In which case, I also felt
that he might welcome a timely bit of encouragement from someone
who had suffered in a similar fashion.

So I wrote him a note, and I told him how I had come through all right,
despite a few minor alarms. I also said that while he was awaiting surgery
in the Alexandra Hospital at Cheadle, a few miles from my home, if he
felt like picking up the phone and giving me a call, I would be more than
happy to have a chat with him. I put the note in an envelope, sealed it,
then drove to the hospital to deliver the note personally.

I realised, of course, that his time would be largely occupied with visits from the medical staff and tests before the operation, so I didn't ask to see him; I simply made certain he was indeed occupying one of the hospital rooms, then I left the note with the woman at reception and headed back home . . . and, of course, I was somewhat curious as to whether or not I would hear from him.

Like me, Souness lived to tell the tale, though not without experiencing a setback, and although I never did receive a phone call or an acknowledgment to my note, I was still very glad to learn that in the long run he appeared to have made a good recovery.

Twelve months after his operation, the career of Graeme Souness at Liverpool seemed destined to be over; certainly betting odds were on his being sacked. During the final week of the season, indeed, the will-he-won't-he-go? saga made headlines on a daily basis, and when it came to the last home game, against Tottenham Hotspur, on 8 May 1993, the portents appeared to be ominous.

'Straight from Souness', the feature which had appeared regularly on pages 2 and 3 of the *Anfield Review*, Liverpool's match-day programme, was missing. Instead, there was a message from the chairman, David Moores, headed 'Thanks to All Our Fans'. In the article, Moores thanked the supporters for the loyalty they had shown throughout the season and he pointed out, rightly, that Liverpool had enjoyed the best attendances in the Premier League, despite the fact that there were no trophies to show for the team's efforts.

He had something else to say: he admitted that the Anfield postbag had been heavy, with many of the fans expressing their disappointment over the season's results. 'Others,' Moores said, 'have asked pointedly what can be done to improve the situation.' To which he gave this answer: 'Everything which is humanly possible.'

Moores added: 'One of my predecessors once said that Liverpool FC was all about winning things and had no other purpose. He was absolutely right.' He went on: 'The board review the situation on a weekly basis, and it must be remembered that we are supporters, too!'

Although by then I had been retired as programme editor for two years, I had still kept my finger on the pulse at Anfield, and I had a pretty fair idea of what had been happening at the club. For instance, I had learned that the programme notes from Moores were a last-minute job, and that there was a bit of a flutter at the printer's, because the

'Straight from Souness' column had not only been written for the final programme of the season (the game against Spurs), but it was practically on the press.

Behind the scenes, at the start of the final week, there were hurried discussions when the matter of Souness's column was broached to chief executive Peter Robinson, and the decision was taken to pull the manager's notes out. Indeed, virtually at the last minute, an eight-page section of the programme, including the Souness column, had to be rapidly rejigged, and the message from David Moores slotted in.

So, almost on the eve of that final home game, it seems that there remained great uncertainty inside Anfield itself about the future of Liverpool's manager. At that late stage, was he staying – or was he about to be 'on his bike'? After all, when you discard your manager's programme notes, after they have appeared on a regular basis for a couple of years, people are liable to draw their own conclusions, and I kept being told during the final week of the season that Graeme Souness was indeed going, and that but for a 'leak' about a Sunday-night boardroom meeting at the beginning of the week, it would have become an accomplished fact, even before the game against Tottenham Hotspur.

The Souness mystery deepened further when, while Liverpool fans were digesting the message from Moores, the manager made a surprise appearance – not at Anfield, for the final game, but at Coventry City's Highfield Road ground. With him was Liverpool's former youth-development officer, Tom Saunders. It was claimed that Souness was checking on a player as a possible signing – this, of course, while the media were even then speculating intensely upon that day being his last one as Liverpool's team boss.

It was not only the media which produced the pressure on Liverpool and Graeme Souness. One of the club's longest-serving and most-respected players, Ian Rush, had something to say. Rush, remember, had been extremely upset several weeks previously about the way in which he had learned he had been dropped from the team to play Sheffield Wednesday at Hillsborough; but he had got over this and made a comeback. Despite his criticism of Souness after having been axed, Rush was not noted for becoming involved in the affairs of the club. His job was to play for Liverpool and give of his best. But he came out publicly and demanded that the club should come clean and say whether Souness was in or out. However, while Liverpool still remained silent, the rumours gathered apace.

Interviewed on the radio after the victory over Spurs, Rush expertly sidestepped some awkward questions. He was asked if he thought Graeme Souness would still be Liverpool's manager after the weekend and – even more pointedly – if he personally wanted Souness to stay at the helm. The Welsh international said it wasn't up to him to decide the manager's future and, as for wanting him to stay . . . well, Rush simply indicated that he would be doing his best for the club and for himself, no matter who was the manager. Soccer diplomacy at its best.

One man who did go against the tide of public opinion that Saturday was Jimmy Armfield, the former England full-back who had managed Bolton Wanderers and Leeds United, and who was working as a journalist (towards the end of 1993, the Football Association handed him the job of head-hunting the next England manager). Armfield, in fact, was at Anfield that afternoon, and he joined in the great debate about Souness. Indeed, he seemed to have a gut feeling that the manager would hang on to his job. Jimmy turned out to be right, too.

Meanwhile, Peter Robinson was telling the press that Souness had gone to Coventry 'of his own choice' to watch a player, thereby knocking on the head any suggestion that he had been 'sent to Coventry' to keep him out of the way of the media men who had flocked to Anfield. Souness himself declared: 'I am still a working manager, and I am here today to do a job.' The word 'still' might have been taken by some people to indicate that Souness himself was unsure how long he would be in charge of team affairs at Liverpool.

That same evening Robinson spoke again, this time in reply to criticism of the way the club had handled matters. He claimed Liverpool had been put under 'unfair pressure', saying, 'It is not our style to be indecisive, and we would like to have handled it differently. We have been accused of indecision, but it has not been like that. We said as long ago as January, after the FA Cup defeat by Bolton, that we would review matters at the end of the season, then make an announcement. The board tried to meet privately last Sunday, but because of a 'leak' we were hounded by the media, and have been ever since. We can understand how our supporters feel because we have not come out with a statement, but we feel we have been put under unfair pressure.'

The 'leak' to which Peter Robinson referred threw up another mystery. Who was the mole who had blown the gaff about that Sunday-night board meeting? But if no one was owning up, chairman Moores made one thing abundantly clear: should the identity of the mole be discovered, his feet 'won't touch the ground'. And I was informed that the leak had provoked something akin to fury among the top brass at Anfield.

So, then, who *was* the 'mole'? That, of course, would be telling; and I am not in a position to divulge names. Yet someone who had close and regular contact with Anfield suggested to me that there could well be two prime suspects, and he did mention names. For various reasons, when I considered matters, both appeared to be plausible; yet, for various other reasons, I had my doubts that either person would have risked becoming a media informant. But somebody did blow the gaff and, after further consideration, I came to the conclusion that someone else might have been the source of the leak – someone whom you might term 'the third man', as in the Harry Lime theme film. To the best of my knowledge, however, no single name emerged as being the culprit, and there were no official developments.

Souness himself, having celebrated his 40th birthday amid such a cloak-and-dagger atmosphere (he wasn't invited to the secret board meeting) phoned his chairman to find out if, as he put it, 'we were all pulling together'. And so many rumours were rife. I was told by more than one person that Moores and Kenny Dalglish had played golf in Marbella, that Kenny had been asked (not necessarily in Marbella) if he would consider a return to Liverpool. I was told he had asked for time, to consult his wife, and that he had rejected a return on the grounds that his family was against such a move. I was also told his right-hand man at Blackburn, Ray Harford, would be going back south – it was said his wife had set her face against moving up north – and that Harford was bound for Chelsea. It was also whispered to me that Souness would be teaming up with his old pal, Kenny, at Ewood Park; that there was no chance of a Dalglish comeback at Anfield; and that Dalglish and Harford were 'happy as pigs in muck' at Blackburn.

Amid such a welter of gossip, it had become virtually impossible to separate fact from fiction. But one of my 'inside' informants was adamant about one thing: according to him, Steve Heighway had been asked by Liverpool if he would consider stepping up from his job as youth-development officer to take over the managerial reins, but that he had declined with thanks.

Now, I have known Steve for more than 20 years, so I would never have embarrassed him by demanding to know if he had indeed rejected the chance to manage Liverpool. However, I believe I know him well enough to feel reasonably certain that, had he been asked, his answer would indeed have been 'Thanks – but no thanks'. Why? Because of the make-up of the man himself.

I got to know Steve very shortly after his arrival at Anfield, and for him, professional football was a whole new ball game. His thoughts had been centred around becoming a teacher, once he had gained his degree and left Warwick University. It took him a fair amount of time to become acclimatised to the rough-and-tumble humour, and the attitude of people who had had no other ambition but to play football for a living and, in particular, to play for Liverpool.

Steve overcame nagging doubts to stay the course and earn the respect of his bosses and team-mates; he became Liverpool through and through. As time went by and Steve took on the job of Liverpool's youth-development officer, I learned that he was becoming increasingly respected by the people whose opinions mattered at Anfield, and that he was regarded as someone who knew his job. So it came as no surprise when I read his name among the list of those being tipped as possibles to succeed Graeme Souness. Even then I doubted very much if Steve would want to take on such an awesome task, flattered though he would surely have been, were he asked. So if Liverpool were seeking a replacement for Souness, they would have to search elsewhere.

Another name on the agenda was that of John Toshack, who had taken Swansea up to the First Division, then enjoyed success in Spain, where he had been in charge of team affairs at Real Sociedad, switched to coaching at Real Madrid, and then returned to Real Sociedad. From my talks with Steve Heighway in his playing days, and from my personal knowledge of Tosh, I knew that he was a deep thinker about the game. When he arrived at Liverpool, as a £110,000 signing, it was said that a hat-trick for Cardiff City had made up Bill Shankly's mind about him – and there was a lovely story attributed to Shanks about their first meeting in Liverpool. The story goes that as Shankly guided him towards Anfield and they stood together on a pedestrian crossing,

Liverpool's team boss brought it to Toshack's attention that 'the traffic stops for us, in this city!'.

Toshack certainly made his own mark with Liverpool, not least as the foil for Kevin Keegan – some folk claimed they had a telepathic understanding. And Toshack the thinker used to take part in the backroom discussions about football in general and Liverpool's previous match in particular. I knew Tosh to be a player with brains, and he was articulate with it. But, as with Steve Heighway, I felt pretty confident that if Graeme Souness did get the chop, John Toshack would not be his successor. I remembered when Joe Fagan had bowed out, and Toshack's name was in the frame for the job then. A member of the hierarchy at Anfield dismissed that possibility to me in such a definite manner that I doubted very much if there would be a change of heart, should Souness go – although one report did suggest that Real Sociedad would not release their manager.

Liverpool hadn't sacked a manager for 45 years, but during the final week of season 1992–93, the media had a field-day; and the consensus of opinion appeared to be that the axe was about to fall. Even on Sunday, 9 May – 24 hours after a scintillating, 6–2 victory over Tottenham Hotspur – the general verdict was that Souness would be sacked.

But, like Jimmy Armfield, one newspaper man, Richard Bott, of the *Sunday Express*, got it absolutely right when he tipped Liverpool's manager to keep his job, although he added a rider to the effect that 'Souness may only receive a stay of execution because of his compensation demands – believed to be £1 million.' Liverpool, it was said, would make an announcement within 48 hours 'after another bewildering day of uncertainty'.

Only a few weeks previously, another sportswriter, Joe Melling, of the *Mail on Sunday*, had published an exclusive story that Graeme Souness and Liverpool would be parting company, with the manager being the recipient of a golden handshake worth half a million pounds. Based on my inside knowledge of the club, I must admit that I found this story more credible than the one which suggested Souness would walk away with double that amount.

Some 12 months before the final act of the 1993 drama (a press conference on the afternoon of 9 May), I had been told that Souness was declaring his readiness to leave Liverpool, if that was what the board wanted, provided he was compensated by a £1 million pay-off. As soon as that story was related to me, I said: 'It won't happen – take my word for it.' I felt sure that I knew my Liverpool. I might not doubt the credibility of my informant; I could see the logic of such a demand from a manager whose contract still had more than three years to run – a lucrative contract which might well bring him that kind of money, were he to remain at the club for his full term. But not for a moment did I believe he would pick up the full sum.

What made me so certain? Well, for a start, one of Liverpool's employees had made his opinion crystal clear when he described the club with the words 'They're as mean as muck'. It was a description I didn't totally endorse although, at the same time, I knew Liverpool were penny-wise and pound-conscious, and I doubted they would part with £1 million to sever the bond with a manager whose contract still had three years to run. They would bite the bullet with that one. Half a million might just be a feasible proposition, especially in view of the fact that, right from the start, Souness's reign as manager had been clouded by controversy – and that, I felt sure, was something the top brass at the club would have abhorred.

Graeme Souness had been a controversial character, on occasion, during his playing days; but from the moment he walked into the building as Liverpool's new manager, in the spring of 1991, he became the focus of gossip and stories which were blazoned across the front and back pages of the tabloid press. The second time around, it became a war of words as the papers criticised Souness, and as he blasted back.

There were stories about his marital problems, stories about his romance with Karen Levy (whom he subsequently married), stories about his heart-bypass operation, about results and the lack of results, about his relationship with the media, with the powers-that-be at Anfield and with some of the players there. Souness sold his heart-bypass story exclusively to *The Sun*, a newspaper reviled by many Liverpudlians because of the way it had handled the Hillsborough disaster. By doing business with *The Sun*, Souness brought upon himself the censure of many Liverpool supporters and, in the final analysis, he found himself having to apologise in the match-day programme as he admitted that, with hindsight, he had been in error. There was an occasion, also, after he had slated his players, when he confessed that, in football parlance, he had gone over the top with his criticism.

Almost immediately after his bypass operation, there was the story about him slipping away for a few hours from the Alexandra Hospital at Cheadle, on the outskirts of Manchester; and there was the story about him having suffered a setback – one which meant that he had to go into intensive care again. Thirty-two days after his operation, which had involved a triple bypass, he went to Wembley with Liverpool – some considered that to be foolhardy, rather than an act of bravery. He looked pale and wan and, after millions had seen the club doctor place a restraining hand on his shoulder as Michael Thomas scored, Souness admitted: 'The doctor was under orders to keep me calm.' He didn't always remain calm, though, whether it was at Wembley or elsewhere.

One of the most overused words heard during the Souness era at Anfield was 'rift'. It was applied to his relationship with the fans, with the media, with some of his own players, with directors and with the footballing authorities. Trevor Francis, who played under Souness at Glasgow Rangers, termed him 'strong, forceful and ruthless'; and another ex-Ranger, Terry Butcher, said Souness was 'not the sort of guy to accept what he sees at a club who, by their own standards, have lost their way a little. If that means treading on egos to get to grips with the problem, then he is the man.'

There are those who would argue forcibly that Souness himself is not short on ego, and a former Liverpool player, Tommy Smith, didn't mince his words as he offered his opinion: 'Nobody is ever going to be bigger than Liverpool . . . unfortunately, it looks as though Graeme Souness is trying.' And one commentator on the Anfield scene suggested that Souness sought virtually absolute power – something no manager, not even Bill Shankly, would ever have got. It was reported that Souness was demanding no less than the right to manage the club from top to bottom and that this included replacing the long-serving Ronnie Moran with his own choice of assistant – though he had already taken another former Liverpool player, Phil Boersma, back to Anfield. An official at another club told me, after his team had played at Anfield, that he had come away with the impression that there was a 'them and us' atmosphere in the Liverpool camp, and certainly Phil Thompson, who had the red blood of Liverpool coursing through his veins, ended up at odds with the manager, because he was sacked.

When it came to signings, the list of ins and outs grew at an impressive rate – more impressive, indeed, than the results Liverpool achieved on the field. Neil Ruddock, Nigel Clough, Mark Wright, Dean Saunders, Paul Stewart (all costing £2 million or more apiece), Mark Walters, Michael Thomas, David James (each costing £1 million-plus), and an assortment of Scandinavians (Torben Piechnik, Stig-Inge Bjornebye), plus a Hungarian international, Istvan Kozma, were just some of the players Souness recruited.

Every signing is a gamble, of course, and after having failed to live up to expectations at Anfield, Dean Saunders was sold to Aston Villa, with Liverpool dropping a considerable chunk of cash – something which, I feel sure, would not have gone down well inside the Anfield boardroom. Not only do Liverpool dislike losing matches, they don't like losing money, either. Saunders, indeed, was said to have been offered to Nottingham Forest (who had been in the original bidding for him) in exchange for Roy Keane. Keane was to cost Manchester United close on £4 million when he did move.

Mark Wright also had an in-and-out spell at Anfield, and he was another to be linked with Forest, with the names of Nigel Clough and Stuart Pearce being mentioned as possibles in a swap deal. Clough, of course, later arrived at Anfield as a £2 million man. As for Kozma, the 27-year-old Hungarian Souness signed from Scottish club Dunfermline for £300,000, the Liverpool manager expressed confidence that the new recruit would be able to cope with the demands of Premier League football. Souness said: 'He's played 30 times for his country, is used to the big-time atmosphere, and my belief, with respect to the players at Dunfermline, is that if he's playing with better players he can be a real influence.' By the time Liverpool met Tottenham Hotspur at the start of season 1993–94, Kozma had made no more than a handful of first-team appearances, and he had returned to his native land.

By then, Souness had sold not only Saunders, but Steve Staunton, Ray Houghton, Gary Ablett, Peter Beardsley, Jimmy Carter, Steve McMahon and Barry Venison, while Swedish international Glenn Hysen had disappeared from the Anfield scene. Souness was to admit later that selling Staunton had been a mistake – 'last season we had such a lot of injuries, and he could have played in so many positions.' Ablett and Beardsley joined Everton, with Beardsley giving Souness a parting vote of confidence: 'I think he will make Liverpool what they were five or ten years ago, when he was a player at Anfield. He has demonstrated he is going to do things his way.' And to those who criticised the sales of Houghton and McMahon, Souness retorted that they had wanted to leave Liverpool.

Questions (and they appear to be valid) were asked not only about sales and signings, but about the relentless crop of injuries Liverpool had to endure during the first two years's of the Souness era. Souness assured fans and directors that training methods hadn't changed since he was a player, but one sportswriter, Colin Wood, who had covered the Anfield scene for more than 30 years, maintained: 'Still an answer is needed – otherwise, Liverpool may never be at full strength, and the wish of Souness to be judged fairly may never be granted.'

Keeping calm had seldom been easy for Graeme Souness, and when he fell foul of authority yet again, towards the end of season 1992–93, he was accused of having used abusive language towards a linesman. By then he had been the target of criticism from the media, and the general view seemed to be that he was on his way out from Liverpool.

That was not the first occasion there had been suggestions of his departure – either of his own volition, or because he had been pushed – because straight after the 1992 FA Cup final he was admitting that someone had asked to talk to him, but that 'I said it was too early . . . I was in a hospital bed, and didn't want to discuss anything before the final'. His name then was linked with the Italian club, Genoa, whose millionaire backer, Aldo Spinely, was said to be ready to pay Souness £1 million a year as a salary, with a luxury car and a villa thrown in as perks. Genoa had despatched Liverpool from the UEFA Cup earlier in the season, and Spinely declared that Souness (who spoke Italian, a legacy from his days at Sampdoria), 'shows incredible determination . . . there are very few trainers in the world willing to give so much of themselves to football as this man'.

Souness himself had already spoken about the pressures of management and how he had been affected by them in the early stages. 'When I was new to this job, I took it home with me. It ruined one relationship . . . I'm not going to allow it to happen again.' His marriage to Danielle had broken up because, she claimed, he had given too much of himself to Rangers. Now, nine months after heart surgery, Souness was saying: 'I try not to let it [the job] get through to the people close to me.'

By the spring of 1993, Danielle was having her say in *The People*, and I'll bet that did wonders for Souness's morale and his image in the

Anfield boardroom – though the *Daily Mail*'s noted columnist, Ian Wooldridge, was moved to express his sympathy with Liverpool's manager because the Sunday tabloid's story was published on the very day the club was about to pronounce judgment on the future of Graeme Souness.

'I have never met the man in my life, and am not particularly bothered whether I ever do,' wrote Wooldridge. 'I simply feel for him because a newspaper encouraged his wife to trample all over him the very weekend that half Liverpool was branding him a failure.' That particular newspaper, I might add, also trampled all over Liverpool chairman David Moores – and myself – and I shall have more to say about that matter later. As for Graeme Souness, in the summer of 1995 he took time off from his new job with Galatasaray to go to the High Court and sue *The People* for libel. It was reported, also, that he would continue to receive payments from Liverpool, despite his move to Turkey. 'Souness', it was said, 'has been paid £6,000 a week since leaving Anfield in January last year, under an agreement which still has ten months to run'. When the libel action ended, the former Rangers and Liverpool manager had been awarded £750,000 damages, although it was announced that Mirror Group Newspapers planned to appeal. As for the Galatasaray job, Souness said it had come 'out of the blue and I'm excited by it'.

CHAPTER 7

LAST-GASP REPRIEVE
Then Souness Goes

I don't want people who just talk about it. People, even so-called stars, can say they are fully committed and passionate about this club. But talk is cheap, and we have a lot of talkers here. What matters is when you cross that white line on the pitch.
GRAEME SOUNESS

GRAEME SOUNESS was under no illusions about what he was taking on when he agreed to become Liverpool's manager. It was 'a monstrous job . . . my predecessors have achieved so much that if we don't win something each season, the manager is bound to be regarded as a failure'. As time went by, he aroused mixed emotions – among the fans, in the boardroom, among his players, and in the media. There came a time when the supporters, polled in a national magazine, voted for or against Souness – with 70 per cent of the opinion that he should be sacked. But, of course, he wasn't.

There seemed to be a chink of light amid the gloom for Liverpool's team boss as he was voted Manager of the Month for January 1992; yet results went against him for a prolonged period after that, as Liverpool hovered too close to the relegation zone for comfort during the following campaign, while there was humiliation in Cup competition.

When Liverpool went out of the Rumbelows Cup, beaten 1–0 by Third Division Peterborough, it was labelled the most shocking result in the club's 99-year history. With Liverpool celebrating their centenary, even worse befell them as Second Division Bolton Wanderers knocked them out in an FA Cup replay at Anfield – a debacle which led Souness to lash his players publicly.

Bolton's victory was termed Liverpool's 'most infamous defeat since non-League Worcester beat them in 1959', and Souness was prompted to complain: 'You can have players with all the ability in the world, but when they go out not wanting to run around and fight for the ball as much as other teams, then you are going to lose. The way the game has gone, you have to look for players with desire, rather than ability.' Then came the stinging words: 'Too many of ours have no real interest or love of the football club. They are only interested in getting another move or another lump of money. My job is to get the people on the pitch to be part of Liverpool Football Club; people who want to die for the cause. I need eleven players like that, not seven, eight or nine. I don't want people who just talk about it. People, even so-called stars, can say they are fully committed and passionate about this club. But talk is cheap, and we have a lot of talkers here. What matters is when you cross that white line on the pitch.'

When it came to the stage where there was only the final League game against Tottenham Hotspur to go, most of the media felt certain that Souness would be going, too. But he survived, despite the fact that he had been in disciplinary trouble yet again. He was already under suspension, so far as UEFA were concerned, and he incurred a fine of £500 after having been found guilty of misconduct following a game against Crystal Palace at Selhurst Park.

Liverpool's manager was not slow to conduct his own defence in the war of words with the media, though, and when asked if he thought he had been fairly treated by the press, he claimed that 'there are those who have been around longer than the rest who feel they are entitled to special privileges'.

That barb stung the *Daily Mail*'s Colin Wood into writing: 'As the one who has been around the longest, all I ask is access, with the rest, to do my job properly.' Wood accused Souness of wanting 'to consign me and the rest of the Mersey media to the deep freeze', and he urged manager and club to 'call off the cold war, bring back the warmth'.

The London media men took Souness to task, as well, with Wood's colleague, Neil Harman, reflecting upon the fact that Liverpool's manager had not appeared for the past three press conferences. Harman wrote that since Souness had succeeded Kenny Dalglish, Liverpool 'have staggered, rather than walked, through the storm'. Harman also wrote of Souness's 'insensitive collaboration with the newspaper despised for its coverage of Hillsborough, the strange sacking of that great servant, Phil Thompson, the dramatic fall-off in season-ticket sales (I am told the so-called "Souness Factor" is as much responsible as the recession and increase in prices), the did-he-or-didn't-he-resign-before-the-FA-Cup-final saga'.

In the autumn of 1992, Colin Wood was writing about 'the atmosphere choking the place' and terming it 'the worst I have felt since my first visit to see Bill Shankly's rising force wallop Wolves 4–0 back in the ice age of February 1962'. And from my personal knowledge of Wood over 30 years, I can vouch for the fact that he doesn't lightly dip his pen in vitriol. For one thing, when you are covering the affairs of a club such as Liverpool day in, day out, you don't go out of your way to antagonise people – not if you've any sense. And Wood has plenty of that. He is also a very responsible journalist, and showed he was prepared to fight for the freedom to do his job.

Souness does deserve credit for quite a lot of things. I have a memory of him driving down from Glasgow, when he was Rangers' supremo, to play in a charity match at Oldham one not particularly nice winter's afternoon. It was a Sunday, and the match was in aid of dependants of two policemen who had been shot at an M62 service station. Souness, like Kenny Dalglish and Phil Neal, was among those who answered the call from Oldham Athletic's manager at the time, Joe Royle. He didn't ask for any reward for playing in the game, and he drove back the same evening to get on with his job at Ibrox.

One of the players he signed for both Rangers and Liverpool was Mark Walters, and he stood up for Souness when he said: 'If I had remained with Aston Villa and not joined Rangers, I wouldn't be at Anfield now. I matured as a player and a person under Graeme Souness at Ibrox. He taught me about preparing for matches. He showed me the value of the right lifestyle if I wanted to get the best out of my ability. On the field, the manager has made me a more intelligent player. I'm more appreciative of my colleagues and have improved my tactical awareness.' Later, however, Walters was debating his future at Anfield after having been farmed out on loan to Stoke City and then Wolves.

Two of the players Souness sold came back to haunt him. Peter Beardsley struck Everton's winner in a Merseyside derby game, and Dean Saunders scored twice as Aston Villa beat Liverpool 4–2.

Souness was reported to have walked out of the post-match press conference, having made a brief reference to Liverpool's injury crisis. But when asked if Saunders' scoring against his old club was 'inevitable', Souness, it was said, 'glared at the questioner and then stalked out'.

Souness was to concede that on occasion he had overstepped the mark with his criticisms of his players; yet he remained true to his beliefs, insisting that come what may, he would never desert the footballing precepts upon which Liverpool's reputation had been founded. 'The purists want to see us, and I intend keeping it that way, no matter how opponents try to stop us. I'll survive or fall going down that road. The way Liverpool play is the right way.'

After Liverpool's FA Cup humiliation by Bolton at Anfield, it was being said openly that 'only the steadfast support of chairman David Moores is keeping Souness at the helm'. But it was also being observed that 'Even Moores . . . faces a tough task persuading the rest of the board that the Scot should stay'. And by February 1993, Moores was sending this message to his fellow-fans: 'Being halfway down the Premier League and out of three major Cup competitions is totally unacceptable. The board have chosen to stay calm, to support the manager and team and do everything else we can to overcome the present difficulties.'

But there was a sting in the tail. 'At Anfield, temporary setbacks apart, no one will ever settle for second-best. We are here to win things, to be famous, to be a source of pride to our fans throughout the world. Whatever it takes to regain that position will be done. No one knows that better than the board and Graeme Souness.'

The manager himself admitted he was 'glad to see the back of 1992 . . . I thought 1993 would be better'. But it most definitely was not, as Paul Stewart joined the list of players pondering their future and Oldham, fighting for Premier League survival, inflicted defeat upon the men from Anfield for the first time in 71 years. That was in the final, fateful week of season 1992–93, when the future of Souness was being discussed almost hourly.

Four days after the Oldham game and 24 hours after the crushing victory over Spurs, Liverpool called the media men to Anfield and announced the shock news: Souness was staying; director Tony Ensor was going; Roy Evans would be promoted to assistant manager; Tom

Saunders would become a director. No mention was made of Phil Boersma's position, although it was later stated that Ronnie Moran, who had served the club for more than 40 years, would be given an extension to his contract. And ultimately Boersma did make his exit from Anfield.

Tom Saunders, former manager of the England Schoolboy team, had pioneered the trail when he became the club's first youth-development officer during the days of Bill Shankly's management. A down-to-earth man, he had performed various roles during his time at Anfield – travelling all over Europe, for instance, on spying missions for the club, as he assessed opposing teams. He had been a talent-spotter, confidant of successive managers, and even after retirement – and a heart bypass operation – he had continued to be involved. On match days, he remained a familiar, cloth-capped figure as he sat in the dug-out. His opinions carried a great deal of weight and he was held in high esteem by the people who mattered at the club. Now, at the age of 70, he was clearly being retained as an elder statesman on the board.

And Roy Evans? Now there was a turn-up for the book. Here was a man who had twice been passed over for the top job, and now, suddenly, he was being named as the No. 2 to Souness. Evans had been at the club since he left school, though he played only a handful of first-team games. He had been signed by Bill Shankly as a 15-year-old, had served Liverpool almost 30 years, much of that time on reserve-team duty, either as a player or on the backroom side. As player and coach, he collected nine Central League medals, and when he was only 26 years of age Bob Paisley was asking him to hang up his boots and take charge of the reserves. After some heart-searching, Evans had agreed. Later, he became trainer-coach to the first team.

After his appointment as assistant manager, he pledged 'maximum support' to Graeme Souness, saying: 'I am a cog in a big wheel . . . I am only part of a team. The manager can discuss his problems with me and we may not always be in agreement . . . football is that way. But his decisions are final, and I will always support them to the hilt.'

Evans also talked about the five managers he had served: Shankly 'fired my enthusiasm'; Paisley's knowledge of the game 'was uncanny'; Joe Fagan 'believed in honest football and simplicity'; Kenny Dalglish was 'the first of our young bosses, and I learned a lot from him'; and Graeme Souness was 'a very determined man who calls a spade a spade'.

Of his own playing career (nine League games, one League Cup appearance and one outing in Europe) Roy Evans conceded: 'I suppose I was not good enough for regular first-team selection, but there was no disgrace in understudying the players who were at Anfield. They were among the best in Britain.' An honest appraisal from someone who had played for England Schoolboys and had been a Liverpool supporter all his life.

And what about Tony Ensor, the director who had decided to walk out of the boardroom? While the press conference was in progress, Ensor sat to one side of the trophy room then, after David Moores had had his say, confirmed that after eight years he had quit as a director 'because of a genuine difference of opinion as to how the club should be run'. He added that he remained a shareholder 'and a supporter of this club', and he sincerely hoped 'that these decisions which the board reached will be vindicated and lead to further success'.

The major decision, of course, was the survival of Souness. The die had been cast, at least for the immediate future, and Moores told the world that the manager would be staying 'for the three years of his contract and, I hope, for much longer than that'. In football, when a manager is given a vote of confidence from his chairman, there is a tendency for people to smirk knowingly – such a vote of confidence is often followed by the kiss of death. But in this instance, Moores had nailed his colours firmly to the mast when it came to expressing support for the manager. And it was clear that he was genuinely backing Souness.

As for the manager, he admitted that he had gone to a board meeting at which things had been said; things 'that made me doubt if I had the support of all the board'. Moores revealed that this had 'sparked off a whole series of discussions within the board and with Graeme. During our discussions, we told him that if he wanted to leave we would pay out his contract in full. He told us very clearly that he did not want the money; he wanted to stay.'

Souness is recognised as a man not short of a few bob, and he also comes across as a proud man. Pride would surely have driven him on, as he sought to stay in his job. It's interesting to speculate what went on in those 'boardroom discussions'; you might wonder, for instance, if David Moores – another with real money – indicated that if the manager went, he would go, too . . . and take his money with him. An unlikely scenario, perhaps, considering his commitment to Liverpool. He was generally acknowledged as Souness's biggest backer in the boardroom, and it had become crystal clear how at least one director, Tony Ensor, felt. And knowing people such as Sir John Smith, Noel White, Jack Cross and Peter Robinson, I simply cannot see any of them having taken kindly to the sort of publicity to which club and manager were subjected during the first two years of the Souness era. In fact, I believe they would have been aghast at some of the headlines they saw, and I can almost hear muttered curses along the corridors of power at Anfield.

Only a matter of weeks before the club revealed its decision to retain Graeme Souness, I asked someone who knew him well (and the innermost workings of the club itself) the jackpot question: 'How long do you give him?' My companion pondered for a few moments, then said: 'Until Christmas . . . but if they're not showing signs of winning something by then, I think he'll be out.' Well, Souness negotiated that particular hurdle, but the forecast wasn't far out – just a matter of weeks, as an FA Cup defeat by Bristol City on 25 January 1994 put paid to Souness's career as Liverpool manager.

After the announcement by chairman David Moores that the 40-year-old Scot had resigned, there came a statement from the man who had just become Liverpool's ex-manager. Souness wasn't present when the resignation statement was made public – he was leaving for a break in Spain. His written statement went like this: 'I took this job believing that I could return the club to its former glory, but this proved to be more difficult than I anticipated. The fans have been very patient, but I feel that their patience is now running out'. In that, he was not mistaken.

David Moores declared that 'for all of us at Anfield and for Graeme himself this is a very sad day. We have understood the difficulties he has faced over nearly three seasons with an unprecedented number of injuries and the need to bring young players forward much more quickly than is usual at Anfield'. But there remained a sting in the tail, as Moores added: 'However, Liverpool Football Club is all about winning things and being a source of pride to our fans. It has no other purpose. With the single exception of winning the FA Cup in Graeme's first season, the results in the league and the other domestic competitions and in Europe have been well below what is expected by the club and supporters'. Indeed, they had been.

Well, some people claim that 'you should never go back', and Howard Kendall discovered that his managerial stint at Everton the second time around brought problems which led to his resignation. And as Graeme Souness walked out of Anfield, maybe – just maybe – he looked over his shoulder, considered the time he had spent as manager of Liverpool, and reflected upon some words spoken by his former chairman and friend, David Murray – the man who took him to Rangers. Not to mention the fate of another Scottish manager, Manchester United's Alex Ferguson. Souness, indeed, might well also have reflected that the dividing line between success and failure can be very slim. As his successor, Roy Evans, reminded people: 'I appreciated the efforts of my predecessor, and am sorry things did not work out for him. His dedication to the job could never be questioned . . . he wanted the club to win everything in sight'.

That could also have been said of Alex Ferguson who, like Graeme Souness, was given money – and even more time – to restore Manchester United to the pinnacle . . . which, of course, meant the Championship. Like Souness, he had been successful in Scotland, having taken Aberdeen to honours and, along the way, demolished the idea that it was impossible to compete with Celtic and Rangers (whom Souness had steered to glory). Like Souness again, he had been known to chuck cups around the dressing-room when his ire had been aroused. And, like Souness yet again, he found himself under some pressure at one stage of his career with Manchester United. One report recorded that by 1990 Ferguson was 'clinging on by his fingertips' and that 'terrace discontent was in the air again'. But Ferguson came good as he saw his players claim the FA Cup in 1990, the Rumbelows Cup and the European Cup-winners Cup – and, finally, the Championship, then the Championship again, coupled with the FA Cup.

The dividing line between success and failure was demonstrated vividly when Aston Villa beat United in the Coca-Cola Cup final of 1994, while United salvaged a last-gasp draw against Oldham Athletic in their FA Cup semi-final, and saw Blackburn Rovers lose a match at Southampton in the Premiership which, according to Kenny Dalglish, could have been a turning point in Rovers' bid to overtake United for the title.

Ferguson got lucky, Souness didn't. And his former chairman at Ibrox, David Murray, admitted that when Souness left Rangers for

Liverpool, 'things were a bit strained at first . . . but I went to visit him at the time of his heart operation'. More to the point, Murray compared Liverpool unfavourably with Rangers, as he saw his supremo depart – it was, said Murray, like comparing hamburger (Liverpool) with steak. He revealed that Souness no longer held shares in Rangers – 'I bought them when he left . . . but we're still friends, although we don't exactly share secrets.' The most telling line delivered by David Murray, however, was this: 'I felt at the time that Graeme had made a big mistake going to Liverpool. I believe I will be proved correct.'

Whether or not Souness himself would confirm this verdict, two things are beyond dispute: he became the most controversial of any of Liverpool's managers; and he was also the first *not* to follow in Bill Shankly's footsteps as a Manager of the Year.

Like other clubs, Liverpool fight shy of washing any dirty linen in public, and while Graeme Souness was a high-profile character in a high-profile job, I can well imagine how, at various times and behind closed doors at Anfield, people must have cringed and shuddered as they saw yet another disparaging headline splashed across the pages of the tabloids. Not that it was all down to Graeme Souness.

I'm utterly certain, also, that from the day Liverpool handed the job to Roy Evans (who, remember, had seen first Kenny Dalglish then Graeme Souness get the nod before him) people such as Sir John Smith and Peter Robinson would be hoping fervently that things would turn out to be different, both on and off the field. Possibly, also, after Liverpool had lost 2–0 at home to Newcastle United in mid-April 1994, they would have been pondering hard on what might have been, had they gone for Kevin Keegan when Dalglish dropped his 'I quit' bombshell. As things turned out, though, they were happy enough when Roy Evans delivered a trophy at the end of his first full term in charge of team affairs at Anfield.

CHAPTER 8

FROM THE KOP TO THE TOP
Roy Evans

Nothing is beyond the bounds of possibility in this game –
especially at Liverpool.
ROY EVANS

AFTER THE roller-coaster atmosphere of the Graeme Souness era, was the appointment of Roy Evans (who had been passed over when Kenny Dalglish got the job, and again when Ronnie Moran's brief tenure of office ended with the arrival of Souness) a safety-first, damage-limitation exercise by Liverpool? No doubt this would be forcefully denied along the corridors of power at Anfield; indeed, chief executive Peter Robinson was soon declaring that the club was 'extremely pleased' with Evans and adding that while 'people might have believed he was too soft for the job, believe me, he is anything but soft'.

I can well imagine Evans being tough enough, yet when I talked to a highly-placed Anfield insider only a few seasons ago and threw Evans's name out as a possible manager, I was informed in no uncertain terms that the job at Liverpool would not be his: 'He likes a good time too much', was how it was put to me. In the dealings I had had with him, Roy Evans had always struck me as someone who knew how to enjoy himself – maybe, even, as someone who didn't take life too seriously – but I also reckoned that if the need arose, he could show a sterner face. And as the surgeon who operated on both Tom Saunders and myself has counselled me, more than once, 'Life is for living.'

At any rate, one might question if, with the naming of Evans as team boss, Liverpool were opting for safety in appointing a long-serving, loyal Scouser who, to the best of my knowledge, had never stepped out of line and who would, at the very least, give the club breathing space, should some be needed. Neither Moran nor Evans had shouted the odds when they had seen others become 'the boss', and if Evans could put the club to rights, so much the better; while if things went wrong . . . well, then, Liverpool would have bought some time to try again. Right or wrong, it's an interesting theory.

To be fair to Roy Evans, he didn't take long to demonstrate that, no matter what doubts anyone had about his succeeding as a manger, he could make tough decisions. In quick time, several of the high-priced players from the Souness era discovered it was no sinecure playing for the new boss. Mark Wright (who, as captain, had lifted the FA Cup) and Julian Dicks were axed from the team even before season 1994–95 had begun; Nigel Clough found himself looking in from the outside; Mark Walters and Paul Stewart were on their way down to the First Division, as they went to Wolves on loan (Stewart later tried his luck with Burnley); and Bruce Grobbelaar was on his way to Southampton.

Five of those six players had been recruited by Souness at a total cost of more than £9 million: Wright, Clough and Stewart at £6 million-plus, overall; Dicks, valued at £2 million in an exchange deal for Mike Marsh and David Burrows; and Walters, at more than £1 million. Ironically, within weeks of season 1994–95 having kicked off, Burrows was back on Merseyside – signed by Everton – and before the season's end he had rejoined Coventry City.

Meanwhile, though Liverpool kicked off by hammering Crystal Palace 6–1, Evans, with 30 years behind him as a red-blooded Liverpool fan and man, was saying: 'I'm not daft enough to get carried away with a result like that.' He had already shown the iron fist with the dropping of Wright and Dicks, not to mention the action taken against Don Hutchison (ultimately sold to West Ham for more than £1 million).

Evans insisted the action he took regarding Wright, Dicks and Hutchison was not a deliberate attempt to prove he could be a tough-guy boss; then he showed that if he could axe high-priced players, he was also prepared to put Liverpool's money where his mouth was, as he splashed close on £7 million on two new recruits, with Peter Robinson talking also about the prospect of a third, big-money signing.

No one needed to tell Evans what was expected of him, and of the side he was reshaping: qualification for Europe, at the end of his first full term – at least. Evans himself talked about the Premiership title being the number-one objective: 'I suppose everyone will say we're not good enough, but this is what I want. Nothing is beyond the bounds of possibility in this game – especially at Liverpool.'

Apart from a relatively modest investment in keeper Michael Stensgaard, as back-up for David James, Evans went into the top bracket of the transfer market to land centre-back Phil Babb for more than £3.5 million and another highly-rated defender, John Scales, for almost as much. These were the first big-money buys since the exit of Souness the previous January. Some months later Evans signed teenage forward Mark Kennedy (Millwall, close on £2 million) and Collymore (Nottingham Forest, £8.5 million).

It had been pointed out that chairman David Moores had underwritten no less than £8 million of a £9.1 million rights issue to gain a controlling interest of more than 57 per cent at Anfield, and certainly the signings of Babb and Scales inside 24 hours were designed to bolster the team's defence – although, with Neil Ruddock already there, the arrival of the two new recruits appeared to make the outlook even more bleak for Mark Wright, while the decision to play Stig-Inge Bjornebye at left-back did not bode well for the future of Julian Dicks.

In point of fact, Dicks was to become expendable and return to West Ham, while Wright approached the end of 1994 as a man on a mission: to make a New Year comeback, after a ten-month spell in the shadows at Anfield. Once upon a time he had been an England centre-back; now the £2.2 million signing by Graeme Souness three seasons previously was striving, at the age of 31, to prove that his career could take off again, after he had been sidelined by Achilles-tendon and calf problems which had necessitated special treatment at the Lilleshall injuries clinic.

His manager – by that time, Roy Evans – was publicly looking upon Wright's return to training as a bonus, not only for the player but for the club. 'The injury has been a bit of a mystery and dragged on a bit but, hopefully, he'll now be fit again early in the New Year.' Wright himself knew, though, that even when he had regained peak fitness, he would still have to battle to oust one or other of Liverpool's three back-line defenders.

If Wright's own story had been one of virtual riches to rags – meaning a downturn in fortune – the transition of Phil Babb from virtual unknown to England's costliest centre-back was a remarkable tale in itself. Babb had started out as a young hopeful with Millwall (where, as an apprentice, he used to clean Neil Ruddock's boots); but he was handed a free transfer by Millwall's then manager, Bruce Rioch. John Docherty, another Scot, had been Millwall's previous manager, and when he fetched up at Bradford City he didn't forget young Babb. He snapped up the 18-year-old and proceeded to play him up front.

I saw Babb playing as a striker for Bradford City, and Docherty was to say of him: 'He did superbly – he had a natural knack of running off the ball, as well as knowing where the goal was.' Babb's scoring ratio was one in two games, although I have to admit I never saw him as a potential star.

On the other hand, a former Leeds United and Scotland player whose opinion I valued greatly – Bobby Collins – thought rather differently. Bobby told me how he had seen Babb in action at left-half and at left-back, and 'I regarded him as a very steady player who didn't have many bad games. But since he got his chance as a World Cup centre-back [with Jack Charlton's Republic of Ireland] he's fairly blossomed.'

John Docherty, whom I met once or twice during his career with Millwall and Bradford City, was always approachable, and he recalled how he switched Babb from left-back to the front line because of injury problems. He also gave the youngster one game at centre-back, 'and he strolled through it'. Docherty said he felt then that Babb might finish up playing in the back-four line, 'but I never thought he would become such a success playing in the World Cup'.

And what did Bruce Rioch (who, by that time, was the team boss at Bolton Wanderers) have to say about the player Liverpool signed for such a huge sum of money? Rioch, articulate and vastly experienced both as an international player and as a manager, recalled that during his days at Millwall the London club possessed its fair share of senior players, 'and we were looking to them to take the club forward'. Talking about Babb, he said: 'It won't be the first time a player has bounced back.' And he added, for the benefit of other young hopefuls: 'Phil Babb's story should serve as an inspiration for all those young lads who refuse to accept that they've been dumped on the scrap-heap.' Which could certainly not be denied. It wasn't the first time, and it wouldn't be the last time, that a player had had to take one step back to go forward two paces . . . although, in this instance, it had been more a matter of a player going backwards or even sideways to make good.

Babb's career took an upward turn when he was transferred from Bradford City to Coventry City, though at the time that deal didn't set the football world on fire. But, as others have discovered, soccer is a game in which things can happen with startling suddenness (Rioch, for instance, became Arsenal's manager after guiding Bolton into the Premiership).

And so, four years after having been given the elbow with that free transfer (shades of Ray Houghton at West Ham and Dean Saunders at Swansea), Phil Babb was making the journey from Coventry City's Highfield Road ground to Anfield and Liverpool were splashing out a cool £3.6 million fee for him. Following hard on his heels was another defender whose career also looked to have been kicked into touch, at one time, John Scales.

At the age of 28 Scales could reflect upon the twists and turns of a road upon which he had embarked with such high hopes – and had them dashed, when Leeds United informed him that he could consider himself free to go. He ended up trying his luck with Bristol Rovers, then Wimbledon were tempted to speculate £70,000 on him. Seven years later he was heading for Liverpool and costing £3 million, with another half-million, should he don an England jersey (which he did).

The signings of Babb and Scales didn't end the search by Roy Evans for further talent (Mark Kennedy was the next big buy), and he handed a vote of thanks to his chairman who, he said, 'has made a magnificent gesture by making £10 million available for players'. Evans added: 'I've been dying to spend it.' It still left Liverpool some way short of the kind of money Kenny Dalglish had been able to splash out, courtesy of Jack Walker, in his bid to make Blackburn Rovers the premier force in the Premiership, although it should not be forgotten that David Moores and his directors also authorised massive spending during the Souness era. However, it wasn't all a drain on the club's financial resources, for Liverpool recouped £1.5 million (and thus made a handsome profit on the player) when they sold Don Hutchison to West Ham.

If Roy Evans felt that he needed to go out and spend around £7 million on defensive cover, he could at least be thankful that up front, alongside Ian Rush, he had inherited a teenager who seemed destined for stardom – Robbie Fowler, one of two genuine, home-grown Scousers in the side (Steve McManaman was the other player who hadn't cost a fee). When Evans played down the opening 6–1 thrashing of Crystal Palace in August 1994, he also counselled: 'We've seen it before at the start of a season, and the form has not continued. We've got Arsenal at home now – they will provide a more accurate measure.'

Young Fowler, scorer of all five goals in a Cup-tie against Fulham the previous season, turned up trumps for Liverpool and Evans in the Premiership contest with Arsenal. In a four-minute spell of lethal finishing he stood the match on its head by hitting a hat-trick. The three goals struck by Fowler were timed officially at four minutes 33 seconds – and within days it was being reported that the 19-year-old was set to receive his reward, in the shape of a contract which would net him £1 million over the next four years.

Fowler, already a magnet for the predatory Italians, had broken into the senior side less than a year earlier, but he showed he had swiftly adapted to the role of being a professional when he declared: 'I enjoy it here, but you have to look after yourself and your family. You're not in football for long. You have to get out of it what you can, while you can.'

No wonder Liverpool were anxious to get him tied up for four more years – and relieved when he said he would take the new deal that was on offer. Fowler followed up his hat-trick with two goals in a 3–2 defeat of Aston Villa, and Dean Saunders (bought by Liverpool for a British-record fee of £2.9 million in 1991 and sold to Villa for £2.3 million) was the first to sing the praises of the youngster who used to clean Deano's boots during the year or so that Saunders spent at Anfield.

Fowler's emergence as a local lad making good didn't improve the chances of £2 million man Nigel Clough – Fowler's room-mate – who, to his credit, admitted not only that the youngster was 'an exceptional talent', but added: 'You don't like it when you're out of the side, but you don't feel so bad when it's players of the quality of Robbie and Ian Rush who are keeping you out.' Nevertheless, with talk of a £1.5 million transfer to Derby County in the air, no doubt Brian Clough's lad intended to keep his options open.

The same probably went for another Souness signing, Michael Thomas (who had cost Liverpool £1.5 million when he left Arsenal). Manager Roy Evans was also keeping his options open, as he knocked on the head suggestions that Thomas would be allowed to go on loan, and indicated that the man whose goal in 1989 had deprived Liverpool of the double still figured in his plans.

While Mark Wright, Julian Dicks, Nigel Clough and Michael Thomas had to play the role of spectators, Evans saw his Liverpool team emerge victorious from their opening three matches of season 1994–95. And the portents looked good for Jan Molby, the Danish international whose career had been dogged by unwanted headlines off the field and a series of injuries which had further interrupted his career at club and international level. He found himself being named by Evans in the starting line-up and gaining praise for his displays.

However, while Liverpool won three matches on the trot, their run came to an end when they took on Manchester United at Old Trafford. Liverpool, by general consent, played extremely well against the Premiership champions, but they lost 2–0, as United cashed in on a John Scales error and on the introduction of Brian McClair for Mark Hughes.

Evans was more concerned with his own tactical decisions, as he admitted after the 90 minutes were up. He had pulled off Molby and sent on new-boy Babb, and he confessed that this substitution decision had been a mistake. Ironically, Evans's United counterpart, Alex Ferguson, said that at the time Liverpool made the switch, he believed that Evans had got it right.

Well, you can't win 'em all, and for Evans this was a reminder (if, indeed, he really needed one) that chasing the Championship and bidding for other trophies would mean a season-long slog, especially with Kevin Keegan's so-far, all-conquering Newcastle United and the Kenny Dalglish-led Blackburn Rovers leading the pack at the top of the Premiership.

The previous term, Evans had welcomed Keegan and his No. 2, Terry McDermott, back to Anfield with Newcastle (who defeated Liverpool that day) by expressing the view that 'nobody can pass through Anfield without learning something which will stand them in good stead for ever'. Keegan was to return the compliment not many months later.

On the last Saturday of September 1994, Liverpool went to St James's Park and ended Newcastle United's 100 per cent run of victories as they came from behind to emerge with an honourable 1–1 draw. Keegan then declared that this was a fair result against a side 'which has been rejuvenated by Roy Evans . . . if we had to lose our record, I'd sooner it be against Liverpool than anyone else. I wanted it to happen against a side which played football the right way, and that was certainly Liverpool today.'

The previous season, after Newcastle had met Manchester United, Keegan had declared that United would become champions again – the rest were looking to pick up the scraps. Maybe, after the draw against Liverpool, he felt his old club was on the verge of a resurgence.

For the first time, Evans deployed Babb and Scales alongside Ruddock, and it worked well. 'The biggest compliment I can pay the players was the way they dug deeper after we went behind,' Evans said. 'It was a bit like *déjà vu* from last week's match against Manchester United, when we lost after having had so many chances. We certainly deserved something out of this game.'

Evans had already shown that, if his accent was pure Scouse, he could face the media and not flinch. When he made his debut as Liverpool's manager for a derby game against Everton (the 150th meeting between the two sides) he admitted that 'this has been a season for shocks . . . we are going through a transitional period, after changes on and off the field'. But, looking ahead, he declared: 'We want those halcyon days back at Anfield, and no effort will be spared in the process.'

On his first Anfield appearance as team boss, when Liverpool played Coventry City (then managed by Anfield old-boy Phil Neal), Evans had declared that 'the pride I feel is almost indescribable. I am a Liverpool lad. I stood on the Kop as a youngster, and understand the football expectations of all our supporters.' And he had some words to spare for the man he had succeeded: 'I appreciate the efforts of my predecessor, Graeme Souness, and am sorry things did not work out for him. His dedication to the job could never be questioned [that couldn't be denied]. He wanted the club to win everything in sight [didn't everyone at Anfield?] . . .' And then Evans added a few words about himself. 'Our army of followers will be asking what Roy Evans can offer.' Here, Liverpool's new team boss took a leaf out of cautious Kenny Dalglish's book, as he said: 'I have been in the game too long to make reckless promises, but I will demand 100 per cent from every player who wears the red shirt.' It could even have been Bill Shankly, Bob Paisley or Joe Fagan talking. Indeed, Evans paid Fagan a tribute which was no more than Joe's due, when he said: 'Joe led us to a treble; Championship, Milk Cup and European Cup. I often wonder if his achievement was fully appreciated, outside Liverpool.' He was probably right to wonder, at that.

For himself, he gave this pledge: 'High standards we have known will be the yardstick for the future, and Liverpool will always be investigating the top end of the transfer market.' Evans was as good as his word and David Moores's money as he speculated nearly £20 million on Babb, Scales, Kennedy and Collymore. There were a few other Evans quotes along the way, too, such as the way he dealt with an inquiry from Manchester City for Ian Rush. Evans said: 'Ian was informed of City's interest because we believed it was the right thing to do. I will keep every player in the overall picture wherever I can. Ian's decision to stay delighted us.' As to Roy Evans's feelings about the place where he had worked for so long: 'Liverpool is a very, very special club, and nothing but the best (to pinch the motto of Merseyside rivals Everton) will ever be big enough.' Then there was another thought: that 'Anfield without European football is like a banquet without wine'.

No question about one thing – the Liverpool supporters could identify with this kind of talk; not least, because they were able to feel that Roy Evans was one of them – a dyed-in-the-wool, committed Liverpool fan. As a kid, he had hopped aboard a No. 68 bus which took him from Bootle to Stanley Park on match day at Anfield. And there his elder brother, Malcolm, was about to introduce him to the famous Kop. That first-time visit lived on in the lad's mind, and it was Roy Evans the manager who declared: 'I joined the Red Army that day.'

Now, of course, the Kop is no more; it had to give way to an all-seater stand, after the final home League match of season 1993–94. But Roy Evans, who once stood on that hallowed piece of ground, has been handed the task of restoring Liverpool to the very pinnacle of English football, not to mention renewed glories on the playing fields of Europe.

It was a mountain which his predecessor had failed to scale, and on the debit side when Graeme Souness departed was the fact that players who had cost millions of pounds were to be considered expendable: Stewart, Walters, Dicks, Wright, Clough, Istvan Kozma and Torben Piechnik had all made their exit or failed to command regular places in the first team. Yet as Evans got down to work, he could reflect that on the credit side there were young players such as Rob Jones, Robbie Fowler, Jamie Redknapp and Steve McManaman who had proved their worth. Plus new faces in Kennedy and Collymore.

One interesting contribution came from Manchester United manager Alex Ferguson, when he was talking about the quest for success. He proclaimed his belief that Scots possessed the main ingredient: 'The big thing is determination, the desire to succeed. We can usually respond to any challenge. I can't define the whole thing, but I know what drives us on. It has to be the hunger to be a winner.'

Ferguson was talking at a time when Arsenal had just claimed the European Cup-winners Cup, to give their then manager, George Graham (another Scot) his sixth trophy in eight years. In turn, Graham said of Ferguson (whose own club had just scored a Premiership-title repeat, with the FA Cup for a bonus): 'Like me, he can often be represented as a dour Scot; but the two of us also share a relentless ambition to keep on succeeding.' The same could also be said of yet another Scot, Kenny Dalglish – and of Liverpool Football Club.

Like Ferguson, Graham and Dalglish, three other men – Sir Matt Busby, Jock Stein and Bill Shankly – were Scottish managers who, in their time, won most of the major trophies in the game; yet it was a Geordie, Bob Paisley, who eclipsed even Shankly and Dalglish (and, so far, Ferguson) when it came to being a winner. Come to that, another Liverpool team boss, Joe Fagan, didn't do too badly, either.

Like Alex Ferguson, Kenny Dalglish hails from Glasgow, and the manager of Manchester United, referring to the ambition to succeed, reckoned that 'so much of it has to do with your background. Your character is formed by the area you come from – just look at those who worked on the yards on the Clyde'. Well, Bob Paisley came from Tyneside, an area also noted for its shipyards in years gone by, while Joe Fagan hailed from Merseyside, where the great liners used to tie up at the docks. As for Graeme Souness, however, in spite of Ferguson's contention about folk from north of the border, he was one Scot who discovered that his ambitions to succeed as the manager of Liverpool were not matched when it came to ultimate achievement (compared to his success with Rangers). True, he saw Liverpool carry off the FA Cup, but that was it, in spite of his undoubted will to continue to be a winner, and in spite of the massive support he received from the boardroom at Anfield – notably from chairman David Moores, who, I am reliably informed, was instrumental in prolonging Souness's stay at the club.

When Liverpool and Souness eventually parted company, it was with the manager taking the initiative, although I did put the question to someone close to Anfield: 'Would there have been a unanimous decision to keep him as manager?' There was some hesitation about giving a direct answer to that one, although Peter Robinson (a director of the club, as well as being chief executive and general secretary) had expressed the view that 'I believe the board was willing to give him further support'. As for a reported £400,000 pay-off for the departed manager, I could get neither a confirmation nor a denial; simply a bland reply that it was 'a settlement palatable to both sides'. Later still, it was reported that Souness, who had left Rangers in the spring of 1991 and made his exit from Anfield in January 1994, was still being paid by Liverpool – the amount was estimated to be £25,000 a month and, it was said, under the terms of his contract, the payments would continue through until 1996, whether or not he took another post.

I was told by my informant that it was 'a complete disappointment that Graeme didn't achieve what we thought he was capable of doing', and one is entitled to wonder if, with hindsight, Liverpool would still have given the job to Souness – or if they would have had no hesitation in asking Roy Evans to take on the task of following Kenny Dalglish. I understand that once Souness had gone and the board got down to considering a successor, Evans's name was not the only one in the frame, although when I put my theory to the test, there was an instant denial that Evans had been a safety-first appointment. I was told: 'No . . . taking everything into account'.

It seems that some big names did come up for discussion, but while 'other names were considered', when it came down to a decision, 'Roy Evans was a unanimous choice'. Football clubs generally strive to play things close to their chest and, in this respect, Liverpool have sought (not always successfully) to get on with their own business quietly. As Phil Neal observed, they would prefer to tell the world only when everything is done and dusted. And with Roy Evans in charge, I knew they would be hoping for a much quieter life.

There's no flash-Harry style about Evans, no flamboyant attitude. His methods have been moulded over the years by the men who were his predecessors in the job. Thirty years after he was taken by his parents to talk to Bill Shankly in the manager's office at Anfield (Evans then was an aspiring, 15-year-old Liverpool player of the future) he could still recall what Shankly told him, in those inimitable, gravel-like tones: 'You're joining the best club in the world!'

Evans, by his own admission, didn't quite come up to the standard set for a regular spot in the senior side, but he contributed a great deal on the backroom side before the fateful day in 1994 – it was a Monday, and the last day of January – when he was offered the job of manager by chairman David Moores. He admitted his feelings 'drifted between disbelief and reality . . . my mind was racing . . . I had to keep calm, think logically.'

It was almost 21 years since Evans had hung up his boots to become just about the youngest trainer in English football. He was then 25, and he had enjoyed success as a player – though not at the highest level. But he had played in all five of Liverpool's Central League-championship-winning sides and, at the start of season 1974–75, managed a couple of first-team outings before taking over from Ronnie Moran, who had been promoted to first-team duty.

When I talked to Evans at that time, he admitted that he had had to think long and hard about switching to the backroom side. 'But you have to look ahead and consider where your future lies.' It was 'a bit strange' to sit and watch a game, but 'I've found that you see more off the pitch than you do when you're on it'. Five years on, towards the end of season 1978–79, the man who, on leaving the St George of England school at Bootle back in 1964, had arrived at Anfield as a young hopeful, was looking back without any real regrets.

He had made his First Division debut against Sheffield Wednesday, enjoyed the experience of playing against George Best (although he never managed a derby-game appearance against Everton), and then came the moment of truth as he realised his first-team days were numbered. 'It's difficult to be honest with yourself,' he told me then. 'But I knew the standard Liverpool set, and so I faced facts and agreed to become reserve-team trainer – although it took four or five times of asking before I finally agreed to hang up my playing boots.'

His first season in charge ended with the reserves claiming the Central League championship, as they had done during his days as their skipper; and there were more successes to follow. But if major first-team honours had eluded him, he could point to one unusual championship honour which he had achieved – across the Atlantic, when he had a spell playing for Philadelphia Atoms, in 1973.

Of course, Roy Evans didn't say no to the offer to become Liverpool's manager, even if he pondered upon the way it had finally

come about. During days gone by, when he was still a young fan, he
had worn pictures of stars like Ian St John and Roger Hunt on his coat
lapels; now, at the age of 45 – and having seen Graeme Souness come
and go – he was being offered the most challenging task of his entire
career at the club he had served all his life.

When he picked up the telephone some time later, it was to give his
father a call. Evans admitted that for his dad, 'the emotion was too
much . . . he cried'. No doubt Roy himself felt a lump in his throat as
he considered just what had happened to him – but when he got down
to it, he came to one firm decision: he would not try to become a copy
of any of the five managers under whom he had served, even though he
had learned something from each of them. 'I cannot be anybody but
Roy Evans,' he declared. 'I will be my own man and honest in my
dealings with people.'

Evans's 19-year-old son, Stephen, who played in goal for Lancashire
Schoolboys, had graduated to the Kop as his dad had done before him,
while his 15-year-old daughter, Stacey, and wife Mary were also avid
Liverpool supporters. The Evans lifestyle, like the lifestyle of Shankly,
Paisley and Fagan, has long been relatively simple – a Saturday-night
out for a meal, a mid-week drink with friends; yes, Roy Evans is indeed
a down-to-earth Scouser.

I'm certain that no one appreciates the situation better than he does.
He may have been handed a contract, but from the very first day he
took charge he was aware that Liverpool needed to stage a successful
salvage operation because, as Peter Robinson acknowledged, the
patience of the supporters is not limitless. One thing in Evans's favour
is that the fans can identify with him as being one of their own. And he
knows exactly what they want – indeed, what they expect: a team
playing entertaining, winning football.

At the start of season 1994–95, Liverpool were quoted by the
bookies as being 16–1 shots for the Premiership title; and the bookies
are usually regarded as knowing what they're about. Roy Evans, when
asked if he really believed his club could regain their glory, admitted:
'We've certainly got to improve a fair amount to get there. But if you
don't believe you can do it, it's pointless starting the season.

'People keep asking what targets we've set ourselves, and I answer
that Liverpool have always said if we get into Europe it's been a
reasonably successful season. Years ago, you could finish ninth and

still qualify; but now it's first, second, third or fourth. We're capable of doing it, if we improve. What I would settle for is a vast improvement in our consistency – but only as a stepping-stone to the title.

'The question almost nobody asks these days is whether we've got a chance of winning it. The answer has to be, "Of course". With players of the quality of Ian Rush, John Barnes and Jan Molby, and youngsters like Rob Jones, Jamie Redknapp, Robbie Fowler and Steve McManaman, we've got a squad which is not the worst in the world. With one or two people topping it up [Babb and Scales for instance] we feel we would have a chance.'

Well, England called up Neil Ruddock, Jones, Barnes and McManaman for the friendly against Romania in the autumn of 1994; Rush would have been a certainty for Wales but for injury; Babb was a Republic of Ireland regular; and Redknapp and Fowler were England Under-21 players. Plenty to build on there.

It had been pointed out that Liverpool (who in season 1978–79 set a League record by conceding only 16 goals in their 42 matches) had leaked no fewer than 55 goals in their 42 Premiership games during season 1993–94, and Evans in turn conceded that the defensive problems still existed, as the club embarked upon a new campaign. Which, of course, was why he plunged into the transfer market for Babb and Scales.

And even after a sound start to season 1994–95, Evans knew that the real test was still to come. He reflected that when he took on the job, 'I tended to think I knew all the aspects of it. But there were far more than I thought. I'm not saying I free-wheeled for the back part of the season, because we were still trying to get into Europe; but I don't think I really took the bull by the horns.

'That's probably a common fault when people take over in mid-season; you don't really get it organised quite how you'd want. You are just going from game to game, trying to get results. I feel more on top of every part of the job now than I did at the end of last season.' He had cause to be optimistic, too, as he viewed the form of Liverpool's rivals.

While Newcastle United and Blackburn Rovers were setting the pace, with Liverpool just behind, Arsenal and Manchester United, along with Leeds United, were faring less well. The Gunners had suffered three defeats in their first six matches; United had gone down three times away from home. And Alex Ferguson had already declared:

'If you lose more than six games, you may as well forget it. We lost only six matches three years ago, and that wasn't good enough, because we were pipped by Leeds.'

George Graham begged to differ, if only slightly, as he said: 'It's difficult to argue against history, but it could be a lot tighter this season. Newcastle are going great guns, Blackburn have a formidable squad, Manchester United will be there, and I don't think Liverpool will be far away. All that suggests a team could lose more than six games and still take the title.' At the same time, just about every manager in the Premiership would have acknowledged that 90 points must be a title-winning target for each of the aspirants.

Ferguson found a backer in Leeds United boss Howard Wilkinson; winning the Championship while suffering more than half a dozen defeats during the season had been done before – 'but not often'. Kevin Keegan sided with George Graham, claiming that eight defeats could still see a team clinching the title. Graham – who was to see Arsenal go down to their fourth defeat, when they lost to lowly Crystal Palace at Highbury – still maintained that the Gunners were in with a chance. Arsenal's League form, however, continued to dip, and Graham's temporary successor, Stewart Houston, was left with the European Cup-winners Cup as the sole trophy target, though they missed out on that.

His Liverpool counterpart, Roy Evans, would have been the first to remind everyone that a match lasts for 90 minutes, and not merely 15, and that while Liverpool had been defeated only once in eight Premiership matches, they needed to maintain that ratio through the remaining 34 games. In fact, they went to Ewood Park to take on Blackburn Rovers, and came away on the wrong end of a 3–2 scoreline.

This time out, Liverpool's £9 million line-up of centre-backs (Ruddock, Babb and Scales) were mastered by the Rovers' £8 million pair of strikers (Shearer and Sutton), and at the end Roy Evans was left to reflect: 'We knew all about Shearer and Sutton, and I would expect our boys to handle them better than they did. I don't think we made them work hard enough for their goals. We defended a bit naively. We've been to Blackburn, Manchester United and Newcastle, played well – and picked up one point out of nine. If we're to have any thoughts about winning things, these are the sort of places where we'll have to start getting victories.'

The television cameras captured the immediate after-match scene: Dalglish, the old Liverpool boss, shaking hands with Evans, his number two, Doug Livermore, Ronnie Moran and Sammy Lee. The Liverpool contingent didn't manage to muster a smile between them. They didn't need telling that a haul of eight points out of a possible 18 in their last half-dozen Premiership matches was far from Championship form. As Evans summed up: 'At the end of the day, we measure our success in points.' And by the spring the Championship was out of Liverpool's reach, although their appearance in the Coca-Cola Cup final gave them the chance to qualify for Europe. A chance they grabbed gratefully, thanks to a match-winning performance from Scouser Steve McManaman. Meanwhile, the Dalglish-inspired Rovers pipped Manchester United for the title – even if they did lose at Anfield in their last game of the season.

CHAPTER 9

THE MAN WHO MISSED OUT
Ronnie Moran's Role

My main concern is to keep the League title here – that's more important than me or anybody else getting the job.
RONNIE MORAN

NINETEEN DAYS after Kenny Dalglish had vacated the managerial chair at Liverpool in such dramatic fashion, the hot seat was occupied for the very first time by a man who had devoted the best part of 60 years to giving total loyalty to the club. Ronnie Moran: lifetime fan, one-time player and, for a long, long time, a valued member of the backroom staff at Anfield.

Moran, blunt to the point of being abrasive at times (he was once chided by *Daily Mail* sportswriter Neil Harman during the reign of Graeme Souness, after he had made a cutting remark to the press), had served under Bill Shankly, Bob Paisley and Joe Fagan. But when Fagan quit the job of managing Liverpool, it wasn't passed on to the man who might well have considered himself to be next in line. Especially if Liverpool ran true to form and kept the job in the family. Instead, Ronnie Moran, the club's senior servant on the backroom side, found himself being asked to stay on and serve under the untried Kenny Dalglish.

True, Moran himself had never managed; but he had gained a tremendous amount of backroom experience under three very able tutors. Yet now he was missing out on the top job, as it went to someone whose skill as a player was universally acknowledged, but whose ability as a team boss had yet to be put to the test. It would have been only natural (and certainly human) had Moran felt snubbed; but to the best of my knowledge he never gave the slightest indication that he resented having been passed over when it came to the top job.

Then came the day that Dalglish so sensationally walked out, and the long-serving Moran actually found himself sitting in the managerial chair – indeed, for an all-too-brief spell, as it turned out, it seemed as if the job might just become his in the long term. But that was not to be.

When the news about Dalglish broke, Liverpool were due to play Arsenal at Anfield on Sunday, 3 March 1991. That was their first home game after Kenny had gone, and Ronnie Moran had been in charge of team affairs for two matches – away to Luton Town, and the Goodison Park second replay against Everton. Liverpool lost 3–1 at Kenilworth Road and Everton won the FA Cup duel by the only goal.

For the Arsenal programme I compiled a piece by chairman Noel White and wrote another article under my own name; together, these pieces replaced what would have been the 'Kenny Dalglish Column'. White said Ronnie Moran had taken over as 'acting manager', and added 'I know you will wish him well'. As had happened against Luton Town and Everton, Liverpool lost their encounter with Arsenal, by the only goal of the game, and by that stage questions were being asked as to how long this state of affairs would be allowed to continue. I had already drawn my own conclusions from a remark passed by chief executive Peter Robinson, immediately after the departure of Kenny Dalglish.

His column had had to disappear from the programme – and something else had to take its place on a regular basis. 'The Ronnie Moran Column'? That was out, because when I asked Peter Robinson if I should contact Moran and do a piece under his name, back came the emphatic reply: 'No.' I didn't pursue the matter any further, although I felt a little bit embarrassed as I wondered how Moran would feel.

There he was, having been put in charge of team affairs; yet he wasn't being given the chance to have his say in the club's match-day programme. However, I kept my own counsel and I also kept my distance from Ronnie Moran – it wasn't up to me to tell him that Liverpool's chief executive had vetoed a 'Ronnie Moran Column'. At the same time, I swiftly came to one conclusion: that whatever decision the club might arrive at, when it came to appointing their new manager, the name of Ronnie Moran was extremely unlikely to emerge at the top of the shortlist. And three defeats on the trot weren't going to help Moran's cause much, either.

Yet by mid-March, when Liverpool played Sunderland at Anfield, Ronnie Moran was being confirmed as the man in charge of team affairs 'until the end of the season' and, after a board meeting, chairman Noel White was going on record saying: 'Ronnie was the first to know of our decision to leave him in charge for now. We rang him to tell him, and he was delighted. He's now looking forward to getting stuck in and getting the results for us.'

Moran's reaction? 'I'm just carrying on as before, but I've got some breathing space to see what it's like. It's great to be in this position after all the years I've been with the club, but it's not based on how long you've been here. It's what happens now that counts.'

What happened was that Liverpool embarked upon a winning run. They followed up a 3–0 victory over Manchester City at Maine Road by beating Sunderland 2–1 at Anfield, and then they inflicted a stunning 7–1 defeat upon hapless Derby County at the Baseball Ground. It augured well not only for Liverpool's title aspirations, but for Ronnie Moran's chances of being confirmed as 'the boss'.

Not until he learned that he was in charge until the end of the season did Moran take it upon himself to occupy the managerial chair as he conducted club business, and even then he insisted his main concern was 'to keep the League title here – that's more important than me or anybody else getting the job. I'm not looking further than that'. Liverpool's win at Derby hoisted them back to the top of the table – but then came defeats at Southampton and at home against Queen's Park Rangers, a home draw against Coventry City, and an astonishing, see-saw battle with Leeds United which saw Moran's men win 5–4 at Elland Road. And once again, questions were being asked about Moran's chances of keeping – or losing – the job of manager.

Moran had added a rider to what he had previously told the media, and it was this: 'If we do win the League, and the club decided to bring in someone else, I'd have to accept it. Given the opportunity, I would still want to stay at Anfield. I don't want to leave . . . I've been here all my working life.' Admirable sentiments which did him credit and demonstrated his total loyalty to the cause.

As it turned out, the match at Elland Road was to be Ronnie Moran's swan-song as caretaker manager, because Graeme Souness breezed into Anfield again. By the time Liverpool were playing Norwich City at Anfield on Saturday, 20 April, Moran was being featured on the front page of the match-day programme – alongside his new boss, as they stood holding a Liverpool scarf between them. Souness's first message to the fans was: 'It's great to be back . . . There is a wealth of experience here in Ronnie Moran, Roy Evans and the rest of the staff, which I intend to call upon when required. Why change a formula which has been the most successful in the history of British football?' Why, indeed?

And then, inside three seasons, Liverpool were looking for a new team boss again, because Souness had come and gone, and as they turned to Roy Evans, chief executive Peter Robinson was talking about 'a more gentle transition, rather than a revolution' (under the Souness regime), and it was being recorded that during the Souness era £20 million had been expended to try to cure Liverpool's ailments on the football field. The writer declared that 'for all it achieved, he might as well have dropped it down the nearest drain'. The result, it was said, was the worst Liverpool season for more than 30 years, with 'a losers' dressing-room littered with over-priced, over-paid players'.

Shortly after the appointment of Roy Evans as team boss, Robinson was giving one of his rare media interviews and coming up with some intriguing answers – especially the one which suggested that, despite all the anti-Souness publicity which had been generated, Evans's predecessor might well still have clung on to his job. At the same time, Robinson didn't duck the issue when it came to assessing just how well (or badly) Souness had spent the club's money.

The club's chief executive declared his belief that Liverpool, having held on to success for so many years, had done things in the right way. And there could be no argument from anyone about that. Then he admitted: 'Unfortunately, it is now obvious that in relatively recent years we started to do some things wrong.' He could say that again . . . and again. For example: 'We did not buy well. And that was something we had always done well in the past.' Now, without any argument, Liverpool's chief executive was admitting, also, that it was absolutely essential that when players were bought, they had to be of the right calibre.

While Robinson didn't come straight out with it and slate Souness for having spent money in a manner which left Liverpool with regrets, he was candid enough to concede that 'we have to be concerned that we spend the money wisely now'. And while 'you can never be certain of getting everything right in a transfer deal, I think you should expect to get it no less than 75 per cent right'.

This, then, was the authentic voice of Liverpool Football Club talking – and in doing so, Robinson was expressing the philosophy which ran deeply through the Anfield club. The philosophy which was based upon obtaining value for money (every single penny of it) to the greatest possible degree. And who could blame Liverpool for thinking like that? Liverpool have long been a conservative club (with a small c), and they hate the thought of losing money, especially when it comes to dropping thousands – or, worse still, hundreds of thousands – on transfer deals in and out. Yes, there was Peter Robinson summing it all up in a nutshell.

Through the years, to the best of my belief, Liverpool had pursued a policy of paying cash up front when they recruited players from other clubs. Not for them a continual state of 'living on tick' and hoping the sun would somehow shine through. However, with the escalating transfer fees and the intense pressure upon them to maintain their pre-eminent standard, they had had to think in terms of millions – and this thinking also had to take in the Taylor Report after the Hillsborough disaster, with more millions requiring to be earmarked for the stadium. Transfer spending during the Souness era had been the most lavish in the club's history; yet, apart from the FA Cup, titles and trophies had been conspicuous by their absence.

When it came to transfers, Peter Robinson was making it crystal clear that the club expected not to lose very much if, having signed a player, it then decided that the time had come for him to move on from Anfield. 'The hope is that the player proves to be everything you wanted; but, if not, you should be able to expect to get back no less than 75 per cent, if he is sold on.' And in nine telling words, Robinson delivered the verdict: 'Clearly, in recent years, we have dipped below that.'

He claimed that the club had always allowed the manager to do his job, and had tried to help and support him in every way, and during my time working for Liverpool I saw no evidence to the contrary. Certainly Souness had been provided with sufficient money to assemble what was virtually a new-look team – and more besides – with the acquisition of a dozen players. And, harking back to the exit of Souness, Robinson reflected that 'it was Graeme's wish to go'. Liverpool's chief executive also made what might be deemed to have been a startling revelation: 'I believe the board was willing to give him further support.' This, it would appear, in spite of the supporters' generally hostile reaction to the manager, after the Bristol City FA Cup debacle.

Robinson, looking even further back, declared that 'it is possible to discern signs of cracks when Kenny Dalglish decided to step down. The team were beginning to age. Replacements were necessary.' One wonders if Dalglish would be disposed to dispute that claim, although it has to be admitted that when he quit Liverpool, he left behind half a dozen or more players whose ages were around the 30 or 30-plus mark. He also left Liverpool at the top of the League table and still in the FA Cup. As for the players who were getting older, even after Souness had gone, Bruce Grobbelaar was still playing in the Premiership (with Southampton); Ray Houghton and Steve Staunton (still in his mid-20s) were considered good enough for Aston Villa; Steve McMahon had given good service to Manchester City; Peter Beardsley was back in the England fold and starring for Newcastle United; and Barry Venison was another England man in Kevin Keegan's team.

As for another old-stager, David Speedie, he had moved on twice – and helped two clubs to gain entrance to the Premiership via the end-of-season play-offs. One of those clubs was Leicester City and the other was Blackburn Rovers, who by that time were under the management of a certain Kenny Dalglish. Speedie didn't hang up his boots until early in 1995, when he became a backroom man.

It's worth looking at the playing squad Graeme Souness inherited from Dalglish, when it comes to assessing Robinson's claim that the ageing team needed replacements. In addition to Grobbelaar, Houghton, Staunton, McMahon, Beardsley and Venison there was the veteran Glenn Hysen and the long-serving Ronnie Whelan. Hysen swiftly disappeared from Anfield, while Whelan stayed around until the autumn of 1994, when he signed for Southend. By that time the injury-dogged Gary Gillespie had moved on, while Steve Nicol was coming up to the veteran stage. However, from the Dalglish era Liverpool still had John Barnes, Ian Rush and Jan Molby (who was to figure prominently in the early teams put out by Roy Evans). When Dalglish departed, also, Liverpool had David Burrows, Ronny Rosenthal, Jimmy Carter, Mike Hooper, Gary Ablett and Mike Marsh – not one a veteran, by any stretch of the imagination. And about to make the breakthrough were players such as Steve McManaman, Steve Harkness, Jamie Redknapp, Don Hutchison and Jim Magilton.

Burrows and Marsh were traded to West Ham in exchange for Julian Dicks; Tottenham Hotspur signed Rosenthal; Arsenal took Carter; Newcastle signed Hooper; and Everton landed Ablett. As for Magilton, this Northern Ireland international was playing Premiership football with Southampton in season 1994–95, after having been sold on to Oxford United by Liverpool.

Altogether, Dalglish left Liverpool with a squad of more than 20 players, and very few of them had vanished from the English League scene at top level by the time Roy Evans was replacing Graeme Souness. Houghton and Staunton, in fact, went to the 1994 World Cup finals with the Republic of Ireland. So it can be argued, with some conviction, that the man who followed Dalglish needed to do little more than carry on the Liverpool tradition of topping up the talent, rather than embarking upon a demolition job.

Robinson came to the conclusion that 'whether we should have had a more gentle transition rather than revolution could be a matter for debate. It had to be one thing or the other. It was impossible to have both.' No argument about that, of course, but Liverpool in the past had always been noted for slipping in players, rather than turning the team upside-down. Still, as he had said, the club had always allowed the manager to do his job, while giving him all possible support.

Six months after the arrival of Graeme Souness, Liverpool had been given a warning from another manager, someone who had played under Souness at Glasgow Rangers. Trevor Francis, then team boss of Sheffield Wednesday, offered this view: 'The days when Liverpool dominated the game are over . . . other clubs like Arsenal, Manchester United and Leeds United have improved considerably. That doesn't mean Liverpool won't win a championship, a cup, or even triumph in Europe . . . but results show Liverpool are not the force they were or, perhaps, are going to be in the future.' The words Francis spoke proved to be prophetic.

With the appointment of Roy Evans as the successor to Graeme Souness came the frank acceptance by Peter Robinson that Liverpool Football Club was facing its greatest challenge in all the 29 years he had been at Anfield. Robinson spelled it out, this way: 'I have always believed that because of our past successes we would be able to maintain our high level of support for about five years before attendances started to dip. We are at the start of our third year of winning nothing, and my calculations could be wrong. Once support starts to go, it could dip very quickly indeed. We have maybe three big buys to make [Babb, Scales, Collymore and Kennedy arrived]. If we get those right, I believe we could be back among the front-runners quickly. But the longer you go without success, the bigger the chance of losing a generation of people who support the club. We have to be successful on the pitch. That's the top and bottom of it.'

Well, Liverpool have always been concerned, firstly, to field a team of winners; and they have always been concerned to give their fans value for money. In return, those fans have backed the club through thick and thin, and this standard of support was reflected even as the days of the Souness era were coming to a close.

During season 1993–94 (Souness remained in charge until the third round of the FA Cup in the January), Liverpool's League gates at Anfield produced figures of 40,000-plus on no fewer than ten occasions, and the aggregate for League matches at home was more than 800,000, giving the club an average exceeding 38,000. Seven of those 40,000-plus gates were clocked up before the FA Cup disaster against Bristol City, and even for relatively unattractive fixtures such as Oldham Athletic and Wimbledon (Liverpool's bogey-team), the attendance figures topped 32,000.

All this certainly demonstrated a remarkable loyalty to the Liverpool cause, and this loyalty was continued with the appointment of Roy Evans as manager. The home League games against Everton, Newcastle United and Norwich City each drew crowds in excess of 44,000. Kevin Keegan's Newcastle pulled in the top attendance of 44,601, while the final fixture of the campaign, against Norwich, drew the second-largest crowd of the season, 44,339. That game, of course, was one of tremendous emotion as the fans stood on the famous Kop terraces for the final time at a Premiership match.

The demolition of the Kop as people had known it for years, to make way for a new stand, meant that crowd capacity was reduced for season 1994–95. Anfield could accommodate no more than 33,000 during the first half of the season, although the development planned was to raise the total to 40,500. But the volume of support remained consistently high, with almost all the seats being reserved for the home fans.

I know Peter Robinson, and I know that he does his homework – not least when it comes to assessing the cash-flow of football. He is not simply an adding machine; he does think deeply about the needs and the wishes of the supporters as well. But he most certainly appreciates the need to keep those supporters coming in through the turnstiles, and the need to win the backing of the up-and-coming generation. He would be the first to recognise that the fans' patience will not stretch for ever; and the way to keep them happy is for the team to keep on producing results. As he said so succinctly: 'We have to be successful on the pitch. That's the top and bottom of it.'

CHAPTER 10

THE MAN WHO PULLS THE STRINGS
Peter Robinson

Winning isn't the most important thing – it's the only thing.
FORMER LIVERPOOL CHAIRMAN, THE LATE SIR JOHN SMITH

LEN SHACKLETON played for both Newcastle United and Sunderland and – now and again – for England, as well. He was a player whose skill and cheek captivated his audiences, and had he plied his trade with Liverpool, the Kop would have loved him when he was in full flow. Shack once told me, though: 'If I were a manager, I wouldn't have me in my team.'

Bill Simmons, still supporting Sunderland at the age of 77, recalled that Len Shackleton's move from Newcastle was at a time when the Roker Park outfit was known as the Bank of England club. Sunderland paid what was then a British-record fee of £20,000 – plus a few odd quid. Bill Simmons said: 'Sunderland insisted on paying extra just to make sure he went into the record books as the most expensive player in history.'

Shack had joined Newcastle from Bradford, and in his first match scored half a dozen goals in a 13–0 victory over Newport. When he left Newcastle, fans organised a petition against his transfer. He could almost make a football talk – one of his party tricks was to flick the ball against the corner flag, then play it as he collected the rebound, exasperating his opponent and defying him to get the ball.

He played for the Football League at Anfield and 'started the ball rolling', as he told me, against the League of Ireland by scoring the first goal, with Jackie Milburn hitting a hat-trick. Two former Liverpool stars, Phil Taylor and Barney Ramsden, were pals of Shack, and when he played at Anfield for Sunderland he enjoyed himself – never more than the day he took the ball through the Liverpool defence until there was only the keeper to beat.

Len recalled: 'I was going to shoot for the bottom right-hand corner of the net, and as I got ready to hit the ball I realised the keeper was going to dive for the shot. As I lifted my foot back, he dived . . . so I lobbed the ball over his body. It was at the Kop end, and when they saw how I'd fooled the keeper, they roared with delight. No Liverpool player could have had a better response to a goal he'd scored. It was a cheeky goal, and the Kop showed they could appreciate it, even though it came from an opponent. When you went to play at Anfield, you knew it was something special, and you seemed to raise your game accordingly.' Then Shack, with that droll wit of his, acknowledged that – after the North-East fans – the Liverpool supporters were the most knowledgeable in the game.

Len Shackleton had a caustic wit, and after I had been instrumental in recruiting him from his job at the *Daily Express* to become *The People*'s man in the North-East, we had more than one set-to, as he savaged some footballing personality in print and I refused to let it go through, because it verged on the libellous. It was Shack who got Brian Clough and Peter Taylor started in management at Hartlepool United, and he paved the way for their promotion to higher things with Derby County. It was Shack – a man who certainly knew his football – to whom I turned when Liverpool were being linked with a potentially expensive signing. When I quizzed Len about this speed merchant, he said dryly: 'Oh, aye; he can catch pigeons, but he canna play football.'

Shack caused a sensation when he wrote a book about football, because the Clown Prince of Football, as he was known, dedicated one chapter to the men who run football clubs. It was headed 'What the Average Director Knows About Football', and there followed a single, blank page. Which brings me to my point, in case you should be wondering why I have devoted such space to Len Shackleton.

There have been many instances of men who have prospered in business, and made a small fortune, going into soccer as directors; and it has amazed me how often they have allowed all their business acumen to fly out of the window. Suddenly, they think they are experts on the game. But I don't think Shack would have included Liverpool's chief executive, Peter Robinson – who is also a director of the Anfield club – in his blank-page condemnation of directors. For a start, Peter Robinson is not your average football director.

He is the man who, for the most part, pulls the strings at Liverpool, and you can take it from me that he is always pulling several strings at one and the same time – and, as a general rule, not once does he fumble with any of them. When I started editing Liverpool's match-day programme, I took over a job which entailed all the writing, all the page layouts, headlines – the lot. I also took on the job of interpreting just what was permissible and what wasn't.

Peter Robinson asked Bill Shankly if he thought he could work with me (I'd known Bill since his days as manager at Huddersfield Town), and was given an affirmative reply. That vote of confidence (I didn't know about it until much later) meant quite a lot to me. But I sensed that Peter Robinson, whom I had also known for many years, would be keeping a close eye on the way I went about the job.

He didn't want the programme editor to be stirring up controversy; he didn't want the programme editor to act as if he were the man in sole command; he wanted to feel happy that I was going about the job in what he considered the correct manner – after all, not only had I been a journalist whose job it was to get stories from inside soccer clubs, but I had worked, and was still working, on a freelance basis, for a Sunday tabloid called *The People*.

Peter knew he could be sure of one thing, though. I wouldn't use my Liverpool connections and pull a fast one in order to get a story in *The People*. For a start, Liverpool played things very, very close to their chest, and rarely did anything come out of Anfield concerning signings and sales until the club was good and ready to let people know. For another thing, Peter knew he could be assured of my loyalty to Liverpool – as I had occasion to remind Kenny Dalglish, years later.

So I kept the two jobs separate – during the week I worked on the programme, and – having spoken to various contacts elsewhere – at the weekend my time was given to *The People*. The arrangement was that if I picked up a story about Liverpool from an outside source – and this did happen – I would check it out, and this arrangement worked well enough through the best part of 20 years. In all that time, I never had a fall-out with Peter Robinson, though I did have a couple of bust-ups with Bill Shankly.

Gradually, Peter relaxed as he saw that I was doing the job in what he regarded as a responsible manner, and he knew that if I had doubts about using something, whether it be a story or a picture, I would check with him. Indeed there were occasions when I knew that while something would be looked upon kindly inside the boardroom, if I used it, that something could also cause complications and, maybe, a complaint from outside Anfield. At such times, I would consult Peter, he would immediately take the point I was making, and he would say, 'Leave it out.' I then left it to him to smooth any ruffled feathers there might be, over the omission.

On one occasion, when I was talking to Peter Robinson about the problems I was having in getting material for the programme from another club, he answered succinctly: 'That's why they never win anything / . . they're just not organised.'

Peter Robinson is known to his staff as PBR. He is undoubtedly a workaholic, and he once confessed to me that the thought of going into retirement 'terrified' him. Not a lot of people have access to his direct line at Liverpool, nor his home telephone number, but I could always ring either. The problem lay in getting to speak to him: it seemed that from early morning until late in the evening his Anfield number was engaged – he was always on the phone, whether it was talking to people around Europe or discussing domestic football matters as they affected Liverpool.

Often, I would ring his home at a time in the evening when I considered it was safe to do so – meaning a time when he seemed sure to be there – only to be told by his wife: 'He's not home yet; try the club.' Or he would have just left Anfield and be on his way home – if he wasn't going to an evening match somewhere.

I first got to know PBR when he was working at a couple of clubs which are considered to be among soccer's minnows: Stockport County and Crewe Alexandra. I remember Peter telling me how he had started at the bottom; he joined Stockport as the office boy in 1953 – 'that was my first job in football' – and he stayed for five years. 'I was assistant secretary by the time I left, to return to my home-town club, Crewe Alexandra, as secretary.

'I remember vividly the day I started at County – we came up against Headington United [now Oxford United] in the FA Cup, and after a draw at Edgeley Park they knocked us out in the replay. At the time I was with County, they had Willie Moir, the former Scotland international [he played for Bolton Wanderers in the 1953 Stanley Matthews FA Cup final] as player-manager, and I can remember County beating Luton Town in the third round of the FA Cup one season. That was at a time when Luton were doing very well.

'In my last season at Edgeley Park, the average gate was 14,000; it was an exciting time, too, because that season decided who would go into the new Third Division and who would finish in Division Four. County qualified for a place in the Third Division.'

Little did Peter Robinson realise then that one day he would be master-minding the administrative side of things at a famous club like Liverpool and travelling all over Europe and even further afield on club business. By the time he was pulling the strings at Anfield his chairman, Sir John Smith, was telling me in no uncertain terms that in PBR Liverpool Football Club had the finest administrator of them all – and not just in this country, but in Europe. Indeed, club officials on the Continent have not been too proud to seek Peter Robinson's advice.

When he moved on to Scunthorpe, I kept in touch with him and I used to drive across the Pennines and visit him at the ground. Sometimes we went back to his home for lunch, and I got to know his wife, Dorothy. Then Peter switched clubs once again, as he travelled south, this time to join Brighton. Eventually, he landed at Liverpool and, in my opinion, there will be nothing to shift him from Anfield now. He spends so many hours of his life at the club that when holiday time comes round, it seems almost to pass him by. One thing I know which he does enjoy, and that is going to Old Trafford – the cricket ground, not the football ground – to take in a Test match.

Even at a club such as Liverpool, of course, there are boardroom politics, and more than once I was made aware that there was a certain pecking order when it came to the directors. Otherwise, feathers could easily be ruffled. The late Sidney Reakes, for instance, was fond of reminding you that he was the club's chairman when the FA Cup first arrived at Anfield, back in 1965. On one occasion I can recall being phoned by Peter Robinson and advised to switch a couple of names on the list of directors featured in the match-day programme – it seemed that the more senior of the two had been doing a bit of moaning. And more than once, when I took the trouble to query something with PBR, he would agree with me that the sensible thing to do was to leave a certain item or picture out of the programme, otherwise we might be inviting complications or potential embarrassment for the club. Peter's reaction in such cases was: 'You can leave the director concerned to me . . . if he's unhappy, I'll sort it out.' Which gives you a firm indication of the power that Peter Robinson wielded and, of course, still does wield.

I worked with three of the men who occupied the chair at Liverpool Football Club: Eric Roberts, who was chairman when I took over as programme editor; John Smith (as he was then); and Noel White. My acquaintance with Eric Roberts was brief enough, because after about a year he was succeeded by John Smith, but I always regarded Eric Roberts as being a thorough gentleman. As was his successor. In fact, I hardly ever had cause to feel unhappy about my relationship with any of the men who occupied the chair at Anfield, nor did I ever cross swords with any of the other directors. I got to know the late Sir John Smith, who died early in 1995, pretty well, while I had known the man who succeeded him as chairman, Noel White, for a considerable number of years even before he had joined the board at Liverpool.

From time to time I would receive a phone call from John Smith about some matter or other and, in any event, I used to ring him at his home on a fairly regular basis, especially when I required a piece from him for the club programme. For example, when Liverpool were playing in a European match at Anfield, or when they were about to pay one of their frequent visits to the place they had nicknamed 'Anfield South' – meaning Wembley.

John Smith was a smooth-talking man who could dictate his thoughts seemingly straight off the top of his head. When I phoned him and said I needed a piece from him for the programme, he would immediately launch into a speech which I took down in shorthand and, in about three minutes flat, I had what I wanted, almost verbatim. One of the things I remember about him, also, was the way he would suddenly terminate a conversation, almost as if time were up and he wanted to get on with something else. In the meantime, he would leave me to get on with doing my particular job.

We got on well together, however, and I soon became aware that he was intensely proud of being a Liverpool supporter, as well as club chairman. He was also extremely jealous of the club's good name, and he told me on one occasion that, for him, Liverpool was 'almost a religion'. He had seen his first match at Anfield as a mere nipper (his father was a shareholder), and he used to recall to me famous players of the previous 50 years and more.

His favourite of them all was the great Elisha Scott, the keeper the fans used to call 'The Cat'; and John Smith (as he still was then) related to me the story of how the Ireland international used to cause one of his team-mates in particular a certain amount of anguish, on occasion. The team-mate was a full-back of repute, too, and he was known as 'Parson' Jackson. The reason for this strange-sounding soubriquet was that Jackson was studying to become a minister of the church, and he used to save his football pay so that it could contribute towards his religious studies. 'Elisha Scott,' John Smith told me, 'had a rich command of choice words, and "Parson" Jackson used to remonstrate with him about this, but to no avail.'

John Smith was the Liverpool chairman through what was termed '17 trophy-laden years' and, of course, he worked very closely with Peter Robinson. Together, they wielded an enormous amount of power at Anfield, and while John Smith – who had a spell also as chairman of the Sports Council – was a very busy man in various ways, he always appeared to be keeping a weather eye on the way matters were proceeding at Liverpool Football Club. Now and again, from remarks that John Smith let drop, I formed the impression that he didn't always see eye to eye with Kenny Dalglish, even though he had been instrumental in ensuring that Dalglish stepped up from player to team boss. But if John Smith had cooled off in his admiration for everything Dalglish did, one thing was sure: both men were working to ensure the continued success of Liverpool Football Club.

There were times when John Smith could appear to be autocratic, times when Kenny Dalglish seemed to be in a somewhat abrasive mood; but there was never any question that either man was capable of doing his own job. By the time Dalglish made public his shock decision to quit, John Smith had become Sir John and Noel White had taken over the chairmanship – although, in stark contrast to Smith's 17-year term, White's tenure of office lasted no more than 15 months, though he had served his apprenticeship as a member of the Liverpool board.

I had known Noel White for a long time, because before joining the boardroom team at Anfield he had been a big cog in a much smaller soccer set-up – at Altrincham, the non-League club famed for putting a

spoke in the wheel of their bigger brethren when it came to jousting in
the FA Cup. Noel White and his friend and business partner at the time,
Peter Swales (later to become chairman of Manchester City), were the
men who guided the non-League outfit behind the scenes during the
post-war years, and White succeeded Swales as Altrincham's chairman
in 1968.

White, indeed, was accustomed to hearing the Scouse accent, since
half a dozen of Altrincham's players hailed from Merseyside, and in
1981 the Robins from Moss Lane were paired with Liverpool in the FA
Cup. Their manager at that time, Tony Sanders, lived at Walton – mid-
way between Anfield and Goodison Park – and their skipper was a
character called John King. In 1979, Altrincham had gone to White
Hart Lane and held mighty Tottenham Hotspur to a 1–1 draw in the FA
Cup; and in January 1995, when the Robins tried their luck there again,
John King was their team boss. A few months later he was running the
club.

In 1981, when Liverpool applied the knock-out blow to Altrincham,
Noel White was still their chairman, but five years later he was joining
the board at Liverpool. It was almost 25 years to the day since he had
first become associated with Altrincham – he had spent seven years as
vice-chairman and general manager, 18 years as chairman. His
association with Merseyside went back many years, too, and in 1976 he
became a member of the FA Council representing the division which
covered Merseyside and Cheshire, where he lives.

White has always been someone who preferred to maintain a low
profile – indeed, he gives the impression of being somewhat self-
effacing – and when he stepped up to become chairman of Liverpool
Football club he made it clear how he proposed to play his new role.
When I suggested to him that he might care to contribute a fairly
regular piece for the programme, he immediately declined, politely but
firmly. He genuinely wanted to get on with doing his job without
fanfare or even any publicity.

When he vacated the chair at Anfield in such a summary fashion, it
caused eyebrows to be raised in other boardrooms and provoked plenty
of gossip and speculation among people in football. To the best of my
knowledge, White has never even hinted publicly that the affair caused
him any problem, but I heard from three different sources that he had
been upset – not least, by the speed with which the switch was

achieved. The way it was told to me, it seems he was making his preparations for the club's annual general meeting when the question was suddenly broached: would he be prepared to step down as chairman, so that David Moores could move up? And I am told it was also suggested that it would be appropriate if Noel White were to propose Moores as his successor.

The speed with which it was all happening was sufficient to make White blink, since he had had not an inkling that such a development was in the air. And, of course, it gave him precious little time to deliberate. However, he felt he had little alternative but to agree with the proposition put to him, so he went along with it, even if it left a somewhat sour taste in the mouth. Given John Smith's 17 years and Noel White's 15 months, it is hardly surprising that people in football were shocked by the turn of events at Anfield.

When I suggested to the chairman of another Premier League club that given similar circumstances, I might well have told Liverpool to stuff their chairmanship and my seat on the board, I received the reply that Noel didn't want to make waves and rock the boat and, knowing him as I do, I could understand this. He has never been one to shout the odds. But I couldn't help feeling a great deal of sympathy for him, and others to whom I talked expressed similar sentiments. Behind the scenes he had worked hard – and he has continued to do so through the trials and tribulations of recent seasons.

While I knew the respective chairmen (other than David Moores) reasonably well, I often felt that various other directors didn't even realise who I was, though they knew me by sight and passed the time of day with me. One of the most senior directors, the late Sidney Reakes (a former chairman) seemed to think I worked for a travel agency which did business with Liverpool – I've got to admit I did bear a passing resemblance to someone who organised trips for the club – and on one occasion Sidney Reakes asked me: 'What have you got lined up for us next?' When he pointed out that he was referring to trips, I managed to mumble some sort of reply and passed it off with that.

I recall a trip to Estoril, in Portugal, which was not with Liverpool, as it happened. I flew out with Matt Busby, who was going on UEFA business, and the then Leeds United chairman, Harry Reynolds, was there, along with Alan Hardaker, secretary of the Football League. We dined together that night in the plush Palacio Hotel. Reynolds, a millionaire who carried his cigarettes in a battered tin, used to say bluntly: 'You get nowt for being second.' Liverpool's former chairman, John Smith, had a saying, too: 'Winning isn't the important thing – it's the only thing.' Bill Shankly put it another way: that football was not a matter of life and death, it was more important than that. Bruce Rioch, whose Bolton Wanderers team sprang a sensational FA Cup upset at Anfield during the Souness era (Liverpool avenged that defeat with their 1995 Coca-Cola Cup triumph) recalled after his side's famous victory: 'I once remember sitting with Bill Shankly when Liverpool happened to have just lost a game. He said he was banning any laughing for a week.'

CHAPTER 11

DAVID MOORES AND ME
The People Saga

David's appointment will help keep the predators at bay.
FORMER LIVERPOOL CHAIRMAN, SIR JOHN SMITH, ON THE
ELEVATION OF DAVID MOORES TO THE CHAIRMANSHIP

'WHAT IS becoming of Liverpool FC?' That was the question posed by
the *Daily Mail*'s chief soccer writer, Neil Harman, at the end of August
1992. He was referring to the match Liverpool had played at Ipswich
Town's Portman Road ground a few days previously and, more
particularly, he was critical of Liverpool chairman David Moores – who,
said Harman, had 'publicly berated football writers in that most civilised
of sanctums, the Ipswich boardroom'. Then Harman asked: 'What would
Mr John Cobbold have made of such appalling behaviour?'

Now for some pearls of wisdom from another noted journalist,
Marjorie Proops, the famous agony aunt of the *Daily Mirror* for many
years. In her autobiography, commenting on a rumour that her then
boss, Robert Maxwell, had wanted to buy her name so that he could
carry on using it after death, Marje retorted that the answer to that one
would have been 'Not bloody likely!' Moreover, she added that she had
never allowed anything that anyone else had written to appear under
her by-line because she considered such an act to be 'highly dishonest.
Absolutely awful.' And, I submit, she is utterly right.

Now who or what, you might ask, is the connection between what
Neil Harman wrote and what Marje Proops said? I will tell you in a
word: *me*. So let us start at the beginning of a saga which involved not
only myself, but Liverpool chairman David Moores, *The People*
newspaper and the man who was its sports editor (Bill Bradshaw), plus
Tony Ensor (who later resigned from the Liverpool board) and the
Press Complaints Commission.

It all started with a telephone call; it ended with an attempt by *The People* to muzzle me, as I became the man in the middle of a dispute with David Moores. It left me smarting with a sense of injustice and regarding Liverpool's chairman with a feeling of something less than approbation.

The phone call? That was made to me by Bill Bradshaw, to ask if I could do a profile for the paper on Moores. I knew what it was all about, of course; at least, I thought I did, as our conversation revolved around remarks chairman Moores was said to have expressed that night at Ipswich. It seemed pretty clear to me that *The People*, probably in the shape of Bill Bradshaw, intended to have a go at Moores. And, of course, this was the paper's privilege.

I told Bradshaw I didn't know Moores (a fairly recent appointment to the Liverpool board, and an even more recent appointment as club chairman); but I said I would do my best to 'cobble something up'. I did my homework and discovered that Moores, a self-confessed Liverpool fanatic, drove around in a Mercedes bearing the registration number KOP 1. He still sported his shoulder-length hairstyle, but apparently had dispensed with the ear-ring which had prompted comment from the chairman of another club.

He was the nephew of Sir John Moores, former chairman at Everton, who had sensationally fired his then manager, Johnny Carey (a one-time Manchester United hero) during a taxi ride across London at a time when the League clubs were gathering for their annual meeting. And David Moores had become chairman of Liverpool Football Club – in quick time, and in somewhat controversial fashion.

It was in 1990 that David Moores, then aged 43, had realised a lifelong ambition by gaining a seat on the Liverpool board. I was told later that his appointment had not come about without at least one expression of doubt, but that it was seen as a means of strengthening the board in financial terms, as Liverpool embarked upon a massive spending spree to make their famous stadium better than ever, as well as complying with the requirements of the Taylor Report in the wake of the Hillsborough disaster.

The late Sydney Moss, who at that time was Liverpool's vice-chairman, said of the new supremo: 'He came here at the age of four, then stood on the Kop when he was old enough. He is not just a supporter, but a fanatical supporter.' Former chairman Sir John Smith put it more succinctly, and phrased it somewhat differently, when he said: 'David's appointment will help keep the predators at bay.'

At the time of his appointment to the board, David Moores had spoken of it as being 'a dream come true', and by the time he had been installed in the chair, in September 1991, he was claiming: 'My feelings are no different from those who stand so proudly on the Kop. Like them, I want success and will contribute to the cause in any way I can. This club is all about players and fans. I make no apology for standing and shouting when Liverpool score.' Fair enough.

It cannot be denied that when David Moores stepped up to become chairman, eyebrows were raised in soccer circles, and there was some sympathy for the man he succeeded, the self-effacing Noel White, who had followed Sir John Smith, an urbane figure with a somewhat autocratic manner. Smith had presided over the club during 17 years which had been liberally adorned with trophies, and both he and White, it seemed to me, were cast in a different mould to Moores.

The club's new chairman declared that his role 'will not change me, the person', and added: 'I will carry on with dignity.' Admirable sentiments, indeed. But Neil Harman, for one, evidently did not consider the Ipswich incident had shown David Moores to be carrying on 'with dignity'. And *The People* story, spread across two pages of a 12-page pull-out section on Sunday, 13 September 1992, kicked off by declaring that Moores had launched 'an amazing tirade on a Merseyside pressman in front of shocked hosts at Ipswich'.

Further, the story went on to ask: 'Shouldn't Moores, of the famous Liverpool pools family, have taken the option offered to every football-coupon gambler? Shouldn't he have buttoned his lip and ticked the box for no publicity?' Again, sentiments which may have been all very fine, as expressed by the person who made them public – except for one thing: they were – wrongly – attributed to me. As were other matters in a story which ran to 27 paragraphs of which I had contributed no more than a dozen or so. That story led to a confrontation between Liverpool's chairman and *The People*, with my name (in a manner of speaking) being taken in vain.

The sequel to the story was that Moores, through his solicitors, demanded from *The People* an apology, damages (to be paid to charity) and costs. There was a similar demand in a letter from the solicitors to me.

What Moores, through his solicitors, complained about was the major section of the story (which I had not written). It referred in detail to the circumstances of the death of his first wife, Kathy, in a car crash in 1977, and to the death abroad of David's brother, Nigel, who was described in the story as a 'playboy'. When I read the story I was incensed, and totally in sympathy with David Moores. As for *The People*, I was more than furious with that paper, because under an extremely bold headline getting at David Moores were three lines of bold type which told the world that all this was a report by Stan Liversedge.

I endorse the Marjorie Proops view – I consider that it was highly dishonest of *The People* to have attributed not only the whole story to me, but also some hard-hitting opinions which I had never even expressed. And I say this while making one thing clear: that I was perfectly prepared to stand up and confirm that I had been the author of the story I had originally sent to *The People*'s sports editor.

What I was *not* prepared to acknowledge was that I had written the material about Nigel Moores and about David Moores's first wife. My contention was – and remains – that the main by-line should have read: Report by Bill Bradshaw. And when it comes to the point where my contribution to the story began, a line should have been inserted to say: *Stan Liversedge writes . . .*

As I read the story on that Sunday morning, I grew livid with anger; then I telephoned Liverpool's chief executive, Peter Robinson, at his home. When I asked if he had seen the story, he told me he hadn't – but, he said, he had already had the chairman on the phone about it, and David Moores was very upset.

I told Peter that applied to me, too, and said I wasn't surprised at the chairman's attitude. I explained that I had had nothing to do with the section concerning Nigel Moores and David Moores's first wife, and asked for the chairman's home phone number, because I wanted to tell him personally what had happened. Peter said the chairman didn't give his number to the press, but he would try to contact David Moores and get him to ring me.

The next day I wrote to Peter outlining what had happened with regard to the story, and asking him to put my letter before the board, so that all the directors would know the situation. I also felt compelled to ring various people in the game – people whose opinions of me I valued – and explain that if they had seen the story, they should not blame me. One Premier League manager, Joe Royle, told me: 'I couldn't understand, when I read it . . . I knew this wasn't like you.' And Peter Robinson had agreed with me, when I pointed out to him that this wasn't my style.

The chairman of another Premier League club to whom I spoke told me later that a member of the board at Liverpool had expressed his disappointment in me, but he wouldn't name the director concerned (though I could make a pretty good guess). And when I heard this I wasn't best pleased.

When I had spoken to Peter Robinson on the Sunday morning, he told me he had assured his chairman that he didn't believe I had been responsible for the story, and on the Monday afternoon my phone rang, with David Moores on the other end of the line. So I explained to him what had happened, and we spent about 20 minutes talking. When I said that I was now considering my position with regard to working for *The People*, David Moores told me: 'That's a matter for you to decide.' And, of course, I agreed. When we parted, it was amicably, and he assured me that he accepted what I had told him.

The next morning, I rang *The People* and complained to the sports editor about the way my name had been used, and when I indicated that I didn't think much to what had been written, without my knowledge or consent, he replied that he thought it was 'a reasonable story', overall. We had to agree to differ, and he said there was a simple remedy for the future: on anything of such a touchy nature, my by-line would not be carried. I was more than happy to agree with him on that point, at least.

Late in September, I received a letter, typed on official, Liverpool-headed notepaper, from Peter Robinson, who thanked me for my letter of 14 September, said David Moores had been extremely hurt and upset by the content of *The People* article, 'but now totally accepts that you were not responsible for the top part of the article'. The final paragraph said: 'Unfortunately, the current standard of journalism, particularly in the tabloid press, is of an extremely low standard.' The letter ended 'With kind regards, Yours sincerely, Peter.'

And that, I felt, absolved me of all blame for what *The People* had published about the tragedy involving David Moores's first wife and the death of his brother. So I embarked on the *QE2* for a week's cruise feeling happier, and having decided that I would make a final decision about continuing to work for *The People* when I got back. But when I returned home, the problems took on a new aspect – instead of being behind me, they were staring me in the face, in the shape of a solicitor's letter. It was a copy of one which had been sent from David Moores's solicitors to the editor of *The People*.

It complained about the reference in the story of 13 September to the accident in which Kathy Moores had been killed. It referred to what it called 'inaccuracies and distortions', and said Moores regarded the reference to 'an appalling family tragedy' as 'tasteless and insensitive in the extreme'. He got no argument from me there.

The letter said Moores did not wish any further publicity, if it could be avoided, but he was 'deeply aggrieved by this negligent and unfeeling treatment of such an event' and, therefore, on his behalf the solicitors sought a letter of apology from the editor and the reporter, acknowledging the errors and undertaking that the matter would not be referred to again in that way.

There was more. As a mark of sincerity, *The People* should donate a suitable sum to charity and pay all David Moores's legal costs. If the matter were dealt with in this way, and promptly, Moores would consider it to be at an end. Meanwhile, all his rights were reserved. Oh, yes . . . the final sentence read: 'A copy of this letter has been sent to Mr Stan Liversedge to whom it is equally addressed.' There was no legible signature – just what seemed to be scribbled initials.

To say that I was astonished at receiving such a letter, after the verbal assurance from Moores and the letter from Robinson, is putting it mildly. I was furious now, not only at *The People*, but at Moores, and I immediately wrote to his solicitors, pointing out – just in case they hadn't heard – that I had already spoken to their client and received a letter from Liverpool's chief executive clearing me of blame. I added a few more things and said I hoped this would be the end of the matter, so far as I was concerned.

Back came another letter, again initialled; it was terse and to the point. 'We consider your observations should be directed to the newspaper who employ you. We await a positive response in respect of our request for an apology, an undertaking, damages to be paid to a charity, and our costs.' By this stage I was steaming, and when I wrote back I made various points and also suggested that the writer should do me the courtesy in future of signing his name and not merely scribbling initials. The next letter I received bore the signature of Tony Ensor.

I rang Bill Bradshaw and we had a blazing row during which he suggested sarcastically that I would be 'a great bloke to have in the trenches' – to which I replied, 'Never mind the . . . . ing trenches – put me through to the legal department!' Then the phone went dead. So I redialled and went through to the paper's legal department myself, to be told that the man dealing with the Moores affair, Arthur Davidson, was on the phone. 'I'll wait,' I said. I was utterly determined not to be sidetracked, either by Bradshaw or by anyone else. And I hung on until Arthur Davidson picked up the phone.

He was calm, he was courteous, and he told me he had just been speaking to Bill Bradshaw. 'I'll bet you have!' I told him. Then I launched into my complaint. Davidson assured me that I need not worry, that I was indemnified by the paper, that it was unlikely the matter would go to court. I made it clear I didn't give a damn about it going to court – I wanted *The People* to tell Moores's solicitors that I was an innocent party and that, so far as I knew, it had been Bradshaw who had written the material about which Moores was complaining.

After that, it became a war of words, with letters flying to and fro like bullets. Bradshaw accused me of having 'a pathetic whinge'; I told him his ethics and mine were 'poles apart'; and I wrote to *The People*'s editor, Bill Hagerty, to demand an apology in the paper. I also said I intended to cease working for *The People* and suggested that, after more than 30 years' service, it would not come amiss if I were to receive an *ex-gratia* payment.

Hagerty replied to say he was inquiring into the matter and would be in touch; but he was obviously having problems of his own, because shortly afterwards he became the first casualty of the new regime at the *Mirror* group when he was fired by supremo David Montgomery. So I then wrote to the next incumbent of the editorial chair at *The People*, Bridget Rowe.

At one point while I was firing off letters, I pointed out that *The People* proclaimed itself to be 'Frank, Fearless and Free', and that it boasted of being 'The Paper that Cares'. I said it had been fearless and free when it came to using my name, but considerably less than frank when it came to admitting publicly that I had not written the offending section of the Moores story.

While all this was going on, I made up my mind to address a formal complaint to the Press Complaints Commission – maybe this was the first time any journalist had done so. They say in the trade that dog doesn't eat dog, but my bitter experience had taught me otherwise. My decision to bring in the Press Complaints Commission sparked off another move, and the wheels were set in motion one Thursday morning with a phone call, not from *The People*, but from Peter Robinson. He wanted to discuss the Moores affair and, it appeared, my decision to involve the Press Complaints Commission. I made it plain that I was going ahead, and I didn't care if the story was splashed in every paper in the land. As I told Peter, while neither Moores nor *The People* was anxious to make matters public, I certainly had no qualms about getting things out into the open. Our talk ended with my telling him that I would keep him posted.

Around six o'clock that evening, my phone rang and a woman's voice said this was *The People* calling. Could I give her my fax number? I said as sweetly as I could that I had recently disposed of my fax machine, and she said there was a letter which *The People* wanted to send me straight away. When it arrived, it bore the signature of Len Gould, the deputy editor, who said he was replying to my letters to Bill Hagerty, 'as I am familiar with the circumstances surrounding this troublesome matter'.

Then he got down to the real business. 'I am happy to acknowledge that the item that caused offence to David Moores was written by Bill Bradshaw.' As for the position with David Moores and *The People*, 'the article is not, and has never been, the subject of a defamation or any other legal action'. No legal proceedings had been commenced, and Mr Moores did not wish to start such proceedings, though he had been upset by the reference to the events of some years ago.

Smoothly, the letter declared: 'In view of our respect for Mr Moores and our good relationship with Liverpool Football Club, we resolved the matter by way of sending him a private letter of apology. That letter is not for publication, neither is there to be any published apology to Mr Moores in *The People* newspaper or elsewhere. The matter has been dealt with in this private way as neither Mr Moores, Liverpool Football Club *nor anybody else involved* [my italics] wishes to give further publicity to it. The matter is therefore, so far as Mr Moores is concerned, finalised to his satisfaction. We have assured both Mr

Moores and Mr Robinson that you did not write that part of the article to which Mr Moores objected. They accept this, and continue to hold you in the highest esteem.'

The letter went on to refer to the Press Complaints Commission and to my situation with regard to *The People*. Like this: 'It would be quite inappropriate for this matter to be the subject of complaint to the Press Complaints Commission or for any further public reference to it to be made . . . I am very anxious to maintain the good relationship you have had with *The People* over the years. I should be very happy if you would continue to contribute to *The People* and I can assure you that we would like to publish your contributions.'

Bully for them. I replied that it was presumptuous to say that 'neither Mr Moores, Liverpool Football Club *nor anybody else involved*' wished to give further publicity to the matter, because I certainly did wish to bring it to the attention of the public. As for Moores and Robinson continuing to hold me in the highest esteem, while I had known Peter for more than 30 years, I had never met Moores and had spoken to him only once, on the phone – so how could he 'continue' to hold me in the highest esteem?

As for the Press Complaints Commission, I took the view that it was extremely appropriate for the matter to be referred to the Commission and, indeed, I had already done so. When it came to working for *The People*, Mr Bradshaw had already expressed the view to me that it would be better if I ceased my association forthwith – ignoring the little matter of my already having decided to quit. So it seemed to me that the sports editor's sentiments were strangely at odds with those now expressed by Mr Gould.

Early in December another epistle from the deputy editor dropped through my letter-box. He was sorry I had not chosen to respond 'more positively' and repeated that 'I hope you will continue to contribute to *The People*. That remains the position of the editor, myself and Bill Bradshaw.'

I got nowhere with the Press Complaints Commission, being told the matter was something in which the Commission could not become involved – a ruling I found strange, since its terms of reference were to deal with complaints by people who had been affected by the behaviour of newspapers. And I had certainly been affected by *The People*'s behaviour. I believe the Commission should have taken the matter up and investigated fully – even if it had come down on the side of *The People* in the end. So far as I am concerned, *The People* sought to muzzle me, after having got me into trouble through no fault of my own. The paper had used my name on a story without my knowledge or permission – a story which, to a large degree, I had not written.

While Len Gould was telling me that the Moores article had never been the subject of a defamation action, the final letter I received from Moores's solicitors phrased matters rather differently, since it told me not only that 'terms for the settlement of my client's claim against *The People* have been agreed and an apology has been received'. It went on to say that 'they have confirmed that although the *defamatory* [my italics] article appeared under your name, you were not responsible for writing those parts which my client found offensive'. The letter concluded with this eight-word sentence: 'Accordingly the claim made against you is withdrawn.'

Let me say now that from the start of this affair, my sympathies had been totally with David Moores – indeed, had he gone on to take *The People* to court, I would have been only too happy to have appeared as a witness on his behalf, as well as speaking up for myself. However, that was not how things turned out, although in the end my name was cleared. Even so, I felt rather sore about the manner in which the affair had developed.

The letter to me, incidentally, was signed by Tony Ensor, the man who later quit as a Liverpool director 'because of a genuine difference of opinion as to how the club should be run'. Ensor said then that 'the precise details are confidential, and I have no wish to embarrass or cause any problems for my former colleagues by saying anything further on that point. The parting . . . was caused at my own instigation because I felt that my strongly-held views were not compatible with continuing to serve as a member of the board.'

Good for Mr Ensor; and when I replied to his letter absolving me from blame over the David Moores affair, I mentioned that it would not come amiss if his client were to express some regret to me for all the hassle I had had to endure. When I stopped working for Liverpool, after almost 20 years, I hadn't expected a gold watch, and I didn't get one, although I did receive a modest pay-off. By the same token, I didn't really expect David Moores to write and tell me he was sorry for the trouble I had been caused, so I wasn't too surprised when there was total silence. Between them, *The People* and David Moores had managed to resolve the affair without it entering the public domain. But now the record has been set straight.

CHAPTER 12

TARNISHED IMAGE
Disasters and Disruption

I am beginning to fear this club could bury itself.
FORMER LIVERPOOL CAPTAIN, TOMMY SMITH

THERE CAN be no argument: the image of Liverpool Football Club became tarnished – indeed, it took a beating over a period of years, as the events of Heysel and Hillsborough, not to mention failings closer to home, impinged upon the public's perception of the club. Liverpool fans bore the brunt of the blame for the tragedy which saw lives lost at Heysel; and from that moment on there was a great deal of work to be done, building bridges and treading carefully, as if walking on egg-shells.

Voluntarily, the club exiled itself from European competition in the immediate aftermath of Heysel, and it took positive steps to build bridges in its relationships with Juventus, some of whose fans never returned alive from the European Cup final in Brussels in 1985. For example, one VIP visitor to Anfield was an 18-year-old girl called Carla Gonnelli, who was allocated a place of honour in the directors' box. She was a Juventus supporter who had experienced at first hand the scale of the Heysel disaster, for it was there that her father lost his life. She owed her own life to a Liverpudlian barman named John Welsh, who pulled Carla and several other Juventus fans from the wreckage in the stadium. Carla, from Ponsacco, near Pisa, made the journey to Anfield with her mother, her uncle and her fiancé, and she spent ten days at Southport, where local hotelier Harry Davies had offered the holiday as a gesture towards restoring good relations between fans in England and in Italy. Liverpool supporters in Southport also helped to arrange Carla's visit.

Gradually, Liverpool's image began to regain some of its glitter . . . then came the disaster at Hillsborough, which cost the lives of 96

Liverpool supporters. *The Sun* newspaper may never be forgiven by many of the Anfield faithful for its treatment of the Hillsborough tragedy; and more than five years on, in the autumn of 1994, Brian Clough in his autobiography raked over the embers and stoked up the fires of controversy once again, with his comments on Hillsborough and the Liverpool fans.

Now, I know Liverpool people – I should do, having lived and worked among them for the best part of 30 years – and they can be funny folk at times, as many of them would openly admit. I know Liverpudlians who will grant you that they will put off until tomorrow what they could well do today; they will grant you that they might have a chip on their shoulder; they will grant you that they can be a law unto themselves. But whatever their faults, I know them to be warm-hearted and caring, especially for each other. And when Hillsborough happened, Merseyside – including the Evertonian half – became a united family. A family united in mourning for those who had perished.

This is not to say that everyone who travelled to Sheffield that April day in 1989 for the FA Cup semi-final against Nottingham Forest was a saint. Grave aspersions were cast upon some of those who had followed their team from Merseyside – aspersions made generally, and not individually. The police also came in for criticism; and yet, at the end of it all, nothing that was said or done could bring back even one of the dead.

Then, towards the end of 1994, Cloughie said his piece: 'I will always remain convinced that those Liverpool fans who died were killed by Liverpool people. All those lives were lost needlessly . . . It was the innocent who were killed on that dreadful day, killed by others who arrived at the stadium later and in such numbers that mistakes were made. If all the Liverpool supporters had turned up at the stadium in good time, in orderly manner and each with a ticket, there would have been no Hillsborough disaster.

'The police bore the brunt of the blame, but I had enormous sympathy with them because they were so outnumbered. Yes, the police made mistakes, but I will forever remain convinced that a major factor was the Liverpool fans who flooded through those gates after the police had become concerned that if they were not admitted quickly there was a danger of people dying outside the stadium.'

Clough's collaborator on the book, it was recorded, was *The Sun*'s sports columnist, John Sadler – and, of course, to many Liverpudlians *The Sun* was a newspaper no longer fit to be bought, after what it had said in the immediate aftermath of Hillsborough. So Brian Clough – whose son, Nigel, was a Liverpool player by 1994 – found himself taking the flak, as Liverpool supporters reacted angrily to his views in his autobiography. Roy Evans spoke up straight away for the Liverpool fans and expressed his confidence that Nigel Clough would not suffer as a result of his dad's appraisal of Hillsborough. Evans declared: 'Any suggestion that the Liverpool fans were totally responsible for the Hillsborough disaster is, and has been shown to be, completely untrue. Lord Justice Taylor made this quite clear at a lengthy and detailed inquiry.

'I am surprised and disappointed at such an ill-founded statement which, in my view, diminishes the reputation of the author and not our loyal fans. It is unfortunate that in some reports unfair reference has been made to Nigel Clough. I know our fans are renowned for fairness and decency, and I know they will continue to judge Nigel on his playing ability.'

A player who had been wearing Liverpool's colours on the day of the Hillsborough disaster, John Aldridge, also hit back at Brian Clough. Aldridge, by that time back on Merseyside after a spell in Spain, and playing for Tranmere Rovers, snapped: 'I can't believe he has even brought this up again. I'm astonished. If these are his thoughts, he should keep them to himself. I believe some fans died at Hillsborough because they were trying to rescue others in trouble. There were heroics from fans that day, and they don't deserve this.'

Aldridge's view that Brian Clough should have kept his thoughts to himself was echoed by many Liverpool folk, and I can say without fear of contradiction that the Hillsborough tragedy has long been an emotive subject on Merseyside. From first-hand experience, I can also say that around the time of Hillsborough, it was indeed a matter of holding your breath, speaking softly and treading extremely warily, as claim and counter-claim were bandied about. If Liverpool Football Club's image suffered in the aftermath of Heysel, one thing emerged for certain after Hillsborough: as editor of the club's match-day programme, part of my job was to ensure that the club did not become embroiled in any kind of controversy. Officials of the club were concerned only to make certain that the grief of those bereaved by what had happened at Hillsborough was not seen to be taken lightly and, as the whole world knows, Anfield became a shrine to which thousands made a pilgrimage. It became a place where the football pitch itself was buried in floral tributes.

Eventually, Liverpool's footballers began to play again; to do the job they were paid to do; and life itself got back under way. After Heysel and Hillsborough, after Fagan and Dalglish, Graeme Souness returned, this time as manager . . . since when there was one controversy after another; not least, as he and some of his players were seen to be at odds. Finally, Souness fell foul of the fans and gave up what had turned out to be an unequal struggle.

At the time that Souness gained a reprieve (the end of season 1992–93), Liverpool Football Club were coming in for some criticism because of the way they had handled matters; and this, despite the protests of chief executive Peter Robinson that the club had been put under 'unfair pressure'. One man who had no hesitation in expressing his views was the *Daily Mail*'s chief soccer writer, Neil Harman.

According to Harman, Liverpool had become 'the game's laughing stock'. He said the Souness affair had dragged on to the detriment of club and manager, adding: 'The club who evoked such sympathy and compassion for their involvement in two tragedies which touched the soul of football, are ridiculed for an inability to get their own house in anywhere near order. Stability and common sense have been replaced by ridicule and embarrassment.'

Harman continued: 'The senior players are a discontented bunch' – he mentioned Ian Rush, Bruce Grobbelaar and John Barnes by name – 'and this seems just the tip of a massive iceberg. The board of directors have grown increasingly anxious at the quality of many of the Souness signings. The manager quite rightly pointed out that Liverpool were dealt more injury blows than most, but the excuse eventually began to wear as thin as their defence.'

Harman recalled an interview he had had with Peter Robinson four months previously, saying: 'It seemed that all was not well. Robinson had steered clear of getting involved, but felt he had to answer suggestions that Liverpool were in the red financially and in turmoil psychologically. He admitted that the club had reached rock-bottom with the FA Cup fourth-round-replay defeat by Bolton of the Second

Division. For that to come from someone of his influence was construed as a severe reprimand.

'For the first time since 1964, Liverpool are not in a position to qualify for a place in Europe. It is a savage financial impediment for them. The club are at a transitional stage. They require someone to handle their situation with care, whereas Souness adheres more to the bull-in-a-china-shop management credo.'

During Souness's reign, which spanned 33 months, the supporters had seen the arrival of no fewer than 15 players, valued altogether in deals which stood at around £21.5 million. During that same period, even more players – 18 – had made their exit from Anfield, and they included two that he had bought, with a third out on loan as he himself walked out through the door. So a total of £12.4 million had been recouped – but money wasn't everything.

As Graeme Souness was acutely aware, results had been patchy, to say the least. Just when it seemed as if Liverpool were climbing back towards the summit, something would happen to halt their progress. Under Souness, Liverpool played 157 matches; they won only 66 of those games, and they lost 45, while drawing 46. Even then, the results alone were not responsible for his departure.

At the end of the day, as they say in football, Graeme Souness failed to establish the kind of rapport with the supporters which managers before him had done. Bill Shankly epitomised that rapport, of course, and Bob Paisley won the fans over. Joe Fagan's swift treble of successes made him a hero, while Kenny Dalglish was already a hero, as a player, when he donned the mantle of team boss. On the day Graeme Souness arrived as manager, he declared: 'I love challenges. I like the aggravation that goes with football management.' He certainly got plenty of that – from the fans, and from the media. When he was under tremendous pressure, he was saying that he had no intention of walking away: 'I've never walked away from anything in my life, and that includes anything to do with football.' But on a Tuesday night, when Bristol City knocked Liverpool out of the FA Cup in a replay on their own Anfield patch, Souness was the target for booing from the Kop, and there were cries of 'Souness out!'.

As he sat in the dressing-room afterwards, he was a beleaguered manager. He said he would think about things 'in the cold light of day'. When the cold light of day dawned, it was decision time – and the decision was that he must quit. This was a contest which, he acknowledged, the fans had won, after a match the players had lost.

Let it be said here that there were times when even the likes of Bob Paisley had to win over the fans. Times, also, when players of the past sometimes fell from grace. Liverpool players and managers have had their spats, too, going back to Bill Shankly's time at the club. When the 1974 FA Cup final came around, for instance, Shankly opted for Chris Lawler as Liverpool's substitute against Newcastle United, whereupon a disgruntled Phil Boersma (the man Souness took back to Anfield) made his exit from Wembley Stadium.

Players like Tommy Smith and Ian St John didn't always see eye to eye with Shankly, either – I know, for example, that there were times when Ian felt Shankly had made a mistake in axing him from the starting line-up. Ian did admit to me later that his pride had been hurt – when he stopped to reflect, he realised that while his brain was still telling him what to do, 'my legs just wouldn't take me any more'. In short, he was coming up against the age barrier every player dreads. In Bob Paisley's time, he and Steve Heighway didn't see eye to eye during the closing stages of Steve's career, and I was present on one occasion when another player, with whom I was enjoying an after-match drink, called Bob fit to bust. Largely because, as the player admitted, Paisley had dropped him from the team.

In the Souness era, we saw half a dozen or more players (Grobbelaar, Rush, Barnes, Burrows, Saunders and Walters) having their say; and in the case of Saunders, the then Welsh team boss, Terry Yorath, clashed with Souness. Yorath delivered this verdict: 'It's no good buying somebody, then telling them they're no good. You have to know your product. At Liverpool, Dean had been going into areas where he can't score goals. He's at his best running on to the ball. I said when Dean went to Liverpool that he was one of the best in Britain, and I still say that – provided he gets the right service, and the people who work with him and coach him gee him up. I think Ron Atkinson is the right type of manager for him.'

Another former club manager had expressed similar sentiments to me about the way Saunders was being utilised at Liverpool, and although Deano became a record marksman in Europe for the Anfield club, he found that League goals were harder to come by. Even so, and despite the fact that he had been given a free transfer from Swansea by John Bond, he achieved success.

Bond himself expressed no regrets at having made that decision, taking the line that no one had ever achieved much by staying at Swansea. As for Everton and Nottingham Forest, they wanted Saunders every bit as much as Liverpool did. Souness it was who won the chase, at a cost of £2.9 million. And after the Yorath criticism, he rapped back with some strong words himself, claiming that had he come out with such talk, he would have been 'hung, drawn and quartered'.

With the passing of time after Souness's arrival at Anfield, there were reports of dressing-room unrest concerning Grobbelaar, Rush, Ronny Rosenthal and Paul Stewart (another £2 million Souness signing). Grobbelaar's decision to play for his country, Zimbabwe, rather than play second fiddle to David James at Anfield, provoked argument between the goalkeeper and the boss.

Grobbelaar, indeed, was at odds with a team-mate, too, on one occasion – it happened when Everton beat Liverpool in a Goodison Park derby game, and the keeper was said to have swapped slaps, as well as words, with young winger Steve McManaman, who had put the ball to Everton's Mark Ward and thus given him the chance to score. Grobbelaar said McManaman should have put the ball out of play . . . but 'No, we never came to blows. If we had, he would be six feet under.'

Souness, far from hammering his keeper, declared: 'I want players who show passion. I want a team of winners, a team who don't like losing. I wish I had more like him [Grobbelaar] out there at Goodison.' And as one observer recalled, 'falling out among themselves is nothing new for Liverpool. Grobbelaar did it with Jim Beglin in the 1986 FA Cup final against Everton.' Beglin, who saw the McManaman incident, said: 'I'm sure they were laughing about it afterwards – that's what we did at Wembley. Mind you, we were drinking champagne, celebrating completing the double.'

Souness himself took some startling action when Liverpool, playing Bolton Wanderers in the FA Cup at Burnden Park, went in for their half-time pep-talk after 45 minutes in which they had distinctly failed to please their manager. Mike Hooper, who at various times found himself first choice, second in line and even down the queue in third place, revealed (after Liverpool had finally managed to salvage a draw) that during the interval 'the manager demonstrated exactly how angry he was by sending 15 cups of tea flying. That said it all'.

Souness came under fire from an old team-mate, too. After Ian Rush had been dropped before a game against Sheffield Wednesday at Hillsborough, the player made it plain that he was disappointed because he had had to learn about this from the media. He said it would have been better had Souness spoken to him first. Rush, in fact, became just one of seven players who, during the Souness regime, captained Liverpool (the others were Steve McMahon, Steve Nicol, John Barnes, Jan Molby, Mark Wright and Ronnie Whelan), and during season 1993–94, the Welsh-international striker spoke up for the manager he had previously taken to task, saying: 'The boss knows people are out to get him, but he can only do so much from the sidelines. He can only help and motivate us so far – it's up to us to go out there and give our best.' Rush talked about 'jealousy at the success we've had in the past' and said Liverpool would prove their critics wrong again. By the start of season 1994–95, the critics were still waiting for Liverpool to do just that.

Meanwhile, a Hungarian international signed by Souness – Istvan Kozma, who had cost £300,000 when he arrived from Dunfermline – failed to nail down a first-team place, then became a victim of a Government-backed clampdown on imported players. Kozma's tally of first-team appearances stood at ten, then he was on his way back home, after 18 months at Anfield.

And while Ronny Rosenthal became a back number – he joined Spurs after indicating that he felt his Anfield days were drawing to a close – Ronnie Whelan was declaring himself 'devastated' when the news broke that he was about to be put out to grass, as it were. 'This club has been my life for so long . . . I know I've not been particularly good in the last four or five games, but the team have not been doing too well in that time. I'm the one the manager has decided has to go, and I have to live with that. But it's a big disappointment.' Having said that, Whelan did manage to make a first-team comeback – only to find, at the end of season 1993–94, that he was still on his way out of Anfield.

David Burrows and Mike Marsh were shunted off to West Ham in the £2 million deal which took Julian Dicks to Liverpool, with Burrows declaring: 'I was pushed out of Anfield. I wasn't getting in the team, and I feel I wasn't treated properly. I don't know what I was supposed to have done wrong – I've always kept my nose clean and worked hard. I played 200 games for Liverpool in five years, but I wasn't seeing eye to eye with Graeme Souness. There's only one winner in that situation at any club, and that's the boss. I didn't want to fall out or get into a slanging match, but I am disappointed to leave.'

There was another angle to it, so far as Burrows was concerned: 'In the last five years or so, the club has declined through changes to the normal routine and the buying of a lot of players.' A newspaper poll revealed that most Liverpool fans were behind the manager in his signings of 'hard men' Dicks and Neil Ruddock, but out of more than 700 supporters quizzed, 91 per cent said they were unhappy with Liverpool's League displays. And while many fans were willing to give Graeme Souness a stay of execution, he would have to deliver a trophy or see his side qualify for Europe by the spring of 1994.

On the playing side, also, Paul Stewart – who some months previously had been worrying about his future at Liverpool, anyway – was making news again, this time after having launched an attack against the then chairman of Manchester City, Peter Swales. The one-time City player had backed the 'Swales out' campaign and declared that he no longer had a soft spot for the Maine Road club: 'Not a bit, especially after some of the things the chairman has said over the last few months. Maybe I will, if he goes, but not until. The only people I have a soft spot for are the fans. They want the man out. It's well noted how he hires and fires people, yet he has the cheek to call players like myself for not having given the club 100 per cent when all the fans know I did.'

No doubt Stewart (soon to go on loan to Crystal Palace, then Wolves and Burnley) spoke with feeling; but his remarks caused Liverpool considerable embarrassment – so much so that chairman David Moores felt compelled to ring Swales and offer an apology on behalf of the Merseyside club. Moores told Swales: 'Paul has made regrettable and embarrassing statements, and the Liverpool board want to be dissociated from the remarks. We are unhappy about his reported statements, and offer our sincere and full apologies.'

Swales reacted with the words: 'It was a most profuse apology, and fully accepted. It's diabolical and wrong for a player to slag off the chairman of another club. I'd like to say a few things, but you keep your mouth shut.'

While that affair caused feathers to be ruffled, the Liverpool fans were showing that they were not unanimously in favour of the signings of Julian Dicks and Neil Ruddock. Dicks arrived with a reputation of disciplinary problems – sent off eight times during his career, missed 13 games through suspension the previous season while with West Ham. Souness defended him, however: 'For me, the most important thing is that Dicks, like Ruddock, is a good footballer, and I think that is sometimes overlooked.'

Ruddock's record? Booked ten times and sent off twice while playing for Southampton in season 1991–92 (once for head-butting Notts County's Craig Short). Southampton put him up for sale, and he rejoined Tottenham Hotspur. Then, in August 1992 he was booked on his debut – against the Saints. That same month, he received his marching orders during the game against Crystal Palace, and 12 months later he was in the dock after former Liverpool player Peter Beardsley had suffered an injury (he was out for six weeks) while playing for Newcastle United in an Anfield testimonial match for Ronnie Whelan. Ruddock, however, was cleared by the Football Association.

With talk of possible legal action by Beardsley, Liverpool's image was hardly being enhanced, but Ruddock reckoned 'people have got the wrong impression of me – I got the reputation at Southampton, where I was booked too often, but the club were only seen on TV about once a season, and people formed an impression from what they were reading. The gaffer at Liverpool brought me in to add a bit of steel, but also because I can play. I like passing the ball and playing the Liverpool way. I'm not just big and strong; I like playing football.'

Ian Rush had this to say about his new team-mate: 'I'd hate to be glancing over my shoulder waiting for him to clatter in with a challenge. I always make sure he's on my side in training, because he doesn't ease up in practice, either!' As for Graeme Souness, this was his verdict: 'Any defender has to have a certain amount of aggression, and he may have let himself down in the past. But I'm only interested in what he's doing for Liverpool, and I've been extremely pleased with his attitude. I expect him to be strong and stand up to be counted, but if it got any further than that, I would be the first to come down on him like a ton of bricks. Neil is an aggressive footballer, and if you took that away from him he would not have been an attractive proposition for me.'

Well, he was an attractive proposition not only for Liverpool, but for Leeds United and Blackburn Rovers, and he was signed back for Spurs by Terry Venables, who has not got a reputation for managing teams that kick the opposition off the park. Souness declared that Ruddock was 'in danger of being tarred unfairly . . . I'm talking about his time at Liverpool. I don't care what he was like before. His reputation has gone before him, and people are quick to latch on to that, which I think is unfair.'

Ruddock received another vote of confidence from his manager when he was chosen to play in the League game against Newcastle United at St James's Park in November 1993 – though Beardsley and company had the last laugh, as Andy Cole struck a hat-trick. That match became even more memorable 12 months later, as Bruce Grobbelaar, by then with Ruddock's old club, Southampton, was facing up to charges by the Football Association, after having been accused of accepting bribes for match-fixing.

There was to be an upswing in fortune for Ruddock when, in mid-November 1994, he was chosen by England coach Terry Venables to partner Newcastle United's Steve Howey at the heart of the defence for the friendly international at Wembley against Nigeria. At the age of 26, Neil Ruddock was not only making his England debut, he was acknowledging the debt he owed to Venables for having come to the rescue after he had been ditched by Southampton.

The head-butting incident with Craig Short had proved the final straw. Ian Branfoot, then the manager of Southampton, tracked down Ruddock to a restaurant and delivered the verdict that he was on his way out. 'The manager rang me to tell me the club were kicking me out. I couldn't finish my meal. I felt physically ill. I was out with the family. Somehow, Branfoot found where I was. The chef took the call, and I didn't believe it was him. It was a desperate moment – it almost destroyed me.' So said Ruddock, looking back on that unhappy period of his career. He also said this: 'On reflection, it was what I needed.' So Branfoot – who himself was to be axed from his job at The Dell – ended up by having done the hard-man defender a favour.

It was Venables who took Ruddock, once of Tottenham Hotspur, back to White Hart Lane. 'It happened just before Christmas. I was pretty low. Then Terry took me back to Spurs, and my life changed course again.' It most certainly did. His tortuous route towards the international arena had involved transfer deals totalling £4 million, and he had gone from Millwall to Tottenham, back to Millwall, on to Southampton, back to White Hart Lane and then to Liverpool.

Ruddock said: 'I don't think any manager other than Terry could have done for me what he has. I'd let myself down . . . he rescued me . . . and convinced me I could play for England. I'm appreciated now for the good things I do, rather than just crunching tackles.' Ruddock admitted that he hadn't watched his diet while he spent six months living in a hotel, after his transfer to Liverpool, and he had put on almost a stone in weight. When he was called up initially for the England squad in February 1994, Venables 'had a right go at me. I needed a kick up the backside, and I got it. It got the best out of me again. The thing about Terry is that you can have a joke with him, but when he does come down on you, it's like a ton of bricks.'

Graeme Souness, criticised for his management methods and what one observer termed 'a grossly-misguided buying-and-selling technique', was brave enough to take a chance on Ruddock when he paid Spurs £2.3 million for the defender. And while (as had happened with Branfoot), Souness ended up making his exit, he could reflect a few months afterwards that, if nothing else, he had had the satisfaction of seeing one of his signings climb the ladder to international recognition – even if another of his £2 million men, Mark Wright, appeared to have all but disappeared from view at Anfield.

It was said that Souness's biggest battle was 'to convince disillusioned fans that while his management policies might be contentious, they will ultimately restore Liverpool to the position of supremacy the club once enjoyed'. One old stager, Tommy Smith, saw it differently. 'He sees himself as a Messiah. But he is leading the club down the drain. He has got carried away in making too many changes . . . but he is in charge, and it is down to him to sort it out. I am beginning to fear this club could bury itself. It seems the whole of Liverpool knows what's wrong, except the club itself.'

Yet Souness, having proved himself a fighter during his playing days, showed he was prepared to battle, too, as a manager; and in the face of strident criticism, at times. He raised eyebrows as he said: 'This is the only job I would ever want in football . . . hopefully, it will be the only job, because I will be successful. I hope to earn the right to stay here longer than this contract is for'. He admitted he couldn't hide his feelings – 'I would be a very poor poker player' – and that he became miserable when the job wasn't going well. 'But this is the job I never dreamed I would have and I think anyone else in football would love.

I've got it at the most difficult time, but I've never walked away from anything in my life, and I will certainly not do that here. I'm delighted I took the job; I'm finding out so much about myself that I never knew – and about a few other people.'

In the end, Souness did walk away, after experiencing what the papers called 'people power'. He had won the FA Cup, he had had one reprieve; but when his team lost another FA Cup-tie in the dark days of January, 1994, it was the prelude to the end. He spent some time mulling matters over, then – after a brief statement about his departure – the job was passed on to Roy Evans.

And as Manchester United, 1994 FA Cup winners, staved off the challenge of Blackburn Rovers (managed by Kenny Dalglish) to stage a title repeat, Liverpool fans and club officials fervently hoped their turn would come again – even if they weren't betting on it. Then, on the eve of season 1994–95, Liverpool were making headline news again – the kind of news the club could well have done without.

Don Hutchison, a 23-year-old Scotland B international who had arrived at Anfield four years previously (thanks to a video which the chairman of his club at the time, Hartlepool United, had sent to Liverpool), found himself in trouble for the third time during his career on Merseyside. This time, he was put on the transfer list, as well as being fined two weeks' wages and suspended from a pre-season tour of Germany and Norway.

Hutchison had been pictured in the centre spread of a Sunday tabloid paper while on what was described as 'a drunken holiday binge in Cyprus'. The paper showed him with his trousers down and a beer label covering his private parts, and the accompanying article accused him of 'flashing'.

The player had featured in the same newspaper the previous year over incidents which had disgusted some female students at a Liverpool night-spot, and he had then been fined two weeks' pay. Shortly before the Cyprus incident, he had been bound over to keep the peace by Newcastle magistrates for being drunk and disorderly outside a pub. Liverpool fined him again, and gave him a severe warning.

Then came the third incident which made unwanted headlines; and Hutchison was summoned to an Anfield hearing with chief executive Peter Robinson, director Tom Saunders, manager Roy Evans and Gordon Taylor, chief executive of the Professional Footballers' Association. Taylor spoke on the player's behalf.

When the verdict was delivered, Robinson said this was the strongest action taken against a player in his 29 years with the club, while Evans declared: 'We will not accept this kind of behaviour from any player. It is a sign of our intent. Incidents like this are demoralising, and not in the best tradition of this club.'

Hutchison had been linked with a possible £1 million move to West Ham – but now, it was reported, he 'has to worry if any club will want to buy him'. Gordon Taylor said the player 'very much regrets what he has done. He is prepared to bite the bullet and pay the penalty. The club have sent out a message that their image is very important to them.'

From first-hand knowledge, I can say that this is very much the case – whether the image of Liverpool concerns what happens on the field or off it. Two other players, Jamie Redknapp and Michael Thomas, who had been on holiday with Hutchison, escaped disciplinary action by the club, since their actions were not considered to be serious cases of misbehaviour – but Liverpool's manager did admit his concern that Redknapp and Hutchison had both risked injury when they went bungee jumping.

Within 24 hours of Hutchison being hauled over the coals, Liverpool were suffering from yet another embarrassing incident – this time defeat at the hands of Bolton Wanderers, who during the Graeme Souness era had humiliated the Anfield club with a 2–0 FA Cup victory. In the pre-season friendly, Bolton gave Liverpool a 4–1 hiding, which provoked immediate action from Roy Evans. And once again, the story made unwanted headlines.

As Liverpool embarked upon their trip to Germany and Norway, they left behind defenders Mark Wright and Julian Dicks – players who, between them, had been valued at around £4 million when signed by Souness. Evans axed the pair, saying, 'I don't feel Dicks is fit enough, and I didn't think Wright's attitude in the game was what Liverpool require.'

The sequel was that Wright went in to see the manager and declared that he wasn't happy with the decision, while Dicks accused Evans of not having the nerve to tell him he was no longer wanted by Liverpool. Dicks, signed only the previous September, and heading for his 26th birthday, said: 'It looks like I've played my last game for Liverpool.'

He described suggestions that he was overweight and unfit as 'absolute rubbish . . . I'm in no worse shape than any of the other lads.

The manager is obviously using this as an excuse because he had not got the bottle to tell me the truth. Obviously he's made up his mind that he doesn't want me in the team.'

This, in fact, wasn't the first time Dicks had indicated he was an unhappy man. Not long before, he had expressed doubts about his future at Liverpool when stories began to appear that Evans was trying to re-sign Steve Staunton, the player Graeme Souness had sold to Aston Villa (and later admitted that he had regretted this decision).

By the end of July 1994, after the embarrassing defeat at Bolton, Dicks was sounding off and claiming: 'I was no worse than any of the other lads at Bolton . . . it's rubbish to suggest otherwise. I don't know what's happening; I just wish people would tell me the truth. If they don't like the way I play, fair enough. Graeme Souness obviously thought I was a good player, but if Roy Evans doesn't want me, I'd rather know.'

Evans said simply: 'It's all about opinions. I have made a decision I think is beneficial for the club. They either accept it for what it is, or they think it's the end. But I don't think anything in football is ever a closed book.' Closed book or not, it was certainly the latest chapter in a catalogue of unfortunate events to have afflicted Liverpool Football Club and done nothing to improve an already-tarnished image. And when it came to Julian Dicks, it turned out that the book had indeed been closed, because he was transferred back to West Ham.

However, in Roy Evans Liverpool did find a genuine champion of their cause – a manager who, as one observer was to say, on the eve of the 1995 Coca-Cola Cup final, 'has done most in his first year to revive a club that had sunk to its knees and point it back towards the game's nobility'. Evans, wrote the *Daily Mail*'s Neil Harman, had transformed Liverpool 'from a team which had become crippled by fear, strife and insecurity to one reaching out for glory in a manner to the bootroom born'. He was no less driven than Graeme Souness had been, 'he simply has a different way of showing it'.

And what did Evans himself have to say? This: 'When Graeme resigned after we'd lost the FA Cup-tie to Bristol City last year, it was all doom and gloom. Everyone was saying Liverpool had gone; it was the end. To me, it was a matter of getting the players to have a bit more faith in their ability, which we knew they had. We tried to make it less intense. I never have and never will slag Graeme off because he was desperate for success for Liverpool, but it came across in a way which made the players fearful. We've tried to take the pressure off, make them more relaxed about it. We want the same results Graeme wanted, but I wanted them to enjoy the game while they're trying to win. If a player makes a mistake, some people think the manager giving him a bollocking is the greatest thing he can do. I don't find that to be the case. Of course there's a time you have to let rip and tell players what they're doing isn't acceptable for the standards Liverpool demand, but I think that can be done only twice a season.'

Evans admitted that after having left out Jamie Redknapp to play Jan Molby and Michael Thomas – 'both senior pros to him' – he and Redknapp had had 'a couple of little ups and downs. Jamie argued his point, I made mine, and he's gone away and rolled his sleeves up. He's learned a lot, and so much of it from John Barnes, who's like an extra coach on the field. Barnes is a great model for Jamie, and Jamie listens. He's always telling him the most important time is when we haven't got the ball – we're all good when we've got it, otherwise we wouldn't be at Liverpool.'

Evans did admit: 'Standards have always been high here; but when we were winning so much, maybe we were a little guilty of thinking it would last for ever, which it doesn't.'

Evans also said: 'I don't think anybody will have the same domination in the League that we had, because there are now five or six teams around the same level who can win the Championship.' And on a personal note: 'I know the impression of me was that I might be a soft touch and I wouldn't be hard enough for the job. It isn't a matter of showing it outwardly; it's having the strength inwardly to deal with situations. I first came on the Kop as an eight-year-old, then I played, coached and now I'm the figurehead. It is special because this is the team I've supported and loved all my life. But it isn't Roy Evans's team; it's Liverpool's team. I'm just shaping its destiny for a while.'

CHAPTER 13

MATCH-FIXING CLAIMS
The Bruce Grobbelaar Affair

*We are determined to keep football above the suspicion of
corruption in any form. We cannot emphasise strongly enough
how ruthlessly it will be rooted out and dealt with, wherever
it appears.*
GRAHAM KELLY, CHIEF EXECUTIVE OF THE FOOTBALL
ASSOCIATION

IF LIVERPOOL FOOTBALL CLUB thought that season 1994–95
would bring renewed hope of success, they had cause to believe their
wishes might come true, as the team achieved some good results during
the early days of the campaign. Yet once again, the club and its
supporters were to be given an uncomfortable jolt as two newspapers
made allegations about players who had been signed by the Anfield
club.

First came the claims by *The Sun* newspaper that Bruce Grobbelaar
had been involved in match-fixing while playing for Liverpool; then
the *Mail on Sunday* followed, with a story about transfer payments
involving two players from Scandinavia – Torben Piechnik and Stig-
Inge Bjornebye – who had been signed by Liverpool. Grobbelaar,
signed by Bob Paisley, had become virtually a fixture between the
posts for more than a decade; the other two players had arrived at
Anfield during the Graeme Souness era.

Grobbelaar, the recipient of brickbats as well as bouquets during his
long and distinguished career with Liverpool, had certainly been a
favourite of the Anfield fans, who referred to him with some affection
as Brucie. Piechnik and Bjornebye had varying experiences – the
former ended up going back to Denmark, while the latter (given the
challenging task of filling the left-back problem spot after the departure

of David Burrows and the installation of Roy Evans as Liverpool's manager) claimed a winners' medal in the 1995 Coca-Cola Cup final.

If it was Bob Paisley who signed Grobbelaar, it was Tom Saunders – now an elder-statesman member of the board of directors – who did the donkey work, as it were, after Bob had asked him to go down to Portsmouth and watch a game against Crewe Alexandra. Tom told me about it not long after the keeper had joined Liverpool (in those days, Tom was the club's youth-development officer, and he travelled all over the place vetting teams and potential talent).

As it happened, when Tom went down to Fratton Park, his original mission was to check on a Portsmouth player; but the object of the exercise didn't have an impressive game. However, Tom's attention was directed towards the Crewe goalkeeper who, as he told me, 'stood between Pompey and promotion'. The home team required two points from the game to go up, and Tom recalled: 'As I watched from my place on the terracing, I wondered . . . As the game went on, the Crewe keeper seemed as if he would stop everything, and I heard one of the home fans say to his companion, 'It doesn't look as if we're going to get two points, the way this fellow's playing.' Pompey didn't either – the score finished at 1–1.

When Tom returned to Liverpool, he told Bob Paisley what had happened, and together they checked the fixture lists. They discovered that Crewe had a mid-week match coming up against Scunthorpe, so it was decided that Tom should check on the keeper again, this time in company with his manager. 'Even during the kick-in before the match he did enough to impress Bob,' Tom told me. 'What stood out was his handling of the ball and his general athleticism.'

However, it wasn't a simple matter of making an offer and clinching a deal. 'When we came to inquire further, we found that signing him wasn't going to be easy – the keeper was registered with Vancouver Whitecaps, in Canada. So the next step was for us to fly to Vancouver, where we spent the best part of a week and watched a couple of games. And though they were playing on an artificial surface, once again the goalkeeper impressed.'

There was one thing in Liverpool's favour; the Whitecaps team boss was Tony Waiters, who had kept goal for Liverpool at one time, and so the clubs agreed to do business. However, Liverpool still needed to get a work permit for Grobbelaar. 'The criterion was that a player had to be an international and, fortunately, Bruce had played for Zimbabwe. Later, he got a British passport.'

On the day that Ray Clemence was signing for Tottenham Hotspur and thus ending a 14-year association with Liverpool, Bruce Grobbelaar was eagerly awaiting his First Division debut and hoping to follow Clemence as the Anfield club's long-term, first-choice keeper. That was early in season 1981–82; and ten years later, he was looking back upon a decade which had seen him virtually unchallenged for the No. 1 spot, having totalled more than 500 appearances and having also been an ever-present in seven seasons out of the ten.

Grobbelaar was well equipped to be a goalkeeper. As he told me, shortly after his arrival at Anfield, both his father and his mother had been goalkeepers, too. 'My Dad played for a team in Rhodesia and had one game for the national side, while my mother was the keeper in a hockey team. I've played in goal since I was a youngster, and I always wanted to be a footballer.' When he was 15, he was supposed to go with another lad to Derby County and, hopefully, sign as an apprentice; but that fell through.

Grobbelaar went into the army to do his national service, and in 1977 when he came out, he moved into South African football for the best part of a year. 'While I was playing in Durban, someone who had contacts with West Brom saw me, and in 1978 I spent five months with the Albion; but I couldn't get a work permit. I went to Bournemouth for two weeks, but returned to Albion still unable to get that permit. Then, on the day I was due to go back home, I was told to take my boots to Derby's training ground – where Vancouver Whitecaps boss Tony Waiters wanted to see me. I went through an hour's training session, then Tony asked me if I fancied going to Canada.

'I explained that I was due to return to Africa that day, said I didn't know what decision to make; so it was agreed that I'd travel home the following day and Tony would contact me in Zimbabwe. He did, and arranged for me to go to Vancouver. I played one full game for the Whitecaps in my first season, 30 games in my second spell with them. Between times, I went back to England to play on loan with Crewe, and I got in 24 games with them. Tony reckoned that my spell in English football would make or break me, and while with Crewe I had a couple of training sessions with Gary Bailey at Manchester United and Peter Shilton at Nottingham Forest.'

The day came, however, when Tony Waiters was on the phone to say he wanted Grobbelaar back in Vancouver, and that was when the showman side of the goalkeeper surfaced. He signed off with Crewe – having been made captain for the day – by scoring from the penalty spot against York City. 'I'd been told that if we got a spot-kick, I could take it, and when I went upfield the York keeper asked me where I reckoned I'd put the ball. I told him I'd shoot to his right – but, as I reminded him after I'd blasted the wall into the roof of the net, I hadn't said whether I'd be shooting high or low!'

Grobbelaar told me how other clubs were said to have been keen on him when he was playing for Crewe, but 'Bob Paisley was the only manager interested enough to fly to Vancouver to see me there, and Liverpool were the only club which persisted in trying to solve the work-permit problem'. Grobbelaar's eccentricities endeared him to the Anfield fans, although his new manager quickly told him to save the clowning – such as doing hand-stands – for more appropriate moments. And during his days with Liverpool Grobbelaar certainly had his ups and downs, as he was blamed for conceding goals after what was termed a rush of blood to the head, as well as lauded for keeping clean sheets.

Ray Clemence once told me of the day he conceded seven goals, during the early part of his career with Scunthorpe; Bruce Grobbelaar told me about the day he conceded half a dozen goals while playing in South Africa against a side which wound up as the league champions. 'We were drawing 2–2 at half-time, and had two players sent off in the second half. Every time I let one in, somebody threw a can of lager at me . . . I walked off with the cans under my arm, at the end!'

Footballers can be superstitious characters and often they develop certain habits which they believe will bring them good luck. There was one habit which Grobbelaar adopted during the waiting time in the dressing-room before a match – he used to kick a ball against the light switches, and a light had to go out before he would stop. He liked to be second in line when the team went on to the pitch – and he liked to be in the thick of the action during five-a-side games.

The man who was his skipper for a considerable spell, Alan Hansen, told me about Grobbelaar's action-man image during those five-a-sides: 'he plays on the wing, and he can be atrocious or tremendous. He can whack a ball from any angle . . . but there are times when he'll miss the simplest of chances.' There were times, too, when he threw caution to the winds while playing in goal, as he came rushing out of his area on what seemed a hopeless quest to get to the ball first – sometimes, he ended up trying to dribble his way out of trouble, at others he was left stranded. He also pulled off some remarkable saves – as Hansen said, his great strengths were 'his reflexes and his agility'.

Hansen recalled, too, how Grobbelaar reacted to the challenge from rivals such as Mike Hooper and the pressure brought about by criticism, after one of his more eccentric displays. 'When he was under pressure, he shrugged it off, even though things were hard for him. He fought back well.' And it has to be said that when things were hard for Bruce Grobbelaar during the second half of 1994, as the stories alleging match-fixing surfaced, he braved the taunts of fans and refused to duck for cover. Even so, as he looked back over his 37 years, he must surely have reflected not only upon his career in football, but upon what might have been . . . because he had to think twice about making soccer his career.

As he told me: 'When I was 19 years old, I was offered a scholarship which would have given me the chance to play baseball in the United States. I chose football instead, and considering how things have gone for me, I've had no reason for regrets. But I would still have liked to be a top pitcher in American baseball. I used to throw in Africa, where I played a lot of baseball, and around that time I had only one sporting hero, the great Babe Ruth, who was the undisputed No. 1 in American baseball.'

As time passed, Grobbelaar took up cricket and rugby union and added new names to his list of sporting heroes: Len Hutton, Jackie McGlew, the Pollock brothers, Graeme and Peter, and Barry Richards and Brian Davidson. He also came to admire Daley Thompson and Nigel Mansell – 'what Thompson achieved in the decathlon over the years is remarkable'. As for Mansell: 'He mortgaged his house so that he could compete in top-level motor racing, and that took some guts.'

When it came to soccer opponents, Grobbelaar singled out John Fashanu and Lee Chapman, who 'put themselves about as much as anyone and more than most, yet they're not malicious with it'. And he remarked: 'We're in a tough sport, and being in goal puts me in a tough situation, because of the physical challenges involved.' He was not to know, then, that being in goal would expose him to accusations of

The horror of Hillsborough, which cost the lives of 96 Liverpool supporters. In the aftermath, Anfield became a shrine as people flocked to lay floral tributes and club favours. And when Liverpool and Everton got down to football business again, you could have heard a pin drop, as people stood in silence and reflected upon what had happened.

Three Liverpool greats: Ian Rush, the man who shattered one scoring record after another, also became the top marksman for goals in derby games against Everton, as they wilted against him at Goodison Park (left, above) and the FA Cup final at Wembley (left, below). John Aldridge (below) signs off with a penalty goal in the 9–0 thrashing of Crystal Palace at Anfield, while Phil Neal proudly displays the Milk Cup.

Up for the Cup and the Championship trophy: showman Bruce Grobbelaar is dressed for the part as he celebrates. By the time he had left Liverpool, however, the man who had won so many medals was fighting to clear his name amid allegations of match-fixing.

The man who cost Liverpool a then record fee of £1.9 million: Peter Beardsley (below), who played against Everton in an FA Cup final, then joined the Goodison club, and finally returned to Newcastle United. Hat-trick hero Dean Saunders, whose goals against Swarovski Tirol in the UEFA Cup made him a record-breaker, is pictured left. He struck Liverpool's two goals in the away leg, and followed up with three of the four they scored at Anfield.

The career of Kenny Dalglish was crowned with success from the moment he joined Liverpool – European Cup, title trophies, FA Cup, plus Manager of the Year awards.

The management career of Graeme Souness, on the other hand, was controversial from beginning to end. The relaxed, smiling figure (pictured at the foot of the page with Ronnie Moran, Noel White and Peter Robinson) being welcomed to the club, is in stark contrast to the tension he felt during match action.

The Kop, dismantled in 1994, was for many fans the essence of supporting Liverpool FC. Another tradition, even more revered, is winning: Roy Evans shows his delight in the club's 1995 Coca-Cola Cup victory.

match-fixing during the time he played for Liverpool. It was a time when he needed the support of family and friends – notably his wife, Debbie, whom he had met in Hong Kong, and married, three months later, in Zimbabwe.

When I talked to Debbie, she told me how, as an air stewardess, she was on a ten-day trip to the Far East, while Grobbelaar was on tour with Liverpool. 'I'd heard of Ray Clemence, but I'd never heard of Bruce. I didn't follow football closely, and while I quite liked Liverpool, West Ham were my favourites.' Though born in Devon, Debbie lived for a long time at Harrow and at Sunbury-on-Thames, but when she got married, it was at a place known by its old African name of Umtali. Talking about her husband, she said: 'Because he's an extrovert, he's an exciting person to be around. He's also superstitious – but he won't say in which way, because he reckons it's unlucky to tell!' Before 1994 was out, Bruce and Debbie Grobbelaar found themselves wondering which way their luck would go.

On the home front, Grobbelaar often turned his hand to cooking – 'he's good at doing steaks and Chinese dishes' – while he became noted more widely for collecting souvenirs such as African hats, spears and skins which were reminders of his homeland. He also became the most successful goalkeeper, in terms of medals, that English football had ever seen. Then, suddenly, he was being accused of the worst crime a soccer star could commit. It seemed impossible he could be guilty, when you considered his record: in his first three seasons at Liverpool there was a hat-trick of Championships, with the League Cup as a bonus, each time; in 1984 there was the title, the League Cup and the European Cup – in that European final against Roma, in Italy's national stadium, he swayed at the hips, bent his knees and generally put off the opponents striving to score in the spot-kick shoot-out. He was in Liverpool's double-winning side in 1986, enjoyed title successes in 1988 and 1990 – and he shared with one-time Bolton Wanderers keeper Dick Pym the record of having won three FA Cup medals.

By general consent, Grobbelaar has always been a showman; a man who sometimes appeared to play to the gallery, although no one doubted that he took his professional duties seriously. Had I been asked if Bruce Grobbelaar would be party to match-fixing, I would have answered, without hesitation: 'No. I don't believe he would.' Certainly he was one of the most popular players at Liverpool, so far as the fans were concerned, and he was often to be seen in the sponsors' lounge after a match, breezing in, maybe presenting a prize to the winner of a competition, and generally making himself agreeable to the punters who wanted to have a chat with him.

Like his team-mates, he had lived through the Heysel and Hillsborough disasters, and after Hillsborough, he and his wife were among those who spent hours comforting the bereaved. When he finally shook the dust of Anfield from his feet, to join Southampton, it was after he and Liverpool had failed to agree about a new contract. Grobbelaar had been offered a further term, but he made it clear he was seeking something better, claiming that in the past he had signed on the dotted line without having done an Oliver Twist and asked for more. This time he wasn't going to put pen to paper simply at the club's behest.

Shortly after his arrival at The Dell, he suffered a cheekbone fracture, yet within weeks he was back in action – and, typically, wearing a face mask which he had painted in the colours of Zimbabwe, where he was a national hero. Indeed, it was while he was *en route* for Zimbabwe and an African Nations Cup-tie against Zaire that he was confronted – at Gatwick Airport – with the allegations about match-fixing.

The Sun claimed that Grobbelaar was involved in fixed games while with Liverpool; that it had secretly filmed the keeper admitting he had 'thrown' a match for £40,000 while playing for the Anfield club; and that a syndicate was believed to have won more than £3 million from betting on Newcastle United to beat Liverpool 3–0 on 21 November 1993 at St James's Park. Newcastle did win 3–0, and Andy Cole was a hat-trick man. Grobbelaar, however, maintained; 'I've never attempted to throw a game in my life.' And the man who refereed that match, Gerald Ashby, made it plain what he felt: 'There was nothing that raised any suspicions in my mind.'

The referee wasn't the only person to express an opinion. From a former England manager, Bobby Robson, came this view of Bruce Grobbelaar: 'Had Bruce been English, he would have won international honours during my time as England's manager. Bruce isn't simply an outstanding goalkeeper blessed with incredible agility – he also gives his team an extra defender.' Well, no one was better equipped to pass judgment on a player's ability than the man who had taken his country to the semi-finals of the World Cup.

And by one of those ironies with which soccer abounds, backing for Bruce Grobbelaar came from a player whose own transfer to Liverpool was being called into question – moreover, a footballer who had been a participant in the match at Newcastle which Liverpool's former goalkeeper was alleged to have thrown.

From Torben Piechnik – now back in Denmark, at Aarhus – came this straight-from-the-shoulder declaration: 'Don't remind me of that game against Newcastle . . . I was made the scapegoat.' Clearly, the match had remained vivid in Piechnik's mind; and with good reason, because he said: 'It was my last game for the Liverpool first team.' Piechnik went on: 'I can say one thing for sure: Bruce did not – repeat not – let in goals on purpose. He couldn't have done anything about those three goals. Bruce couldn't go into a game and let another team win to make money. He loves the game and hates to lose. He's such a competitor.' Thus the verdict from a player who, since he had left Liverpool, had no axe to grind.

Four other matches were highlighted and analysed in the press; Liverpool versus Manchester United on 4 January 1994 (when, after United had stormed into a 3–0 lead at Anfield, Liverpool battled back to force a 3–3 draw); Norwich City versus Liverpool on 5 February 1994; Coventry City versus Southampton on 24 September 1994; and Manchester City versus Southampton on 5 November 1994. Former Liverpool manager Graeme Souness said of the United game: 'They punished us for every mistake.' United boss Alex Ferguson called it one of the games 'of a lifetime'. As for the goals, Grobbelaar was beaten by a Steve Bruce header, a curling shot from Ryan Giggs and a long-range Denis Irwin free-kick.

So far as the other three games were concerned, Norwich and Liverpool drew 2–2; Southampton beat Coventry City 3–1; and the Saints drew 3–3 at Maine Road. With regard to the Coventry–Southampton match, referee Kelvin Morton recalled that when Coventry scored, 'Dublin latched on to an error in Southampton's defence, then chipped over the advancing keeper. To me, there was nothing suspicious that day.' According to a match reporter, 'the entire Southampton defence reacted too slowly to stop Dublin'.

In the match at Maine Road, Manchester City came from behind to draw, and their first equaliser was allowed to stand although defender Jeff Kenna (who was later transferred to Blackburn Rovers) believed he had cleared the ball off the line. According to a match reporter, Grobbelaar's reaction 'was one of annoyance that the goal counted, and he ran up the pitch gesticulating and shouting at the linesman and referee'. The reporter, however, reckoned that the keeper 'was clearly at fault with the Peter Beagrie goal that made it 3–3'.

Grobbelaar, who went to Zimbabwe and helped his national team beat Zaire, returned to take his place in goal for Southampton against Arsenal, as the Saints' director of football, Lawrie McMenemy, declared that 'Bruce totally denies all the allegations'. Further evidence for the defence came from Martin Johnson, described as Grobbelaar's personal assistant, who said: 'Throwing a game is just not in Bruce's character. His trademark has always been his professionalism.' Liverpool's chief executive, Peter Robinson, said the club had contacted the Football Association at the earliest possible moment and promised full co-operation for the investigation. Robinson added: 'We welcome the investigation.' And, knowing him as I do, I would have expected nothing less from him.

Nevertheless, the Football Association – having been presented with evidence by the newspaper (whose representatives were pictured on television handing over the material to Graham Kelly on the steps of the FA) – decided there was a case for Grobbelaar to answer. Chief executive Kelly announced that after four days of studying the evidence, it had been decided to charge the keeper with accepting bribes and with conduct liable to bring the game into disrepute. Meanwhile, he would be allowed to carry on playing. Kelly declared: 'As far as we are concerned, he is innocent until proven guilty. We cannot pre-empt or pre-judge anything. We have bent over backwards to be fair to him, but there is a *prima facie* case for him to answer.' Roughly translated, *prima facie* is the Latin for 'at first sight'. The allegations included videotapes – seven hours of them – and, according to David Davies, the Football Association's Director of Public Affairs, the Association's lawyers had studied 'a considerable amount of material' and a judgment had to be made on whether or not there was a case to answer.

Grobbelaar's reappearance on the English soccer stage ended with a 1–0 victory and the keeper admitted afterwards: 'I thought my debut for Liverpool all those years ago was hard; but it wasn't a patch on today. If you thought I was under more pressure than ever before in my career, you were right.' Grobbelaar made some fine saves, while Arsenal missed a penalty – the Saints' goalkeeper saw Paul Dickov blast his spot-kick over the bar. There were two strokes of irony about that match, too. Southampton's winner was scored by Jim Magilton who, as a young hopeful at Liverpool some seasons earlier, had cleaned the boots of Grobbelaar and other senior professionals; and the Gunners' manager at the time, George Graham, who said, 'I think Bruce wrote the script today – he had a blinder', was to find himself soon afterwards being sacked by Arsenal after having been linked with allegations of a kickback. Grobbelaar's verdict on his team's victory was this: 'Nobody would have believed it, if I had said that Jim [Magilton] would be the man to get that goal. He hadn't scored for Southampton before; then he comes up with this one.'

As the Grobbelaar story ran on, it was reported that four months before the bribery allegations, the keeper had admitted that despite his well-paid career through more than a decade with Liverpool, he had no savings. When he appeared in court at Wrexham, accused of drink-driving, he was given 28 days to pay a £250 fine and his solicitor told the court Grobbelaar's only savings were for his children's schooling. It was later reported, also, that Grobbelaar and his former business partner, Chris Vincent, had been involved in a Zimbabwe safari-holiday company which had crashed with debts estimated at £140,000. It was claims by Vincent which *The Sun* had spent two months investigating before publishing the allegations about Grobbelaar.

As the weeks went by the George Graham story blew up – and, with it, one concerning two Scandinavian players who had been signed by Liverpool. One was Torben Piechnik, from Copenhagan; the other was Stig-Inge Bjornebye, from Rosenberg. Piechnik had cost Liverpool £550,000 (a figure confirmed by Peter Robinson), but Copenhagan secretary Frank Mathieson was quoted as admitting 'there is some difference between the nett amount and what we received from Liverpool'. He added: 'We got our money promptly, although I am not prepared to say how much, and we are happy with the way things were handled'. I have no doubt Copenhagen were happy with the way Liverpool conducted their side of the business, because I know how the club operates. Robinson insisted: 'We complied with every rule . . . the full agreed fee was paid to both FC Copenhagen and Rosenberg for Piechnik and Bjornebye in one payment each. We are not aware of what the clubs did with the money, once they received it. We acted quite properly'.

I believe every word he said, because I know he is a stickler for going by the book in such matters, and he would never be a party to anything which contravened the rules. Robinson did concede: 'I have heard what has gone on since. Whether at the end of the day it will all be right or wrong I don't know'. But I am certain neither he nor Liverpool Football Club could have had anything to fear, in any investigation. As for the players, Piechnik dismissed the allegations as he spoke of 'newspaper rubbish', while Bjornebye insisted there had been no irregular dealings concerning his transfer. 'There were no problems. Hauge (Norwegian agent Rune Hauge) was involved, but I made a point of contacting the Inland Revenue myself to ask for their advice.'

According to the *Mail on Sunday*, the annual report of FC Copenhagen listed sale of players at £250,000. That year, the paper said, Piechnik was the sole major transfer from the club. It was reported that no fewer than 23 transfers were being investigated by the Premier League commission set up, though member Rick Parry claimed: 'I don't believe the game is rife with corruption.' One man who, it was said, was not surprised at claims that foreign deals involving agents were throwing up irregularities was Gordon Taylor, chief executive of the Professional Footballers Association. He said: 'We feel a lot of foreign players are being brought in not because they are better than what we have here but because of the way that, on some of them, money can be manipulated.

'I think the business of players coming in and transfer fees being paid far in excess of what the selling club receive is a disgrace and a flagrant breach of the rules. Vast amounts of money are going out of the game, and that is why we need an independent monitoring body.' Asked if he believed the Premier League inquiry would unearth the truth about the transfers, Taylor replied tersely: 'Don't hold your breath. They have had information on various things for some time now.'

However, Taylor's opposite number at the Premier League, Rick Parry, pledged that the latest allegations would be investigated fully, while Graham Kelly declared: 'We are determined to keep football above the suspicion of corruption in any form. We cannot emphasise strongly enough how ruthlessly it will be rooted out and dealt with, wherever it appears.'

It was on 14 November 1994 that Grobbelaar was charged by the Football Association with bringing the game into disrepute and accepting a 'consideration' for influencing match results; and by mid-December it was reported that Hampshire police were conducting investigations with the help of Merseyside police. By that time, also, allegations about the transfers of Piechnik and Bjornebye had surfaced, and the Premier League was preparing to inquire into these matters.

The commission consisted of Rick Parry, Robert Reid QC, and Steve Coppell, then the chief executive of the League Managers' Association and a former chairman of the Professional Footballers' Association. Parry made it plain that 'the integrity of the game is more important than any one person or any one club. If it means half a dozen managers going to the wall, so be it. Our remit is to get to the bottom of what's gone on.'

Meanwhile, Grobbelaar's solicitors said the decision to issue writs against *The Sun* had been taken after consultation with a QC. 'We have explanations for all the allegations relating to bribery,' they said. And the bottom line was: 'We intend to take this matter all the way.' They called for the Football Association inquiry to be halted, pending completion of police investigations, with solicitor David Hewitt claiming it would be 'intolerable and contrary to natural justice' for a tribunal to be held on matters still being investigated by the police. The FA, for its part, said it was 'mindful not to do anything which might prejudice criminal investigations'.

While Grobbelaar's solicitors claimed the Football Association had still not told the player which game he was accused of throwing, Rick Parry was admitting that when it came to the inquiry into transfers from Scandinavia, 'we can't get any information from the Inland Revenue, because they aren't allowed to discuss the affairs of individual tax-payers'. But 'if we feel we have to go to Norway and speak to the Norwegian FA, we will do that. It is important we deal with these matters urgently, but we must also make sure we get the results right. It is a time for cool heads and clear thinking. Football currently has the image of being buffeted from one crisis to another, but underpinning all these allegations is our desire to put into place a long-term structure for the Premier League'.

While it is true that the Inland Revenue will not talk about individuals, it is also a fact that when inquiries are made, they are painstaking and ongoing – sometimes for years – and it has long been conceded that football has come under scrutiny from the tax men. The Inland Revenue, indeed, has its own 'special branch' – a team of inspectors who have dug, and continue to dig, into the affairs of clubs and people in football. The investigators are not only open to what might be termed 'information received', but they keep a sharp eye on stories which appear in newspapers or are reported on radio and television. Sometimes their inquiries reveal that, like the iceberg, far more lies beneath the surface than meets the eye.

The Premier League's inquiry team decided to send someone to Norway to interview agent Rune Hauge, whose name had been linked with the transfers of players from Scandinavia to English clubs. Hauge, however, maintained: 'I have to keep quiet if I am to continue in this business . . . it is important I keep the trust of those I work with. That means complete confidentiality.'

Rick Parry said the commission 'will not be rushed into conclusions – there is a great deal of information to be gathered and examined. Our intention is to establish the facts.' Police sources indicated that with regard to their inquiries into the Grobbelaar allegations, no news could be expected before the end of January 1995 at the very earliest, and by the middle of the month there was a new twist in the saga of transfers from Scandinavia, because it was revealed that Rune Hauge had flown into London from Oslo and 'slipped into talks' with members of the Premier League's commission of inquiry. Jeff Powell, who had scooped the world when he broke the story of Don Revie's defection to the Middle East, claimed another exclusive when he revealed that 'what both parties hoped would be a top-secret assignation in a West End hotel lasted almost five hours'.

Powell asserted that 'many household names' would be anxious to know how much Hauge 'has felt able or obliged' to assist the investigators, but Rick Parry offered no clues as he said: 'I'm sorry, but I cannot say anything about our talks with the Norwegian gentleman.' Meanwhile, Hauge himself was reported to have been retained on a list of agents officially approved by FIFA.

Then came news that Bruce Grobbelaar, along with Hans Segers, John Fashanu, Fashanu's girl-friend, Melissa KassaMapsi and

Malaysian businessman, Heng Suan Lim had been arrested, then released without charge. All had protested their innocence and been granted police bail. As for Graeme Souness, he was reported to have filed a libel writ against a newspaper as he dismissed allegations centred around the signing of Piechnik as 'completely untrue' and, through Mayfair-based solicitors, added: 'Libel proceedings will be issued immediately against the concerned newspaper and against any other newspapers or broadcasting organisations which repeat the allegations, either explicitly or implicitly.'

And as football came under ever-increasing scrutiny, Liverpool could be grateful for one thing, at least – that in his first full season as manager, Roy Evans had given the fans something to cheer as he steered the team to the final of the Coca-Cola Cup and thus had the chance to make the spring of 1995 memorable for the right reasons. It all ended well, too – two-goal Steve McManaman emerged as man of the match after an enthralling final in which Liverpool got the better of Bolton Wanderers by the odd goal in three, and Evans had the satisfaction of knowing that he had ensured Liverpool were once more back in Europe. But, typically, he said he still wanted them to finish in one of the top four places in the League. And they did.

CHAPTER 14

HUMAN DYNAMO
Kevin Keegan

*Keegan has a Doncaster childhood and a Scunthorpe
upbringing. Yet he seems to have been born with Liverpool in
his soul.*
JOE MERCER

SOME PLAYERS have left an indelible mark at Anfield; Kenny
Dalglish, Ray Clemence and Kevin Keegan, to name but three.
Kenneth Mathieson Dalglish had a trial with Liverpool when he was
only 15 years old, and he declined an invitation to return. 'I felt I was
a bit too young to leave home, at the time,' he recalled many years later,
when he was starring for Liverpool as a player. When he made his way
to Parkhead, the home of Celtic, it was sitting on the top deck of a
No. 64 bus, and it turned out to be a bus ride to footballing fame.

A fellow-Scot and team-mate of Kenny also had a trial for Liverpool
at the age of 15, although the Anfield club ended up paying Partick
Thistle £100,000 for him. His name was Alan Hansen. After he had
joined Liverpool he told me how, in his formative years, he put golf
before football. 'I was crazy about the game, and by the time I was 16
I was playing off a handicap of two.' His idol then was the Golden
Bear, Jack Nicklaus. Hansen was accomplished in other sports as well
as golf and soccer, but ultimately he became one of the finest
footballers ever to grace a Liverpool jersey.

Hansen was to repay his transfer fee over and over again, as did Ray
Clemence, a more modest £20,000 signing from Scunthorpe. Years
later, Clem said he joined Liverpool believing he would claim a first-
team place in a matter of months – he thought Tommy Lawrence was
aged around 30 and on his way out. But he discovered that Lawrence
was no more than 28, and Clem was kept waiting two and a half years

before playing his first match in senior football. He was to total more than 650 appearances for Liverpool.

Alan Hansen told me how he worked in an insurance office – for just six weeks. 'I didn't take to that at all!' he said. Ray Clemence spent some time during the summer months as a deckchair attendant at Skegness before joining Liverpool. And Kevin Keegan – like Clemence, recruited from Scunthorpe – worked for a spell in a brassworks at Doncaster, where he used to climb over the wall at the Belle Vue ground to watch the Rovers play.

Keegan made an altogether swifter entry on to the First Division scene, after having been signed by Liverpool five days before they went to Wembley for the FA Cup final in 1971. At the time, he was pictured sitting astride a dustbin, and in a relatively short time he was to have the footballing world at his feet. He turned out to be a human dynamo, destined to star at home and abroad. That was Joseph Kevin Keegan, the son of a miner; born at Armthorpe, near Doncaster, and a bargain buy by Liverpool at £35,000. He became an idol of the Anfield faithful (especially those fans who stood on the Kop) in next to no time. Overall, he won 63 caps, captained England 29 times and was named European Footballer of the Year not once, but twice.

When Keegan made his first-team debut, he was a marksman with the game only 12 minutes old. He claimed an England Under-23 cap after only 22 First Division appearances, and his first season was rounded off with his being voted the managers' choice as the Young Footballer of season 1971–72. Needless to say, Bill Shankly had a few words of wisdom to dispense about his latest find. Like this: 'Kevin's qualities? He does everything right. Off the field he's a quiet and unassuming fellow who's blessed with a good deal of common sense. He's alert, alive and knows right from wrong.'

Keegan himself recalled how he was invited for a trial at Scunthorpe. The invitation came from a defender who was an opponent in a Sunday League game. The defender also happened to be a part-time scout for Scunthorpe. Two trial games later, and Keegan was signing forms as an apprentice in December 1968. The Scunthorpe manager then was Ron Ashman, whom I got to know well, and he recalled that Keegan not only had talent – 'you didn't have to be an ace scout to see that he had what it took' – but 'what struck me was his refreshing approach to the game and to training. I knew we would have to let him go, eventually, and I was glad that it was to Liverpool.'

It was Joe Mercer, that shrewd judge of soccer talent, who said: 'Keegan has a Doncaster childhood and a Scunthorpe upbringing. Yet he seems to have been born with Liverpool in his soul.' And Ronnie Moran, then in charge of Liverpool reserves, recalled that he had Keegan in his squad for three friendly games (as the pre-season matches got under way, Kevin switched from midfield to the front line). In a practice match, he hit a hat-trick against the reserves, and he never looked back after scoring on his debut against Nottingham Forest (a match Liverpool won, 3–1).

According to Moran, Keegan 'oozed enthusiasm, had good control, strength on the ball and a determination which kept him in the top flight here. He proved himself all over again with SV Hamburg, Southampton and Newcastle United'. Keegan was 'in a hurry with his career' and, for the most part his days at Liverpool were glory days; not least, the 1974 FA Cup final against Newcastle United when he was a two-goal marksman in Liverpool's 3–0 victory over a side which included Terry McDermott and Alan Kennedy (both later to wear Liverpool's colours). There was the odd, best-forgotten occasion, too; such as the Wembley day a few months later when Keegan and Leeds United's Billy Bremner tangled and received marching orders.

That was during the Charity Shield match which heralded season 1974–75. Referee Bob Matthewson, from Bolton, issued 'Off you go' orders to Keegan and Bremner, and even before he had left the scene each player had discarded his shirt – not surprisingly, much was made of this in the Sunday-morning papers. The affair hadn't finished with that, of course; there remained the matter of punishment from the Football Association. And when the commission met it decided the offence had been of sufficient gravity for Keegan and Bremner each to pay a stiff penalty: suspension for 11 matches, and a £500 fine apiece. Keegan himself expressed words of regret about the incident, and he took his punishment like a man – as, indeed, did his Leeds United opponent. It was clearly a salutary lesson for both players.

Strangely enough, however, when I think of Kevin Keegan some of my most vivid memories concern his days with SV Hamburg, Southampton and Newcastle United. There was, notably, a game at

Anfield on Saturday, 28 November 1981, when he skippered the Saints, and Liverpool lost as Steve Moran scored the only goal.

It was a match I didn't even see because at the time it was being played, I had just come out of the operating theatre after open-heart surgery and was in intensive care. The previous day, I had gone to the hospital for an angiogram, expecting to be sent home and given the verdict later as to what was going to happen to me. Instead, I found myself in a hospital bed that Friday afternoon, being confronted by a surgeon who told me: 'You've got a badly blocked artery, and I'm proposing to operate tomorrow morning. You've nine and a half chances out of ten. How does that grab you?'

Once I had taken in the implications, my first thought was to let Peter Robinson know the situation – there was a programme coming up, and suddenly a new (and, I hoped, temporary) editor was required. They allowed me to make a phone call to Anfield – though I had to be wheeled to the phone and remain sitting in the chair – and Peter got a shock when I explained what was about to happen. I told him I would arrange for a stand-in editor, and phoned a newspaper colleague who took on the job while I was out of action. And that was how I came to miss seeing Keegan and company at Anfield and, of course, why 28 November 1981, is a date which will linger in my memory as long as I live.

I don't know if I was the first Liverpool employee to undergo open-heart surgery, but I do know that two more Anfield names were to follow me. Tom Saunders, the club's youth-development officer, was operated on by the same surgeon who saved my life, and Graeme Souness was the other. Souness arrived at Liverpool the first time around after Kevin Keegan had departed for SV Hamburg, and both men had their trials when they returned to Anfield.

I recall how Keegan came back with Hamburg – where he had overcome some considerable problems in settling in, for various reasons which were not his fault – and, while being given a warm welcome, was still made to suffer. Liverpool and Hamburg were meeting in a Super Cup game, and Keegan and his team-mates finished up on the wrong end of a 6–0 scoreline – with Terry McDermott, who became Keegan's right-hand man at Newcastle, having hit a hat-trick. And both Keegan and McDermott were to suffer together when they returned to Anfield in the colours of Newcastle United, this time for an

FA Cup-tie. Once again, Liverpool came out on top – indeed, they more or less cruised through the game, scoring four goals.

That was the night which, apparently, decided Kevin that his days as a player at top level were numbered, because he discovered that he was up against an opponent – Mark Lawrenson – who was not only a few years younger, but who had the legs on the one-time Liverpool star. Keegan and his team-mates hardly got a kick, and Kevin was left to mull over the way he had been out-run – remember, when he wore the red jersey of Liverpool, he had been accustomed to winning any stamina duel hands-down.

Bob Paisley, who had originally vetted Keegan as a possible signing for Liverpool, told me that when Kevin left for Hamburg it was because he felt he needed a new challenge – in which case, Bob believed, if a player no longer had his heart in what he was doing, then the best thing was to hand him a vote of thanks for services rendered and wish him all the best at his new club. When Paisley was asked by Bill Shankly about Keegan, Bob answered: 'Take him.' Shankly did.

At that time, the idea was that Keegan would be the replacement for Ian Callaghan who, having shown signs of struggling after a cartilage operation, seemed to be on his way out. In fact, Liverpool got a bonus, because as Keegan blossomed, so Cally regained his fitness and his form, and went on to give six more years' service. Ian was switched to a midfield role, Kevin was pushed up front; and both of these moves turned out to be winners.

It seemed that while he was at Scunthorpe, Kevin had been given a right-sided role in midfield and wasn't exactly delirious with joy about this. Bob Paisley and Joe Fagan noticed, when they checked him out, that he always seemed to be veering towards the left side of the park. After a while, Shankly and his backroom team came to realise that, in any event, Kevin could not have replaced Cally as a right-sided midfielder and, of course, Keegan and John Toshack built up what was almost a telepathic understanding in attack.

According to Bob, Kevin was the major partner; Tosh had brains and aerial ability, and he got into the right positions, though his mobility was limited. Kevin used his speed and his extraordinary stamina to cover the ground and be there for the knock-downs. Once, the players' telepathic partnership was the subject of an experiment on TV, though they had limited success in that instance, but between them

– and with Steve Heighway's contribution – they certainly struck gold and goals.

Toshack was a 95-goal marksman for Liverpool, Steve struck 76 and Kevin totalled exactly 100. And according to Bob Paisley, Keegan's display in the 1977 European Cup final – his swan-song for the club – was his best-ever for Liverpool. Bob told me: 'He refused to be intimidated and simply got on with the game – and that didn't always happen with him. There were times when, after taking a lot of stick, he reached flashpoint and boiled over. On the night, Kevin took Berti Vogts – a brainy player – out of the game. Kevin and Steve covered every blade of grass, drawing defenders away and making room for other Liverpool men to get through. Our third goal, the penalty, came when Kevin left Vogts standing. Berti had had a lot of running to do, and maybe this had taken its toll – at that stage of the game it showed. Kevin's remarkable stamina enabled him to leave the German stranded, so that Vogts' final resort was a foul – and that meant a penalty.'

Although Keegan departed for Hamburg, Real Madrid were the first club in for him; but it was SV Hamburg who stepped in to secure Keegan's signature, although Bob felt Kevin must have suffered some pangs of regret the night Liverpool beat Hamburg 6–0 at Anfield. Bob told me: 'It must have been galling to someone as competitive as Kevin to see his old team-mates running rings round his new team-mates.'

Naturally, there were comparisons when Kenny Dalglish arrived, but from Bob Paisley's point of view, it wasn't just a case of replacing Kevin Keegan. It was the fact that Kenny looked a typical Liverpool-type player that made Bob invest £440,000 of the club's money in him. 'He was consistent, he did the simple things . . . his timing was immaculate, his head ruled his feet. If Kevin had the greater speed and physical strength, Kenny had the speed of thought which gave him the ability to read every situation. He was the coolest striker I ever saw – some of his goals were fashioned almost clinically.'

Keegan bowed out as a Liverpool player in front of 57,000 spectators in that European Cup final in Rome, and he was lured back into English football by the then Southampton manager, Lawrie McMenemy. Arthur Cox, then the team boss at Newcastle, persuaded Keegan to throw in his lot with the Magpies, and it turned out to be a master-stroke by Cox. Arthur had tried earlier on to take a striker to Tyneside – he wanted Andy Ritchie, when Andy left Manchester

United for Brighton, and he signed Mick Harford, though that move didn't work out as Cox and the player had hoped. Cox (who told me that 'all this club needs is someone to light the touch-paper') did sign Imre Varadi, and the player they called Ferrari, because of his speed, did get among the goals.

But when Cox paraded Keegan at a press conference, that was when things at Newcastle United really took off. Along with Chris Waddle, Peter Beardsley and Terry McDermott, Keegan played a major role in shooting the Magpies back to the First Division. And while he was reputed to be earning £3,000 a week, he certainly gave value for money, just as he had done at Scunthorpe, Liverpool, Hamburg and Southampton.

Apart from being an unselfish player for Beardsley, Keegan literally ran himself into the ground, and there were times after a match when, back in the dressing-room, the Newcastle physio had to peel the sweat-stained shirt off Keegan's back because the player himself was too drained to do so.

Keegan still kept his home in Hampshire, and lived in an hotel in Gosforth during the week. On occasions when Newcastle had to travel south – say, to Oxford or Cambridge – for a Saturday game, Kevin would go with the rest of the team on the coach, while the physio drove Keegan's Jaguar car to Newcastle's pre-match headquarters. At that time Keegan was promoting a product called Brut 33, hence his car-registration number, KK33.

After the match, Keegan would drive home, then be up around five o'clock on a Tuesday morning, arriving at Newcastle's training ground in time for work. And he and McDermott often showed they had retained their sense of humour, as well as their working partnership. On one occasion as the Newcastle players were waiting to start training, a jeep rolled up and from it two figures emerged in army-type camouflage – then they began to act as if they were firing guns. The 'commandos', of course, were Keegan and Terry Mac.

I was in Keegan's company one evening before a Newcastle home game, and we were standing in the foyer of the official entrance, talking. When I glanced down, I spotted a five-pound note which was partially obscured by Keegan's foot. I bent down to retrieve the note, starting to say that someone must have dropped it . . . then, as I reached for it, the note suddenly vanished . . . up Keegan's trouser-leg. It had been planted for some unsuspecting mug like myself.

Keegan is well known for his interest in racing, and he and Terry McDermott could claim some credit, indirectly, for thousands of punters winning money when the Grand National steeplechase was staged at Aintree – not the 1993 fiasco, but a race which went the full distance some years previously.

It happened because they knew the jockey, Neale Doughty, and – unfortunately for him – he had collected a whole series of injuries (neck, back, collar-bone, ribs) which, it seemed, might well prevent him from riding in the world's most famous steeplechase. So Keegan and McDermott arranged for the jockey to undergo what amounted to a crash-course of treatment by Newcastle United's physio.

The treatment worked so well that Doughty was able to saddle up and ride a horse named Hello Dandy, which left all its rivals behind on the testing Aintree course; but while the jockey gave full credit to the physio for having got him fit, the latter had to admit that he had placed only the most modest of bets on Hello Dandy, because he had heeded the words of Neale Doughty too well. The jockey had expressed his confidence that Hello Dandy would stay the course, but when it came to tipping the horse to win, he had cautioned: 'Don't put your house on it.'

Arthur Cox, who presented a rather dour image to the general public, was cast in a similar mould to Bill Shankly, and I always had the feeling that this was probably a major reason for Kevin Keegan deciding to move from Hampshire to Tyneside – for him, it must have been like working under Shanks again. One time, when there was talk of Newcastle making a trip to the Middle East, Cox's favourite player and his sidekick, McDermott, turned up dressed as Arabs, and while I don't know what Keegan is like now, as a manager, I cannot imagine he'll have lost his sense of humour.

Once Newcastle had achieved promotion, Keegan bowed out, to an emotional farewell, and it seemed he had turned his back on football for good. Another former England international, Francis Lee, revealed that when he and Kevin were chatting on one occasion, he said the only club for him would be Manchester City, while Kevin reckoned Newcastle United could be the only ones to tempt him back into the game. And they did, too – although it appeared his comeback would not be for long, as he apparently walked out after only 38 days in charge. However, the will-he-stay-will-he-go? saga ended with Kevin agreeing to sign for three years and apply himself to the considerable task of taking the Magpies into the Premier League. And the record books show that he and Terry McDermott achieved their objective.

I must confess that I hadn't really envisaged Kevin Keegan as a manager, not least because, firstly, he had been out of football for eight years and, secondly, he was wealthy enough to be able to do without the hazards and aggravation of being a manager. I wasn't alone in taking such a view, because Keegan's former sparring partner at Liverpool, John Toshack – who knew the pitfalls inside-out – expressed similar sentiments, 15 years after he and Kevin had been the scourge of opposing defences as they wore the colours of Liverpool.

Tosh was forthright as he said: 'I didn't think he had it in him.' And, to be honest, neither did I. Toshack reckoned that Kenny Dalglish 'was always going to make it. Of the two, he struck me as the one who would become a successful manager because of his thinking and the type of fellow he is. Kenny is very deep, thinks very carefully before he acts. Kevin is strong-willed, single-minded – once he makes a decision, it's very difficult to change him. What they have in common are their Liverpool backgrounds, the enormous respect they get from their players, and an absolute determination to be winners.'

Toshack said of Keegan: 'He was never the most gifted player [my sentiments, too], but I've never known anyone work so hard at his game. He made himself great. He never seemed the type to go into management – he has been persuaded by the only job that would have lured him back.' Oddly enough, after he had been installed as Newcastle's team boss, Keegan persuaded his old manager, Arthur Cox, to rejoin him at St James's Park, in a backroom role.

One man who did give Kevin Keegan a resounding vote of confidence was Liverpool's chief executive, Peter Robinson, who was labelled by one sportswriter as 'the king-maker at the palace of Anfield'. Robinson was said to have picked out Keegan as managerial material a dozen years earlier. Robinson said of him: 'Kevin was dedicated to his football, had a very good personality and seemed to have all the right ingredients. I've always admired him as a player and as a man. I'd have total confidence in him. I'm sure it's the right appointment by Newcastle, and he will make them successful.'

And as Middlesbrough went down, so Newcastle passed them on their way up in May 1993 – they were runaway leaders of the First Division, with 96 points (eight ahead of runners-up West Ham), and ready to flex their muscles against the likes of Liverpool in the Premiership. Some people reckoned that Kevin Keegan had used up a huge ration of managerial luck in his first year or so at St James's Park – Newcastle had been threatened with relegation when he arrived – and certainly the acid test faced him as the Magpies embarked upon season 1993–94.

In fact, he gained his revenge upon Liverpool for those defeats when he was with Hamburg and Newcastle, because at St James's Park an Andy Cole hat-trick demolished Graeme Souness's team, and when Liverpool met Keegan's men in the return game in April 1994, Anfield's new team-boss, Roy Evans, saw his side go down 2–0. It was a deserved victory for the Magpies, too.

Not surprisingly, Keegan received a special welcome from the fans who had idolised him from the Kop, and Evans was sporting enough to say: 'Kevin's doing a similar job to Shanks, and in less time, because it took Shanks two and a half seasons to lift Liverpool back to the First Division. Kevin took over a team which was dropping towards the Third Division, and now they're challenging for a place in Europe. To turn it round like that is tremendous. There's a bit of Shanks in his mannerisms. He gives 100 per cent, and if he believes in something he'll go to the ends of the earth to achieve it.'

The Kop, of course, was not to remain as it was for much longer – two more weeks – and the bulldozers would descend as Liverpool replaced the famous vantage-point with a 12,000-seater grandstand. In their time, famous soccer personalities had stood on the Kop terracing as Liverpool fans: Steve Coppell, Phil Thompson, and even Bill Shankly. And the Kopites who saw Newcastle do the double over their own team were not slow to show their appreciation of the way the opposition had gone about the job. Indeed, the fans from Geordieland also played their part in what, for Keegan especially, was a moving occasion.

He said afterwards: 'The highlight of the game was not our two goals or the three points we won. It was when our fans made the Kop sing "You'll Never Walk Alone". It was as if they couldn't come here and go home without hearing it sung in all its glory. It was very emotional, and something I'll remember for ever.'

Possibly, also, Keegan was moved to think about the might-have-beens . . . he might have dismissed talk of his taking over the England job as Graham Taylor's successor, but another Graeme – Graeme Souness – had walked out of the exit door at Liverpool. True, Roy Evans had been handed a three-year contract; but if Keegan was a player in a hurry when he landed at Anfield, Liverpool had become a club in a hurry – a hurry to restore the glitter and the glory days of Shankly, Paisley, Fagan and Dalglish.

No disrespect to Roy Evans – and everyone associated with the club wished him well in his efforts to achieve success – but if things had worked out differently, it might have been Kevin Keegan who was asked to take on the task of getting Liverpool back in the big-time. In the event, while Keegan at first seemed set to leave Newcastle very shortly after having become their team boss, by 1994 he was being rewarded with a ten-year contract and, as the Magpies made their bid to claim the Premiership-title trophy in season 1995–96, he was splashing out £10 million of Newcastle's money inside a week to land striker Les Ferdinand and defender Warren Barton – with the promise of two more signings to come. Like Evans and Liverpool, Keegan and Newcastle wanted success.

CHAPTER 15

THE LIVERPOOL LADS
Homegrown Talent

It hurts like hell what happened to me.
PHIL THOMPSON, AFTER HIS SACKING AT LIVERPOOL

THE STORY of Liverpool Football Club is interwoven, to a considerable degree, with the story of the Liverpool Boys team and, indeed, with the story of local lads who made good as professional footballers at Anfield. It goes back many years. For instance, a youngster called Tommy Bromilow, who captained Fonthill Road School, presented himself at Anfield in season 1919–20. He had his football boots tucked under one arm, and he asked Liverpool for a trial.

Tommy Bromilow got one, and he stayed to become a member of the Liverpool teams which won the First Division Championship in seasons 1921–22 and 1922–23. Capped five times for England, he totalled 374 games for Liverpool. And later, there was another Tommy, Tommy Smith, who was to total 633 appearances in Liverpool's colours. Alongside him were Chris Lawler and Ian Callaghan, while a player called Jimmy Melia also made his mark.

During Bob Paisley's time as a player, Liverpool's captain for a spell was Jackie Balmer, and he totalled ten goals in three successive matches. That was during an era when, in season 1946–47, Liverpool claimed the League Championship – a feat they were to repeat often during later years.

Jimmy Melia, Ian Callaghan, Tommy Smith and Chris Lawler all came to prominence during the Bill Shankly era, while Phil Boersma also played a role in the scheme of things. Later came Phil Thompson and Sammy Lee, and currently Liverpool have local-lads-made-good in Robbie Fowler (who scored all five goals in a game against Fulham) and Steve McManaman (a hat-trick hero against Sheffield Wednesday and the two-goal marksman who won the Coca-Cola Cup for Liverpool in 1995).

When Jimmy Melia, who played for St Anthony's School, was heading for a career at Anfield, he was chosen to play for Lancashire Boys and for England Boys, and in season 1952–53 – as a member of the Liverpool Boys side – he scored 27 goals. Melia was a mere stripling of 17 when he made his debut for Liverpool, and he played an outstanding part in their return to the First Division. Then, after 268 games and 79 goals for the club, over a span of ten years, he still brought Liverpool a £50,000 fee when he was transferred to Wolves.

One of Melia's team-mates was full-back Gerry Byrne, a 1965 FA Cup-final hero as he played on in extra time against Leeds United, keeping his broken collar-bone injury a secret, and he and Melia teamed up together to play for England against Scotland on 6 April 1963. Byrne was one of those Liverpool players who was later to land a job on the backroom side at Anfield, although in his case it wasn't on the coaching staff. When he finished as a player, after 330 appearances, Bill Shankly was prompted to say of him: 'When Gerry had to hang up his boots, it took a big chunk out of Liverpool. Somehow, something was missing . . .'

The man who became Liverpool's record holder, in terms of appearances – 850 between seasons 1959–60 and 1977–78 – was Ian Callaghan and, in effect, he enjoyed two careers with the club; first as a winger, then as a midfield man playing wide on the right. He also proved that you can come back when almost everyone else has written you off. Cally joined Liverpool as an amateur, won England Youth and Under-23 honours, went on to figure in a World Cup squad and collect medals galore. And all this after having made his club debut at the age of 18, as a stand-in for the revered Billy Liddell.

Cally was a player universally liked – I never heard anyone say a bad word about him – and by the time he reached that 850-game milestone in his career he had been awarded a testimonial and continued to remain a key figure in the first-team squad. Remarkably, he had played in more Cup-ties than many footballers had had games in their entire career: 79 appearances in the FA Cup, 42 in the League Cup, and 89 in European matches – a grand total of more than 200. In addition, he was heading for his 650th League game.

When, in April 1978, Ian Callaghan was admitting to having been disappointed not to finish on the winning side in the League Cup-final replay against Nottingham Forest, it was suggested that it might have been his final chance to complete his collection of honours. His reply: 'When I went to Wembley for the FA Cup final in 1974, people were saying it could be my last appearance there. Since then, I've been back several times with Liverpool and played again for England, so I'll just keep on doing what I've been doing for quite a while now, taking each week as it comes.'

There were people who claimed that Cally didn't score enough goals (he totalled 69 during his 19-season career with Liverpool), but he made many more for team-mates, and he would not have remained at the top for so long had he been 'just another player'. He was a team man through and through, and he always found time to give a helping hand off the field, as the late Ken Addison, who for many years was in charge of the Liverpool Development Association, pointed out when he told me: 'When it comes to lending a helping hand in off-the-field activities, no-one responds more quickly than Cally. We get requests for players to attend all kinds of functions and visit people who, for one reason or another, cannot get to games. Cally has always been a willing volunteer – so much so that at times I've felt embarrassed at the calls on his time. A lot of people have good cause to thank him for the trouble he has taken in making their lives a bit brighter – not least in perking up folk when they've been in hospital.'

Ian Callaghan was one of the quiet ones at Anfield, as was Chris Lawler, whom Bill Shankly dubbed 'the Silent Knight'. Chris rarely said two words if one would suffice, but on the field he certainly let his feet do the talking for him. In 1957 the Southport Schools Football Association invited a Liverpool Under-13 team to play the home youngsters at Haig Avenue, and Liverpool officials chose as their captain a slim, poker-faced lad aged 13, Chris Lawler. When the 90 minutes had ended they were thinking they had just been watching a future England centre-half in action. Lawler did become the England Boys centre-half, though when he graduated to the full England side it was at full-back. He reeled off a remarkable sequence of hundreds of games without having to drop out through injury – his tally for Liverpool was 546, and he totalled 61 goals.

Ian St John used to tell a lovely story about Chris Lawler and Bill Shankly, as he recalled an incident which happened during a training session at Melwood, where the players were put through their paces during the week. 'I'm reminded about it every time I see Chris,' Ian told me, and he went on to explain: 'Chris was carrying a bit of a knock, and this particular morning as we were starting to get down to some shooting practice, Bob Paisley told Chris to do a bit of jogging . . . "but watch your ankle". So off Chris went.

'Enter Bill Shankly, and he arrived just in time to see Chris making his way from the main group of players. Shanks used to hate hearing about players being injured at any time – if he opened the treatment-room door and saw a player on the table he'd duck away. And when he saw Chris moving off on his own, he rasped out, "Where's that malingerer Lawler going?"'

What made the occasion so laughable was that, as Ian said, Chris at the time was going all out to play his 250th consecutive game for Liverpool – a remarkable record of consistency. Yet I could just see Bill Shankly having his say when he spotted Lawler apparently taking things easily, for once. I remember how, like Lawler, Phil Neal clocked up match after match, and I know that other players did their utmost to steer clear of the treatment table at Liverpool, not only because they didn't want to lose their place in the team, but because they knew how Shanks was likely to react.

Indeed, I can think of three Shankly signings who didn't meet with his total approval after they had arrived at Anfield; not because he felt that they were lacking in ability, but because he reckoned that they spent more time than was absolutely necessary having treatment for injuries which, in his opinion, they should have been shrugging off. When Shanks and I talked about these particular players, his recognition of their skill was tinged with some rather grudging praise as he pondered on their – to him – injury-prone habits. One thing was for sure, though – Chris Lawler could *not* be counted among their number, and neither could Ian Callaghan, who was once treated all the way home on the train from London, as he battled to take his place in the line-up for another big match a few days later. He made it, too.

Chris Lawler, like Gerry Byrne, Tommy Smith, Phil Boersma, Phil Thompson, Steve Heighway and Brian Hall, was to serve Liverpool in a capacity other than as a player, because after moving on to Portsmouth (then managed by former Liverpool team-mate Ian St John) and back north (to play for Stockport County), he returned to Anfield to become reserve-team coach. However, he relinquished that job in the end and, as with some others, the parting of the ways was less amicable than it might have been.

As a schoolboy, Chris Lawler played for St Teresa's, while Tommy Smith was a pupil at the Archbishop Godfrey School. With Ian Callaghan, he and Lawler formed the cornerstone of Shankly's rebuilt Liverpool side, after the great team of the 1960s had been broken up. It was Shankly who said of Tommy Smith – a lad born to play for Liverpool – that he was not just a hard man, but a player who possessed tremendous ability. 'The way he has been playing, it will be a disgrace to football if he doesn't collect at least one international cap, before he finishes.'

Capped ten times at England Under-23 level, Tommy finally made it as a senior international, when he played against Wales, in 1971. Like Ian Callaghan, when he left Liverpool he had a spell playing for Swansea, under the management of John Toshack. While with Liverpool he totalled 48 goals in his 633 games. Ironically, it was when Chris Lawler finally dropped out of the Liverpool team mid-way through the 1973–74 season that Tommy Smith emerged from the shadows again.

Smith, one-time skipper and an automatic choice for the No. 4 shirt, slotted into Lawler's No. 2 spot and kept his pal out when Chris was fit again. Then, in season 1974–75, when young Phil Thompson (then staking his claims to a regular place) became a cartilage victim, Smith and Lawler teamed up together again. And, at a time when Smith was thought to be on his way out, he played an important part in Liverpool's greatest success, up to then – the triumph in the European Cup final of 1977.

There was an occasion when Bill Shankly observed dryly that Tommy Smith 'would start a riot in a graveyard'. And, indeed, Tommy, even as a youngster, showed that he had an inborn sense of professionalism. The incident happened in 1958, when he was playing for his school side in a Cup-tie.

In those days, of course, there was no such thing as substitutes; and Tommy Smith knew his football rules and regulations, as he soon showed the match officials. During the game, an Anfield Road opponent injured a foot and, at the interval – after some discussion between the masters – it was agreed that a replacement should be allowed. The masters hadn't reckoned with Tommy Smith, though – as the reserve player was getting changed, in readiness to reinforce the Anfield Road side, young Smithy (the Archbishop Godfrey team's captain) strode up: 'Excuse me, Sir, but you can't do that – substitutes aren't allowed,' he told one of the masters. The master mused for a moment, then he had to admit that this was indeed the case, and so Tommy Smith had both made and won his point. The reserve retired from the scene and the lad who had been injured came back on to the field to line up again for Anfield Road. Tommy might well have wished he'd kept his mouth shut, however, because Anfield Road still managed to win the tie.

It was Bob Paisley who told me that 'when you see Tommy Smith go down, then you know he's been hurt'. And when Phil Thompson lost his job as reserve-team coach at Liverpool, he admitted that he had been hurt. It cost Liverpool close on £30,000 as they coughed up the cash in compensation, before the matter of Thompson's dismissal was finally settled.

Thompson had always been regarded, like Tommy Smith, as Liverpool through and through. As a lad, this Kirkby-bred Liverpudlian used to stand on the Kop and cheer his heroes; as a fully-fledged professional, he captained both club and country, and he totalled more than 460 appearances for Liverpool. According to Shankly, Thompson was a player with 'matchstick legs'; but if his frame was slim, he was all heart, and he could get in a tackle with the best of them. Capped 42 times, he spent a dozen seasons at Anfield as a player, returning to become a backroom man after a brief spell with Sheffield United.

The *Daily Mail*'s Neil Harman wrote of Thompson's sacking that it was 'one of the most undignified decisions ever taken by Liverpool', while Thompson himself described the parting of the ways like this: 'It hurts like hell what happened to me. The reasons for my dismissal [by Graeme Souness] were nothing like I think I deserved. I don't think anyone has told it properly yet.'

So far as I am aware, the sacking of Thompson never became a matter which was publicly aired in detail since, in the end, Liverpool agreed to fork out thousands of pounds to compensate their former employee – who, let it be remembered, at one stage had been mentioned in some quarters as being a possible future manager of the club. There was little doubt that Thompson felt hard done by when he got the sack.

He and his former team-mate, Tommy Smith, went on BSkyB's *Footballers' Football Show* to air their views, and Smith offered this opinion: 'Nobody is ever going to be bigger than Liverpool . . . unfortunately, it looks as though Graeme Souness is trying.' Smith added: 'I watch Liverpool all the time. They're frightened to do anything for themselves in the first half and have to wait to be told by the manager at half-time what they should be doing.'

When the then vice-chairman, Sydney Moss, was tackled about what was happening at Liverpool, it was recorded that he looked 'desperately uncomfortable' as he talked about 'a little lapse' and added: 'How can such magic disappear overnight? It will be back . . . we will come again.'

Meanwhile Tommy Smith – who, as a player, never shirked a tackle – had something to say not only about Souness, but about his predecessor, Kenny Dalglish. While at Anfield Kenny had made 'some strange team decisions – Liverpool had a tradition for playing flamboyant football, but he became cautious in what he did. He had his reasons for going. He was ill – it was as simple as that. He was obviously under a lot of strain and finding it difficult to cope. But he's a nice lad, and he's done a lot for Liverpool.'

Smith then was talking on the eve of Kenny's return to Anfield as manager of Blackburn Rovers, and he said: 'If nothing else, he deserves a big welcome back.' And Everton's then manager, Howard Kendall, recalling the news of Kenny's decision to quit his job at Liverpool, admitted that while he was shocked at the time, 'I understand the reasons for him leaving. There are times when you feel you've done enough.'

Phil Thompson had his own memories of Dalglish, because not long before, Kenny had returned to Anfield for a Rovers' reserve game which they won 3–0. The gate that foul November night (when it came to the weather) was a mere 2,000, and John Barnes was making a comeback after injury. And as Thompson, who had held down the job of reserve-team coach under Kenny, looked ahead to Dalglish coming back a second time (on this occasion, for a first-team game) he observed: 'This will be different. I'm sure he'll feel the emotion of what will be a very special occasion for him. He has provided supporters with tremendous memories, and I'm certain they won't let him forget that.'

Thompson, of course, was speaking as someone who had been born and bred on Merseyside and whose whole life had virtually revolved around Liverpool Football Club. He was to experience what it was like, also, to walk out through the door at Anfield. And Dalglish, who saw his senior side beaten by a narrow margin on his return, spoke afterwards of his own feelings. 'I said, when I left, Liverpool Football Club would never leave me, although I was leaving them; and I don't feel any different, after today.'

It was a former Everton player, Duncan McKenzie, who once said to me: 'You don't have to like someone to play in the same team as him.' And many players have discovered the truth of this. There were times, also, when players who wore the famous red jersey found themselves at odds with team-mates, and no doubt long-serving Ronnie Moran (a Liverpool Lad who was recommended to the club by the local postman) can recall plenty of occasions when hard words were spoken. I found Ronnie himself to be a bit short on words when I asked him about his debut for Liverpool, and I happened to mention that Derby County, their opponents that day, had won by the odd goal in five. Ronnie growled at me 'Oh, I don't remember things like that.'

Liverpool have certainly had their share of home-produced players, through the years: Jimmy Case, Terry McDermott (though he was signed from Newcastle United), John Aldridge (who came from Oxford United), David Johnson (a debut marksman every time out while at Everton, he joined Liverpool from Ipswich). Gary Ablett, like Johnson and Johnny Morrissey, played for both Liverpool and Everton, while Steve McMahon made history as he became the first player to skipper both Merseyside clubs. And, of course, while Rob Jones was a £300,000 signing by Graeme Souness from Crewe Alexandra, this youngster's grandfather, Bill, played 278 games for Liverpool – and kept Bob Paisley out of the 1950 FA Cup final.

Tommy Smith's father was a fervent supporter of Liverpool, and there was nothing he wanted more than to see his lad playing for the first team at Anfield. Unhappily for Tommy, his Dad didn't live long enough to witness that proud day. It was Tommy's mother who took her son to see Bill Shankly, and thus set him on the path which led to footballing fame. While David Fairclough became a football reporter for a national Sunday newspaper, after his playing days had ended, so Tommy Smith became a regular columnist for the local evening paper, the *Liverpool Echo*. And, of course, during his spell on the sidelines, as it were, he took notice of what was happening at Anfield.

Even before the era of Graeme Souness, there had been some changes on the backroom side. Chief scout Geoff Twentyman, a former player who clocked up close on 200 first-team games for Liverpool, parted company with the club as he made way for another ex-Liverpool centre-half, Ron Yeats. Oddly enough, Twentyman was then recruited by Souness, who was still at Rangers, while when Souness became Liverpool's manager he took Phil Boersma with him from Ibrox.

Tommy Smith also saw the departure of his former team-mate, Phil Thompson (who was replaced by Sammy Lee), and by the time that Liverpool had lost to Bristol City in an FA Cup replay at Anfield in January 1994, the one-time Anfield Iron was poised to strike. Like Thompson, Smith was Liverpool through and through, and after the humiliation of that Cup defeat, he didn't mince his words, nor spare Souness's blushes.

Through the medium of his column, Tommy Smith declared that the FA Cup defeat was 'the final slap across the face to fans whose season used to start boldly in August and finish magnificently in May with either a Championship lap of honour or a colourful day out in front of Wembley's twin towers.' And Smith predicted: 'The tidal wave of discontent is likely to swamp manager Graeme Souness today. And I for one will not be sorry to see him go.'

Smith pointed out that during a period of 12 months he had never wavered in his views about Souness, 'despite a certain amount of criticism from people who claimed I was conducting a witch-hunt'. And he maintained that 'the vast majority of Liverpudlians have been on exactly the same wavelength as me'.

He recalled how Anfield had once been 'an impregnable castle . . . suddenly all-comers fancy their chances. And that includes clubs who previously would have crumbled at the thought of walking out in front of the Kop'. Smith offered the opinion also that 'if ever a man penned his own dossier for disaster it was Souness'.

He pointed to the exclusive story sold to *The Sun* newspaper, after the manager's heart bypass operation; to the sale of players 'who still had something to offer' – Smith argued that replacements who arrived were no better and, in some instances, 'less talented'. He summed up:

'The end product has been a series of embarrassing defeats against clubs that should not have stood an earthly against the Reds.'

The final accusation was that Souness 'seemed to rule by fear. It has caused so much discontent within the camp that senior players who were previously inspired to keep their grumbles and grievances in-house were going public and venting their frustration in the Press.' Smith said, also, that 'we had the unprecedented experience of a first-team player, John Barnes, actually apologising in the Anfield programme for speaking his mind about the manager'.

Smith recalled the progress the club had made with its off-the-field activities: facilities 'now second to none'; the 'magnificent' new Centenary Stand: the visitor centre and museum – 'a credit to the club and the directors' – and the prospect of the new Kop Stand which would 'rise into the Anfield sky – a monument to the glories of the past 30 years'.

Tommy Smith then declared: 'Souness has had everything going for him. The board have backed him with millions of pounds to spend. The club should be bombing along in all areas; instead, it suddenly finds itself on the verge of parting company with the manager, with close on four months of the season remaining. It's an action replay of last summer, when Souness came within an ace of leaving the club. At that time, he pulled off a Houdini act. I simply can't see it happening again.' And it didn't, because Souness himself gave up.

Smith delivered another wounding charge, as he said that Souness 'was told to change the public's perception of him as a manager without a real feel for the city – strange for a man with working-class roots and who once played for and captained the club with such distinction. On the surface, Souness has remained aloof and distant from the very fans at the grassroots that he should have been nurturing.' And another stinging sentence: 'You are nothing without the total support of the people.'

The former Anfield Iron declared that 'the club is still the greatest in the world . . . anyone who kicks Liverpool in the teeth is kicking me in the teeth as well'. And he expressed a wish that 'if Souness goes, I hope Liverpool can get back to the old way of doing things by appointing Roy Evans and Ronnie Moran as co-managers with a real feel for how things should be done. The fans deserve the best. The players need direction and inspiration. I sincerely hope today that we are about to take a giant stride back.' And if Ronnie Moran failed to figure as number two in Liverpool's new-look, managerial line-up, at least Tommy Smith got half his wish when Roy Evans was appointed team boss, with a three-year mandate to get the club back on the rails.

Evans, signed as a 15-year-old by Bill Shankly, had played for the Lancashire and England schoolboy teams, had been a committed Liverpool supporter all his life, and had made his League debut against Sheffield Wednesday in March 1970 in a line-up which included other local lads Chris Lawler, Tommy Smith, Ian Callaghan and Doug Livermore. When Evans made his managerial bow at Anfield, for the League game against Coventry City on 26 February 1994, he told the fans: 'The pride I feel is almost indescribable.' Evans, from Bootle, also declared: 'I am a Liverpool lad. I stood on the Kop as a youngster, and I understand the football expectations of all our supporters.' Evans also told the fans that 'the high standards we have known will be the yardstick for the future, and Liverpool will always be investigating the top end of the transfer market'. He recognised 'the magnitude of the task', but insisted that 'the job holds no fears for me'. He had good and experienced men all around him, and said boldly: 'I am in charge of my own destiny.'

By one of football's strokes of irony, the man in charge of team affairs at Coventry then was Phil Neal, who had won eight League-Championship medals during a glittering playing career at Anfield. When he hung up his boots he took charge of Bolton Wanderers from 1985 to 1988, had a spell assisting Graham Taylor and Lawrie McMenemy at England level, and arrived at Highfield Road as the number two to manager Bobby Gould. When Gould quit, Neal stepped up, and by 1994 he was back at Anfield as the opposition's team boss.

It had been Liverpool's decision to name Kenny Dalglish as their manager in 1985 that provided Neal with one of the major disappointments of his footballing career, because he had held hopes of being the man to succeed Joe Fagan. In fact, Liverpool's chief executive, Peter Robinson, later admitted: 'I can't say his name was not discussed at the time, but at the end of the day the coin came down on Kenny's side.'

No one had more inside knowledge of the workings of Liverpool than the 42-year-old Neal, who as a player had collected 17 medals. As well as eight Championships, he figured in four European Cup triumphs, and on the fateful evening of the Heysel Stadium disaster, he was the Liverpool team's captain. When he landed the Coventry job his first task was to take his team to Ewood Park – where the manager of Blackburn Rovers was Kenny Dalglish. If there had been some awkward months during Neal's closing spell at Anfield, they had long since been shelved, along with any feelings of bitterness he might once have harboured. His philosophy was simple: enjoy life. He recalled Joe Fagan's advice to his players: 'Joe used to tell us we had no worries when we went out on to the pitch to play. Pack up your troubles and forget everything else for 90 minutes.'

So the wheel had turned full circle for Neal, who had returned to Liverpool as a manager, albeit the manager of another club. And after his own experience in management (he was later to leave Coventry) he knew as well as anyone that you need luck as well as ability to keep your sanity in a job which, to say the least, is hazardous.

By a remarkable coincidence, when he arrived at Liverpool as Bob Paisley's first signing (a bargain, at £65,000) in October 1974, the man who gave the first team talk he ever heard at Anfield was Roy Evans, then in charge of the reserves. Phil recalled, much later: 'Overall, it was like listening to Bob Paisley, Joe Fagan and Ronnie Moran – Roy was steeped in the same Liverpool traditions. He's knowledgeable on the game, straightforward with players, and certainly not short of Scouse humour.'

Phil Neal, whom I have known and respected greatly through many years, might have added that Liverpool's latest team boss would be needing all the Scouse sense of humour that he possessed.

CHAPTER 16

SEEING STARS
Rush, Barnes, Beardsley, Nicol and Grobbelaar

When I lose, it hurts inside . . . Some players go round the dressing-room before a game screaming and head-butting walls, but I sit quietly in a corner and concentrate on the next 90 minutes. It doesn't mean the other guy wants to play more than me.

JOHN BARNES

THROUGH CLOSE on 20 years, I talked to many of the players who graced the Liverpool jersey; among them some who had cost a small fortune, while others had been signed for what might be termed peanuts. Obviously, there are too many names to be mentioned in detail, but there are some who demand inclusion in a book such as this, and it will come as no surprise when I kick off with two modern-day players whose names have become synonymous with Liverpool Football Club. One is Ian Rush, the other is John Barnes. Surprisingly, the former kicked off as an Everton supporter, while the latter used to admire the likes of Pelé, Franz Beckenbauer and Wolfgang Overath before he became an international himself. Rush, from Flint, in North Wales, told me how he contracted meningitis as a six-year-old and spent three weeks in an oxygen tent. 'The weight just rolled off me,' he said, and he's remained lean (and hungry for goals) ever since.

As a youngster, he went with his pals to watch Everton, although the first League match he saw was Liverpool in action against Tottenham Hotspur at White Hart Lane. He made his mark as a schoolboy when, at the age of 11, he scored 72 goals in a season when Deeside Primary Schools won all 33 of their matches. He was a target for Burnley, had trials with Wrexham and Chester, who sold him to Liverpool for £300,000 at the start of the 1980s. Then he joined Juventus for £3.2 million and returned to Anfield for £2.8 million.

When I talked to Ian before he left (he said farewell to the Kop by scoring the winner against Watford), I would have put money on his stay in the land of the lire being short. He told me that Tracy, who became his wife, was learning to speak Italian, while 'I've got a phrase book' – I just couldn't imagine this likeable lad with the Scouse accent conversing in Italian, and I felt sure he would miss Merseyside. When he did come back to Liverpool, he told me he didn't regret having gone, but it was plain that he was glad to be back. And what a tremendous servant he has been to Liverpool.

There was a time early in his Anfield career when he felt he wasn't making progress quickly enough, and when he talked to Bob Paisley he was given this reply: 'Score goals'. So he took Bob at his word – and his record now speaks for itself. In five seasons out of six, before he joined Juventus, he was Liverpool's top League marksman; in derby games against Everton he holds the record which was once the property of the legendary Dixie Dean, whose tally was 19 goals. Rush struck twice, to equal that record, in his final derby game before moving to Italy, and on his return he carried on scoring against Everton: two goals in an FA Cup final, two more at Goodison Park, to make it 23 in 24 derby games. Remarkably, not one of those goals had come from the penalty spot. And by 1995 he had reached the 25-goal mark.

He's been a hat-trick specialist, too – his first came when he played for the Welsh Schoolboys against the Republic of Ireland in 1978, and in Italy he hit three goals against Pescara. He did his old team-mate, Kenny Dalglish, no favours either when, in November, 1994, he dumped Blackburn Rovers out of the Coca-Cola Cup with a superb hat-trick at Ewood Park – this, on his 600th appearance for Liverpool. In the League, he scored five goals against Luton Town, four in games against Everton and Coventry City, three goals (twice) against Notts County; and there were hat-tricks also against the likes of Aston Villa and Leicester City. Ipswich Town, Barnsley, Swansea City and Crewe Alexandra were other victims in Cup-ties, and in the European Cup he hit three goals against Benfica, netting also in the penalty shoot-out as Liverpool won the European Cup in Rome in 1984.

Four goals against Everton in season 1982–83 equalled an individual record which had stood for 47 years, and in a World Cup qualifier against Belgium he captured the Welsh-international record with this, his 24th strike. He also hit a hat-trick for Wales in a 6–0 win over the Faroe Islands, and with three dozen FA Cup goals was heading for Denis Law's record tally of 41 – a record he equalled, in season 1994–95, when – as Liverpool's skipper – he also collected the Coca-Cola Cup.

Rush played his 500th game for Liverpool against Norwich City, at Carrow Road. It was his 29th birthday and Bob Paisley, the most successful manager in English football, was there to witness the occasion. Paisley was then aged 70, and a director of Liverpool, and he recalled how Rush had made his First Division debut in December 1980, eight months after his arrival at Anfield.

Rush failed to score that day – he also failed in a number of attempts during the following ten months, and reached a state of such anxiety that he went to see Paisley, who recalled: 'He was struggling . . . he was probably too unselfish at the time. That's often the case with a young player, particularly with one coming into a successful side. He tended to look for others and lay the ball off when he could have had a go himself. I told him to be a bit more selfish, and it wasn't long before the penny dropped.' The goal famine ended when Rush went on as a substitute against the Finnish side, Oulu Palloseura, on 30 September 1981. Ten days later, he was scoring his first goal in the First Division, against Leeds United.

Even when he was being labelled less than a hit, after his costly move to Juventus, he still managed to tuck the ball away 14 times, and while his return to Liverpool was not easy – he had been weakened by illness – he found his way back to fitness and form, culminating with those two FA Cup-final goals against Everton at the end of the season.

He claimed his 200th League goal with a classic header in a 4–1 success over Middlesbrough, and as he headed towards that Roger Hunt record of 286 goals overall for Liverpool, he was encouraged by the words of 'Sir Roger' himself, who forecast: 'I'm sure it's only a matter of time before he overtakes me. As long as he avoids serious injury and maintains his current rate, he should do it within the next two years. It looks to me as if he is now back to the form he showed before he went to Italy. It took him a while to settle on his return, but now he's as sharp as ever. I think he's the best in the modern game, and his record proves it. He's so quick – he's a natural goal-scorer and also a great team player.' A verdict echoed by Kenny Dalglish.

Hunt added: 'The game has changed a lot since my day. It's quickened up and tightened up. There was more attacking when I played, and more chances. I reckon Ian would have scored more goals then than he has done now – it's all the more credit to him that he's got his goals in this era.'

Remarkably, Rush had to try, try and try again to find the net against Manchester United, but he finally managed it in March 1992 in a match which Liverpool lost 2–1 at Anfield. However, on 18 October 1992 Rush was on the mark at Old Trafford to help Liverpool secure a 2–2 draw, and that became his 287th goal in all competitions for the Anfield club.

Approaching his 500th appearance for Liverpool, he had scored against the Cypriot team, Apollon Limassol, in a European Cup-winners Cup game, to take his tally to 285 – he had already struck four goals in the first leg (a 6–1 romp at Anfield), which meant he had topped Hunt's record of 17 goals in European competition for Liverpool. So his second-leg goal meant he needed just one more to equal Roger's all-time record. It came in a Coca-Cola Cup-tie at Chesterfield, after the under-dogs had given Liverpool a scare in their own Anfield citadel.

There, Chesterfield had forged a 3–0 lead, to the bewilderment of the home side, not to mention the Kop, although Liverpool hit back to make the final score 4–4. In the return, Liverpool won 4–1, with Rush driving in a dagger-blow as he equalled Hunt's 286-goal feat. Generously, Roger paid him this tribute: 'Ian and Gary Lineker have been the best strikers over the past decade, and with the introduction of the new back-pass rule Ian will capitalise on the slips by defenders. The new law could prolong his career . . . he'll score a lot more before he hangs up his boots.'

Kenny Dalglish called Rush 'one of the best finishers, if not the best, that I've seen. His contribution to the club has been massive.' Indeed it has – and when I talked to Ian on his return from Italy, he had this to say: 'I didn't need much persuading to come back. I'd spent seven years here, and I missed it a bit because of the fans and the people around the club. Juventus was a good career move, but if I go anywhere again from Liverpool it will be a step down. Hopefully, I'm here to stay.'

During the Graeme Souness era, when Rush and his manager were seemingly not on the same wavelength at one stage, there was talk about the Welsh star moving 'across the park' to Everton; but that was soon snuffed out. Rush even played for Liverpool as captain, under Souness's management – indeed, he spoke up for Souness at a time when Liverpool's boss was a target for the snipers, after a run of five defeats in six League games and not one League goal in a month.

Rush, in fact, had good things to say and criticisms to make about Souness: for instance, after having been dropped for the first time in his career (before a match at Hillsborough) he lashed out: 'It would have been better if the manager had chosen to speak to me first.' Rush had learned of his omission from the media, an hour before kick-off. He declared: 'I'm upset about it, but I'll be fighting to get back.' And he did.

His anger at having been axed cooled shortly afterwards when the striker, then aged 31, celebrated the birth of his second son with the words: 'It's gone from being one of the most disappointing days of my life on Saturday to the best day of my life on Sunday, along with the one when my first son was born.' Rush, who hadn't even been named as a substitute at Hillsborough, maintained: 'I'm at the club to stay, unless told otherwise. I've been here 11 years and, hopefully, I'll continue to be here. When I signed a new contract last year I intended it to be for three years . . . and that's what it will be, if it's up to me.'

It was then March 1993 and 12 months later Rush was still at Anfield. However, he could look back on two other trips to the steel city of Sheffield which had left him feeling less than happy. Three weeks after a 3–1 defeat by Sheffield Wednesday (he had been demoted to substitute), Liverpool met Sheffield United at Bramall Lane and Rush (by then the captain) was replaced by Mark Walters close to time. It was reported that Rush 'spent the last eight minutes with arms folded, pointedly standing several feet from the bench'. He admitted: 'It always hurts when you're the one taken off. I don't know why it was me – that's up to the manager. As to whether we talk about it later, that's between him and me.'

The day Liverpool beat Spurs 6–2 at Anfield, Rush scored twice, and he was raring to go again, as season 1994–95 got under way, with more than 300 goals behind him. One opponent, Leeds keeper John Lukic, paid him this compliment: 'He's the best first line of defence in the business. His high work-rate is a feature of his play. He learned his trade and picked up the tricks from playing alongside Kenny Dalglish. Young Robbie Fowler is learning in the same way from Rushie now.'

The Liverpool fans flocked to Anfield during season 1994–95 as Rush staged his testimonial match. Celtic provided the opposition, and the Welsh international was rewarded with a gate of close on 26,000 people who produced record receipts estimated at quarter of a million pounds gross – which beat the previous highest take for a Liverpool testimonial, that of Kenny Dalglish, who was reported to have pulled in a crowd which paid £150,000. It was a night for Rush and his wife Tracy, and their sons Daniel and Jonathan to savour to the full, and Ian admitted that the sheer emotion of the occasion made him feel nervous in a way he didn't feel when playing in an 'ordinary' match.

Those 25,856 fans saw Liverpool score a 6–0 victory over the opposition from Parkhead, and the icing on the cake came when Rush himself contributed goal No. 6. In 601 appearances for Liverpool since he had been signed from Chester for £300,000 in 1980 he had scored 330 goals, topped the all-time record for his country with 28 goals and, at 33, was still first choice for his club, as well as for Wales.

By the time the FA Cup came around on 7 January 1995, Rush was revealing that he had once been 'robbed' of a goal which would already have enabled him to share the 41-goal record with Denis Law. It had happened 15 years previously, when he was still playing for Chester, and team-mate Brynley Jones had claimed a goal. Rush said: 'My first Cup goals were for Chester against Workington at Sealand Road. I scored twice, but I was only credited with one – Brynley claimed the other. He tried a shot, and although I turned it into the net, he claimed it. I was only 17 or 18 at the time and, as a kid, I wasn't really in a position to argue.'

Ian Rush followed Ian Callaghan, Kevin Keegan, Emlyn Hughes, Terry McDermott and Kenny Dalglish (who claimed the honour twice) as Footballer of the Year, and after him came another player whose talents have delighted the Liverpool faithful: John Barnes, whose two awards were sandwiched by the one which went to Steve Nicol.

Barnes has been something of an enigma, when you look at his career with club and country, but for someone who was spotted by a

Watford fan while playing football for a Middlesex League club called Sudbury Court, he hasn't done too badly! And despite his laid-back style, at times, he meant it when he told me on one occasion: 'When I lose, it hurts inside.'

In another interview, Barnes said: 'Some players go around a dressing-room before a game screaming and head-butting walls, but I sit quietly in a corner and concentrate on the next 90 minutes. It doesn't mean the other guy wants to play more than me.'

It was former England manager Graham Taylor who labelled Barnes and Paul Gascoigne 'the two greatest talents this country has produced in 15 years' – yet it was said more than once that Barnes never shone for his country as he has done for Liverpool. Indeed, he has known what it's like to be booed by England fans at Wembley.

At the age of 29, John Barnes was fighting to make a comeback after an 18-month battle to overcome an Achilles-tendon problem, and he managed it. He once told me he had never envisaged a career in soccer, but with Liverpool he became one of the highest-paid professional footballers in the land (at a reputed £10,000 a week), and now it seems as if his once-golden dream of making his mark abroad can be forgotten, largely because of that interruption which was caused by injury. By the spring of 1993 he was approaching the end of his second one-year contract at Anfield, and negotiating a lucrative new deal intended to ensure that he stayed with Liverpool for the rest of his career.

Like Rush, Barnes has done a stint as Liverpool's captain, and – again like Rush – he had his differences of opinion with Graeme Souness. Indeed, Barnes ended up apologising to Liverpool's then manager through the medium of the club's match-day programme. More of which later . . .

At a time when he had won 76 England caps, Barnes was ready, willing and able (he is an articulate man, as anyone who watched his TV programme on South Africa would appreciate) to talk about playing for club and country. He declared: 'I'm very, very hungry to do well for Liverpool and England. I'll admit to being concerned about the England stigma that's now attached to me. Of course, my international form has disappointed me. At Liverpool, I get the ball 20 times in a game, maybe lose it ten times, but produce six good crosses and perhaps a goal, and that means I've had a good game. For England, I only get the ball six times. In proportion, I'm as successful, but people think I'm not in the game.' Barnes believed that 'players like Glenn Hoddle, myself, Nigel Clough and Chris Waddle have sometimes been seen as a liability'.

At that time, John Barnes was also saying something about Graeme Souness and the talk that Liverpool players were suffering more from injuries under the training routine. 'Despite the popular view, we're not all injured because of his training methods – in fact, we trained harder under Dalglish.'

And he mused upon what life for him could have been like. 'When I go home to Jamaica I see the shanty towns and realise it could have been me. If my father had not been posted by the army to England, none of this would have happened.'

By May 1993, when the future of Graeme Souness was being widely debated, it was being suggested that it was being undermined even further by the grapevine gossip that John Barnes would make his exit during the summer, should Souness still be in charge of team affairs. At one stage, Barnes publicly admitted: 'Yes, Souness and I have had our problems, and until recently we weren't speaking to each other. He wants to be a winner, but when things don't go well he blames the experienced players in order to protect the youngsters. I can understand that, to an extent. I don't want the burden of Liverpool's past to rest on our promising young players. It could destroy them. But the whole team hasn't functioned, not just the experienced players. We've had such terrible injury problems that on occasions he has criticised the experienced players after a game, and I've sat down with the only other experienced man in the side and said he must mean you and me!'

Barnes talked about the changes having been rung. 'People are now realising that clubs have been discarding their players far too early. When Peter Beardsley left Liverpool, everyone assumed he wasn't playing well, but that wasn't the case. Everyone's raving about him now, but he's not the new Beardsley. He was playing like that when he left Liverpool.'

Barnes believed – and said as much – that 'Souness has found the English game a bigger problem than he thought. He saw us play four or five matches, where we lost a few, and decided that the team had to change just on this basis. But the English Premiership has become far more competitive since he left the scene.'

Quizzed about the signings of Neil Ruddock and Julian Dicks, Barnes answered: 'In football, the manager reflects the team, and the team reflects the manager. When Souness came to Liverpool he thought the team wasn't tough enough. I didn't think we needed to be tougher, because the side had recently won the League and was clearly one of the best teams in the country.'

That John Barnes interview was given shortly before Liverpool met Bristol City in an FA Cup replay. Having drawn 1–1, Liverpool got a second bite at the cherry on their own ground, with Souness saying in his programme notes: 'The FA Cup is fraught with danger . . . one-off games are full of surprises. Cup-ties have thrown up hundreds of hard-luck stories . . . and we don't want to see ourselves in that position tonight. City are bound to approach this replay with confidence, after meeting us twice in 11 days and creating enough chances to win.'

Twenty-two pages further on, and there was a headline: 'Barnes says sorry to Graeme Souness'. In the accompanying article, Barnes claimed that the newspaper interview produced a piece which was 'totally unbalanced'. He maintained: 'We spent 90 minutes discussing my life, my career, my England situation, my past injuries, Liverpool FC and other issues. The article, however, made it appear as though I had devoted the large part of my time to making criticisms of our manager, Graeme Souness. That was not the case. It was my intention to discuss football in a broad sense, which we did, but I was shocked at the outcome. I feel I owe an apology to the manager, the club and anybody else who felt embarrassed by that article.' The programme piece concluded that 'I owe this explanation . . . and regret that the article placed an emphasis on the Liverpool manager. It was never my intention to offend any of them.'

In fact, there was more emphasis than ever placed upon the manager, once the Cup replay had ended, because a goal by Bristol City's Brian Tinnion had put paid to Liverpool's Wembley ambitions and, within days, Souness had made his exit. It was said that 'people power' had finally forced him to go. John Barnes remained at Anfield and returned for pre-season training in the summer of 1994 hoping his and Liverpool's problems would be a thing of the past, and some six months later, as Liverpool drew an FA Cup-tie at Birmingham, he had shrugged off some Brummie jeering and was able to savour these words from manager Roy Evans: 'John may not be the same guy bursting forward that he used to be, but he's a great influence on the younger players. He was fabulous again today. They wanted to play at 100 miles an hour, we wanted to play at our pace; and John made sure we weren't rushed out of our stride.'

Meanwhile, another player who had given the club long service – and who also had not seen eye to eye with Graeme Souness – had packed his bags, taken himself off to Southampton . . . and was fighting to clear his name. During season 1993–94 Bruce Grobbelaar had had to face up to the fact that his days were numbered, after having declared: 'I want to play for Liverpool until I lose my smile . . . or until they put me out to grass. To be a goalkeeper you need to be a bit crazy and have a skin as thick as a turtle shell, because you'll always get flak.' He added: 'I'll carry on taking all the stick they dish out, just so long as I can keep on enjoying the good times.'

By the summer of 1994 he hadn't quite been put out to grass, but the smile was wearing a bit thin and he and Liverpool failed to agree on a new deal. The writing appeared to be on the wall as Grobbelaar declared: 'My contract ends on 30 June, and I've not spoken to the club about a new one. I have no security for myself and my family, and we'll have to wait and see what develops. The saddest thing for me is that I have always accepted what they have offered. I've never held out, but that won't happen this time.'

So Grobbelaar made his exit from Anfield, after more than a decade – most of his time there having been spent as the No. 1 goalkeeper. He had seen off the challenge of others, notably from Mike Hooper, who ended up being signed by Liverpool old-boy Kevin Keegan for Newcastle United, and regained his place after having seen David James being given his chance. At the end of the day, however, Grobbelaar found himself taking the same route that many other old favourites had taken: out of the door and away from Anfield . . . and finding that he was to be the centre of more controversy, as he took with him so many memories – some good, some bad.

Like Grobbelaar, another player who became a firm favourite of the Anfield faithful moved on – and, by doing so, he caused more than a few people to ponder upon the wisdom of Liverpool letting him go. His name: Peter Beardsley. He became the player clubs and country seemed to discard, and then lived to regret it. When Kevin Keegan persuaded him to rejoin Newcastle United in 1993, he did so saying that for his money, Peter was still the best player in the country, even in his 30s, and the transfer fee of £1.5 million showed that Keegan was ready to put Newcastle's money where his mouth was. Beardsley amply repaid that faith.

Anyone who had formed the opinion that Beardsley was past his sell-by date was swiftly made to revise that view, and as his former clubs, Liverpool and Everton, struggled to make an impact in top-flight football during season 1993–94, Newcastle soared up the table to show that they were capable of challenging for a finishing spot which would gain them entry into European competition.

Peter Beardsley was a Newcastle United player during the mid-1980s when I first came across him, if only briefly. I knew, even then, that he was a quality player. As Newcastle United, inspired by Keegan, Beardsley, Terry McDermott and Chris Waddle, surged towards the First Division, Beardsley kept his feet firmly on the ground. He might be edging towards star status, but he was no big-head; as a member of the backroom staff told me: 'He was always ready to help out any way he could, at any time. He didn't think he was above helping to carry the team skips out to the coach when we were playing away.'

Beardsley was bought by Dalglish for Liverpool in July 1987 for a then record fee of almost £2 million, and he became the toast of the Anfield faithful as he helped his new club to carry off the League title and go to the final of the FA Cup. During his second season at Anfield, Liverpool went so close again to achieving the classic double, and in Beardsley's third term at the club they were hailed as League champions.

When Liverpool had signed Beardsley, I interviewed him for a programme feature. His signing had been heralded, or so it seemed, months before his arrival, but he gave me the background to this, as he recalled a match Newcastle had played at Anfield on a winter's day the previous January. The Magpies had lost to Liverpool, but Beardsley had played his heart out. 'At the end of the game, I went over to where the Newcastle fans were standing, in the far corner of the ground, and after acknowledging them I made my way towards the tunnel. The Liverpool fans in that area gave me an ovation, and I applauded them in return.'

It had all been unrehearsed, of course, but almost immediately the rumours began to circulate: Peter Beardsley for Liverpool. 'It's amazing how stories like this originate,' Peter told me. 'But, of course, there was nothing to it at the time.' As the weeks passed, the stories began to link both Tottenham Hotspur and Manchester United with Beardsley, but when I asked him how Liverpool had managed to win the battle for his signature, he answered without hesitation: 'At the end of the day, Liverpool were the only club actually to put their money down.'

That was straight enough, and it summed up the kind of attitude Peter Beardsley has towards football and, I imagine, towards life itself. When he went back to Newcastle, after his spells with Liverpool and Everton, I discussed his return to the north-east with someone who knew him well as a player, and this was the verdict: 'Peter has always looked after himself physically, and in my view he can go on playing at the top level for another four or five years. I saw him at close quarters when he was at St James's Park after his return from Vancouver, and he was a manager's dream. He trained conscientiously, he lived the right way, and I can't speak too highly of him. Kevin Keegan wasn't buying a player who was on his way out when he signed Peter – he was getting value for his money.'

Born in Long Benton, a suburb of Newcastle, Beardsley had harboured ambitions about wearing the black-and-white stripes of Newcastle United – in fact, he did have a trial with the Magpies when he was a youngster, and was offered a contract. But Carlisle also offered to set him on the road to stardom, and he signed for them.

At Carlisle, Peter came under the influence of coach John Pickering, whom he rated as having been the greatest influence on his career. 'He worked hard to make me a better player.' As for Beardsley's relationship with Kevin Keegan when they were team-mates at Newcastle, he told me: 'Kevin was a big help, playing alongside me. He was very unselfish – so much so that he took many of the knocks for me. He took the attitude that he was coming towards the close of his career, while I was just starting, and he was prepared to go for the high balls and take the knocks for me.'

Kenny Dalglish became the eighth team boss under whom Peter Beardsley had served, because after Martin Harvey and Bobby Moncur at Carlisle, there were Bob Stokoe (who transferred him to Vancouver Whitecaps), Johnny Giles (then managing the Whitecaps), Arthur Cox (who signed him for Newcastle, at a bargain-basement fee of

£150,000), and then came Jack Charlton and, finally, Willie McFaul (who had been the Magpies' goalkeeper and served on the backroom side for many years).

Beardsley said of Arthur Cox: 'He was brilliant.' And he rated Dalglish one of the three best players he had ever seen – Bobby Charlton and Johan Cruyff were the others. Beardsley told me: 'George Best must have been some player at his peak, too – I played against him in the North American soccer league, when he was with San José Earthquakes, and you could tell that he still possessed those touches of class which go to make up a great player.'

It can be said, as a generalisation, that very few players who cost £1 million or more move on again for a similar kind of fee, once the buying club is ready to part company with them. A fair number of players have cost £1 million and in a relatively short space of time faded almost into obscurity. Trevor Francis was one of the very few who commanded £1 million each time he moved, as he left Birmingham for Nottingham Forest and moved on to Manchester City, then Sampdoria. Peter Beardsley joined that select company when he took the short-cut across Stanley Park to Everton, and then was persuaded by his old team-mate, Kevin Keegan, to return to Newcastle. Forgetting the £150,000 Newcastle paid for him the first time around, Peter Beardsley has made three moves for a total of more than £4.5 million – a figure which speaks for itself.

By the end of season 1987–88, Peter Beardsley had played in almost 50 games for Liverpool and scored close on 20 goals. He was certainly repaying Liverpool's massive investment in him. And he has continued to repay the transfer fees paid by the other clubs he has served with such distinction.

I feel certain that he would not have chosen to leave Anfield, had it not become clear that he was for sale, and despite the fact that Kenny Dalglish, the man who had signed him for Liverpool, sometimes used him as a number in the squad game, rather than as an automatic and integral part of the starting line-up. As it was, Everton's manager at the time, Howard Kendall, knew a good thing when he saw one, and he didn't hesitate to part with more than £1 million when Graeme Souness gave the nod that Beardsley was for sale.

Kevin Keegan didn't hesitate to snap up Beardsley, either, for another £1 million-plus fee, and so the little Geordie returned to

Newcastle, even though it was clearly a wrench for him to leave his home in the Southport area. Before long, he was back in the England team and starring for the Magpies in a manner which had one manager, Frank Burrows, singing his praises. Burrows had seen his own side, Swansea City, demolished by Newcastle in an FA Cup-tie, and afterwards he said of Peter Beardsley: 'His touches have such vision and subtlety. It's ten years since, as Sunderland's coach, I attended lunches where he always seemed to be receiving Player of the Month prizes. He's 34 now, but looking better than ever, and deserving his England place. How long can he go on? I'd expect him to be still looking the part if I returned in another ten years!'

Meanwhile, another former Liverpool stalwart, Steve Nicol, had made his exit from Anfield, after around 13 years' service. Signed by Bob Paisley in October 1981 and described then as 'one for the future', he soon showed he could play equally well in either full-back position, at centre-back or wide on the right or left of midfield – and score goals. He also became a regular in Scotland's international side. A bit of a joker, Nicol was nick-named 'Chipsy' or 'Zico' by his team-mates (he was a great one for chips and crisps, while the 'Zico' appellation was a reference to the one-time Brazilian ace). Nicol, like Beardsley, gave Liverpool 100 per cent, no matter where he was asked to play and, indeed, both men typified the all-round qualities of what Bob Paisley used to call 'a Liverpool-type player'. For a while, it seemed as if they didn't make them like that any more, but come 1995 the team Roy Evans was able to turn out at Wembley demonstrated that the glory days might not be too far distant again.

CHAPTER 17

BOGEYMEN AND ENEMIES
Wimbledon and Manchester United

We'd better get it sorted out – otherwise, we'll be
dead and buried.
BRUCE GROBBELAAR, AFTER A WIMBLEDON
VICTORY AT ANFIELD

NO CLUB in recent years has turned out to be more of a bogey menace to Liverpool than Wimbledon. They went to Wembley in the FA Cup and defeated the men from Anfield; they scuppered their hopes of glory in a Coca-Cola Cup shoot-out; and they have done the business in League encounters – even at Anfield. That was the ground where they scored a 3–2 victory which provoked the then Liverpool keeper, Bruce Grobbelaar, to accuse senior players of betraying the club's heritage as he said: 'I'm sick and tired of watching people who don't want to die for this club. If their hearts aren't in it, they can jump in the Mersey, as far as I'm concerned.' Grobbelaar, declaring that 'we'd better get it sorted out soon, otherwise we'll be dead and buried', had been restored to the side at the expense of David James – and, typically, he didn't duck the issue when he was called upon to accept the blame for Wimbledon's second goal, which came as he charged out of goal to punch a cross off John Fashanu's head. The keeper was left stranded, however, as Robbie Earle lobbed the ball over him to put his team two up.

Grobbelaar accused the older players in the side of 'not doing their job . . . We're not making it easy for the young ones at all.' Neither did Wimbledon make it easy for Liverpool as a team – indeed, they never have made it easy for the men from Anfield. What, for example, was Kenny Dalglish saying about the Dons back on Saturday, 26 March

1988? At that stage of the season, remember, the FA Cup final was still weeks away, and when it did come round, the contestants turned out to be Liverpool – and Wimbledon.

On that Saturday in 1988, however, Liverpool's team manager was looking back and expressing his undiluted pleasure that at long last, he and his players were back on home ground for the first time since the beginning of February, thanks to a rearranged fixture. Liverpool's opponents that day were Wimbledon, and Dalglish had this to say about the Dons: 'We haven't forgotten that Wimbledon took three points from us on their first-ever visit to Anfield, last season [it was a 2–1 victory for the Dons that day]. So there's an incentive for us to reverse that result, for a start.' Which Liverpool did.

Then Dalglish went on to say: 'When Wimbledon pipped Portsmouth for third place a couple of years ago, the critics claimed that the newcomers to the First Division wouldn't be able to live with the kind of competition they would meet. Wimbledon gave their answer by picking up 66 points and finishing sixth from the top.'

As the world of football now knows, Wimbledon have been giving their rivals in the top flight their answer in their own kind of way ever since – especially Liverpool.

In 1988, Kenny Dalglish reminded people that Wimbledon had reached the semi-finals of the FA Cup that season, for the first time in their history, and pointed out that they could even finish up meeting Liverpool at Wembley in the May. 'Having said that, though,' reflected Kenny, 'I'm not tempting fate!'

It has to be admitted, however that when Liverpool and Wimbledon did come up against each other in the FA Cup final, the men who played for Kenny Dalglish did tempt fate, on the day. And the Dons have turned out to be bogey-men since then, as well, so far as their rivals from Anfield are concerned.

By the tail-end of 1993, Wimbledon had despatched Liverpool from the Coca-Cola Cup in that penalty shoot-out, and manager Graeme Souness was departing on the team coach without having a word to say to the media. He did speak up a couple of days afterwards, when the speculation about his future was beginning to surface once again. And yet, like Kenny Dalglish, he went out of his way to give Wimbledon credit for sticking to their style and playing to their strengths – he didn't accuse them of using unfair methods to win matches.

No matter what disasters befell Liverpool when they came up against Wimbledon during the time when Dalglish and Souness were in charge at Anfield, neither man turned on the Dons and raged against them, as some others have done. There were no sour grapes. Dalglish made it clear: 'I'm not among those who have criticised Wimbledon's style of play – and I'm not going to start now. We play our way, they play theirs, and if the styles contrast, that's no reflection on them. Quite simply, Wimbledon play to their strengths, and I feel it's wrong for people to be critical of them for doing that. The way they play has proved successful for them, and in a footballing sense they are always liable to prove a threat. In fact, you can anticipate that when Wimbledon are in action, there's always going to be plenty of excitement when it comes to goalmouth incidents.'

Dalglish reflected, also, that 'Wimbledon had their own way of going about things when the FA Cup semi-final draw was made. They were out training and got through their work before they thought about the next stage of the competition'. In fact, the Dons were drawn against Luton Town at White Hart Lane while Liverpool were paired with Nottingham Forest at Hillsborough, where John Aldridge produced a couple of telling strikes to Forest's single counter. His second goal was acknowledged to be one of the finest goals ever to win a semi-final. Meanwhile, in typical gritty style, Wimbledon had come from behind to conquer Luton, so the stage was set for the Wembley duel with Liverpool.

It was a final graced by the presence of the Princess of Wales, and most people expected it would end with Liverpool claiming not only the Cup but completing the classic double. But on Saturday, 14 May, in the heat bowl that was Wembley, the underdogs triumphed against the odds – as might have been expected, considering that the omens for Liverpool hadn't been good at the start of the week, when (against Luton) Gary Gillespie and Nigel Spackman had been hurt in a clash of heads. Both were in the Wembley line-up, though each wore a protective headband, and once play had begun, there were signs of an upset when a foul on Aldridge went unpunished and when a scoring strike by Peter Beardsley was ruled out.

Worse was to come, as Wimbledon – playing their usual rumbustious game, ever-ready to 'welly' the ball as close as possible to Liverpool's goal – carried out the tactics laid down by manager Bobby Gould, who explained his philosophy this way: 'I was a forward, and I believe you should play the ball forward as quickly as possible. We try to pressure our opponents in their own area.'

The Beardsley 'goal' came after the Liverpool man had shrugged off two challenges to stick the ball past keeper Dave Beasant, only to find that referee Brian Hill had blown for a foul and was awarding Liverpool a free-kick. Hill later conceded: 'There was every opportunity to play advantage and, perhaps, in hindsight I might have done.' But the whistle had gone – and with it, a goal and, maybe, Liverpool's chance to turn the screw.

Minutes later, it was Wimbledon who were awarded a free-kick and, as winger Dennis Wise pumped the ball towards goal, Lawrie Sanchez soared to get his head to the ball and glance it past Bruce Grobbelaar into the right-hand corner of the net. So, come half-time, Liverpool were trailing and had it all to do.

The second half saw Liverpool fans poised to cheer a penalty goal, as John Aldridge was brought down inside the area. But while Wimbledon were less than happy about the award, they were soon dancing with delight. Aldridge, who had scored from 11 spot-kicks that season, sidefooted the ball with his right foot, and his aim was true . . . but there was the giant frame of Beasant, leaping across goal to turn the ball away. He performed more heroics, notably when Aldridge seemed a certain scorer – this time Beasant flung up a hand and, somehow, managed to deflect the ball for the clearance to be made, as John Barnes raced in for the kill. And on another occasion Beasant stuck out a foot to foil yet another goalbound effort. So, by a mixture of good fortune, goalkeeping heroics and sheer persistence, Wimbledon managed to prevent Liverpool from scoring the one goal which, surely, would have opened the floodgates.

When the whistle went to signal the end, the Sanchez goal was the Cup-winner; Beasant had become the first keeper to save a penalty in a Wembley final, and the first keeper to skipper an FA Cup-final side. He took his bow as man of the match, and collected the Cup from the Princess of Wales.

There was one heart-warming sequel which showed that there can be sentiment in football. Liverpool substitute Jan Molby gave his medal to reserve-team keeper Mike Hooper, who had played in the third round at Stoke and made a save which kept Liverpool in the competition.

Now move on to September 1992 when Graeme Souness was manager and saying publicly: 'I'm not a critic of the way Wimbledon choose to play. It's vastly different from our style, but every club has the right to decide upon its own tactical formula. Frankly, the success they have had with limited resources is a testimony to Joe Kinnear and the managers who were there before him. They did come through all four divisions, and they're a hard nut to crack in the Premier League.'

Souness said Wimbledon's game 'is based on getting the ball into our 18-yard box as quickly as possible, being brought down by their big men and creating shooting positions. We know defenders will launch the ball upfield and attempt to put our midfield out of action. But I don't go along with people who say Wimbledon do not attempt to play football – they do try to build up their moves.' As they had done the previous season, the Dons won, 3–2.

If it was Dave Beasant who foiled Liverpool at Wembley in May 1988, it was another goalkeeper – Hans Segers – who emerged as a hero for the Dons in December 1993 when they despatched Liverpool from the Coca-Cola Cup in a replay at Selhurst Park, after having gone close to claiming outright victory at Anfield. And Souness had spelled it out, right at the start: 'The winners will take a place in the last eight, and another vital step towards European qualification.'

Once again, he said that while Wimbledon's style 'has courted controversy over the years, we at Anfield have no complaint. The contests between us have been highly competitive, played in a sporting manner. Whatever pattern they choose to follow is their own business, so long as they play within the laws of the game. They hit opposing teams on the break, their set-pieces are good.'

And yet again Wimbledon showed they had not gone to Anfield to roll over and die; after 90 minutes they were walking off to the sound of cheers from the Kop (for them) after the home fans had booed their own players. They had scored after a disputed Liverpool penalty goal; John Fashanu had had a goal disallowed; and, by general consent, they had outplayed Liverpool. Joe Kinnear said: 'We've played them five times since I became manager, and we've not been beaten.'

What happened to Liverpool in the replay left Graeme Souness speechless – he refused to comment to the media men as he dashed for the team coach after what had been a long, long (and deeply disappointing) night for Liverpool's manager and players. Because a game which had gone into extra time had ended in a penalty shoot-out, with victory going to Wimbledon. And this time it wasn't Dave Beasant who was the man of the match, but keeper Hans Segers.

In the 90-minute span, Dean Holdsworth and Robbie Earle had scored for the Dons, while Neil Ruddock had kept Liverpool in the game. The match was two minutes into injury time when Segers, trying to get to a cross from Steve Nicol, punched the ball into his own net. He said later: 'It was my fault – I lost my footing in the sand and before I knew it the ball was in the back of the net. I felt terrible about it. I apologised to the others afterwards, because it meant we had to play another 30 minutes.'

But by the end of play, Segers was being hailed as a hero. During extra time he had prevented Liverpool from taking the lead for the first time, as he saved a penalty from John Barnes, after John Fashanu had fouled Mark Walters. And so the tie went to a spot-kick shoot-out.

Ruddock beat Segers, Fashanu beat Grobbelaar; Jamie Redknapp missed, Holdsworth scored; Barnes didn't fail with his kick, Vinny Jones missed, making it 2–2. Up stepped Walters and, as he had done against Redknapp, Segers saved. Brian McAllister made it 3–2, Robbie Fowler levelled the score . . . so it was down to a 21-year-old, Neil Ardley. And he beat Grobbelaar to clinch the tie for Wimbledon, whose players raced around the pitch waving outstretched arms as if they were aeroplanes in flight.

A headline in the *Daily Express* next morning said simply: 'Chopped Souey'. And while Souness stayed silent, Wimbledon team-boss Kinnear reflected: 'It's a tragedy when a team goes out on penalties, but I think we deserved to win. We were cruising in the first half, and should have been four up.' That victory meant the Dons had extended their unbeaten run against Liverpool to half a dozen League and cup matches. And no doubt Graeme Souness would have been the first to appreciate the Kinnear comment that 'you age a lot through a game like that'.

For the umpteenth time since he had become Liverpool's manager, speculation was fuelled that Souness's job could be on the line again. It was speculation given an added dig by comments from one of his former Liverpool team-mates, Mark Lawrenson, who claimed that Souness might be close to quitting Anfield. It was recorded that 'Merseyside buzzed again, as it has so often in the two and a half years since Souness took charge at Anfield, that Liverpool were about to part with their controversial manager'.

There was no question about one thing: Liverpool's exit from the Coca-Cola Cup had been a bitter blow, because had they gone all the way and qualified for Europe, the Anfield coffers would have benefited by many thousands of pounds. As it was, Liverpool's best hope now was the FA Cup – although their manager proclaimed his belief that a high-enough finishing place in the League could still put them into Europe.

When the Dons went to Anfield, two weeks after the Coca-Cola Cup penalty shoot-out, they struck another blow as John Fashanu silenced the Kop with an equalising goal – and that was the eighth successive match in which Liverpool had failed to beat what was termed 'their hoodoo side'. True, it was keeper Segers who was the Dons' hero again – he received an ovation from the Kop – but for all their attacking flurries, Liverpool could not avenge that Cup defeat.

If Graeme Souness was left to suffer again, he wasn't alone in finding that Wimbledon were Liverpool's jinx team. His successor, Roy Evans, didn't take long to discover that Wimbledon would not be an easy proposition for the men from Anfield when, towards the end of season 1993–94, they visited Selhurst Park again. This time out, it did look as if the hoodoo would be banished, with Liverpool leading 1–0 and the match two minutes into injury time.

Then John Fashanu was challenged by Steve Nicol on the edge of the box; Gary Elkins took the resultant free-kick and, as the Liverpool players were still disputing the award, the ball was deflected off Nicol so that it sped past David James and into the net, to preserve that impressive, if mystifying, record of the Dons. That 1–1 result left Roy Evans saying ruefully: 'We thought we had broken the jinx. We didn't think it was a foul and, to compound things, the shot went in off Nicol.'

As Evans looked ahead to his team renewing their rivalry with Wimbledon in season 1994–95, he could take consolation from the fact that the burly Fashanu was no longer with the Dons – he had joined Aston Villa in a £1.3 million transfer. And the hoodoo was banished, once and for all, because when Liverpool tangled with Wimbledon at Anfield towards the end of 1994, they scored three goals without reply (though the Dons had been cruelly hit by injuries). Liverpool well and truly became top dogs early in 1995, as they triumphed in the FA Cup against their doughty rivals – although not without a scare; because at Anfield, in the fifth-round tie, they had a let-off two minutes from time when, with the score 1–1, Robbie Earle's blistering shot came back off the inside of a post. However, in the replay, it was Liverpool captain Ian Rush who made the headlines, as he slid in his 41st FA Cup goal (to equal Denis Law's record and clock up his 334th goal in 618 games). That goal came after John Barnes had struck, and the 2–0 scoreline remained after 90 minutes, as testimony to Liverpool's second success in a dozen encounters with the Dons. It was another southern club, Tottenham Hotspur, who shattered Liverpool's Wembley visions, leaving Rush to wait for another season before he could become the FA Cup's top marksman of the century.

If Liverpool at last gained the upper hand on the Dons, they also helped to put paid to the championship ambitions of the club one observer had termed 'the sworn enemy' – Manchester United – as they scored a 2–0 success over Alex Ferguson's team at Anfield in the spring of 1995. Three years previously, United had lost by a similar scoreline at Anfield and seen their title hopes demolished as Leeds came though to capture the championship. In 1995, it was between United and the Blackburn Rovers side managed by Kenny Dalglish – and as Liverpool beat United, the home fans chanted Kenny's name. United then were aiming to repeat their League-FA Cup double of the previous season, after having taken the Premiership title 12 months earlier, when they had claimed the championship for the first time in more than quarter of a century. So Alex Ferguson then was hailed as a worthy successor to Sir Matt Busby, formerly a Liverpool player who had opted to become manager of impoverished United, rather than take a backroom job at Anfield. His decision caused a rift for a while – had he stayed at Anfield, would Bill Shankly ever have become manager of Liverpool?

That's an intriguing question which can never be answered; but what can be stated without fear of contradiction is that while Liverpool and Everton still enjoy (and that's the correct description) their rivalry, Manchester United remain the real enemy, the team Liverpool fans want their favourites to beat above all others. Officials of the respective clubs have claimed, with truth, that the Anfield – Old Trafford relationship is friendly; but the supporters don't see it that way, and the simmering resentment, jealousy – call it what you will – has surfaced at times.

During the mid-1980s, when United visited Anfield, an incident involving the use of an aerosol spray made headline news. It happened in February 1986, and at a Christmas party in 1994 I was reminded about this by a United fan. He spoke with some feeling about the high regard in which he had held Bill Shankly – and with even greater feeling about that aerosol-spray incident. Clearly, he had a long memory, as he recalled: 'It happened as the United players got off the team coach, and at least one of them – I think it was Clayton Blackmore – got the spray in his face and couldn't play.'

Naturally, Liverpool Football Club swiftly expressed regret about what had happened, and I did a piece for Kenny Dalglish which appeared in the *Anfield Review*. It was short and very much to the point. Dalglish told the world: 'On behalf of the players, myself and everyone else at this club, I would like to say that we totally disown the person or persons responsible for the aerosol incident which happened before the match against Manchester United. If this is how such people are going to behave, we don't want them anywhere near Anfield.

'Like the players of any other club which visits Anfield, the players of Manchester United came here simply to do their job to the best of their ability – just as Liverpool's players do, and at the end of the day if a visiting team proves better than us, then that's how it goes. But please: no more incidents such as the one that happened recently. This club can do without people who behave like that.' As it happened, the match ended in a 1–1 draw.

Fortunately, incidents such as that one have not marred more recent encounters between Liverpool and United, and there was a happier follow-up some months later, as related by a Liverpool supporter living in Worcester.

She made it her business to write and tell me: 'After all the recent publicity concerning ill-feeling between Liverpool and Manchester United fans, I thought this little incident might encourage our real supporters who love the game. My family are all Liverpool supporters, and four of us travel regularly to watch Liverpool play. My brother-in-law, however, is a Manchester United supporter, and a few weeks ago he phoned me to ask if my sister, who lives at Bicester, near Oxford, and who is a Liverpool fan, could get him a ticket for the Oxford – Manchester United match.

'She lives more than 19 miles from Oxford's ground, but she travelled there, bought him a ticket, then arranged for him to call at her house on match day to collect it. And I feel it's refreshing to hear of a Liverpool supporter going to those lengths to help a Manchester United fan obtain a ticket so that he could cheer on his team.'

So there are two sides to every story, although it is still a fact that the rivalry between the supporters of Liverpool and Manchester United matches – maybe exceeds – the rivalry between the players when they come up against each other. And when United went to Anfield during season 1993–94 and forged a three-goal lead, the home fans were mortified. Only a Liverpool fight-back which, after 90 minutes, had salvaged a 3–3 draw, restored the self-respect of the Anfield faithful and renewed their belief in their team. Even so, they had been forced to recognise that, coming up to the mid-1990s, United had usurped Liverpool's title as the No. 1 club in the country. Which was a galling thought for the Merseysiders. Their consolation is that, as yet, United have failed to come even close to matching Liverpool's overall record (notably in Europe) during the past three decades. And, of course, Liverpool fans fervently pray that they never will.

One glance through the League-honours list through the past 30-odd years tells the story eloquently enough.

Season 1963–64: Champions – Liverpool (United second)
Season 1964–65: Champions – Manchester United
Season 1965–66: Champions – Liverpool
Season 1966–67: Champions – Manchester United
Season 1967–68: Champions – Manchester City (United runners-up,
                                        Liverpool third)
Season 1968–69: Champions – Leeds United (Liverpool runners-up)
Season 1969–70: Champions – Everton
Season 1970–71: Champions – Arsenal
Season 1971–72: Champions – Derby County (Leeds second,
                                        Liverpool third)
Season 1972–73: Champions – Liverpool
Season 1973–74: Champions – Leeds United (Liverpool runners-up)
Season 1974–75: Champions – Derby County (Liverpool runners-up)
Season 1975–76: Champions – Liverpool

Season 1976–77: Champions – Liverpool
Season 1977–78: Champions – Nottingham Forest (Liverpool runners-
up)
Seasons 1978–79 and 1979–80: Champions – Liverpool

The pattern continued through the 1980s, with Liverpool and Everton claiming the lion's share of the Championship prizes: Liverpool in seasons 1981–82, 1982–83 and 1983–84; Everton in season 1984–85; then Liverpool, Everton, Liverpool, Arsenal, Liverpool, Arsenal, Leeds United – and, on a spring day in 1993, at long, long last, Manchester United – who, 12 months on, rubbed it in by doing the double.

Liverpool fans did have something to smile about during season 1993–94 as Aston Villa pipped United for the Coca-Cola Cup and, in the European Cup, the so-called no-hopers from Turkey, Galatasaray, put paid to United's publicly proclaimed ambitions. In season 1994–95, also, there was a spring in the step of Liverpool fans as United were hammered 4–0 by Barcelona in the Nou Camp Stadium and beaten 3–1 by Gothenburg in Sweden, to demolish hopes of European Cup success at the second time of asking.

Older Liverpool supporters can recall a season, too, when (under Ron Atkinson) United reeled off ten straight wins in the League before being held to a draw by Luton Town. The pundits then talked about the title race being over by Christmas, but Liverpool demonstrated that a race is never lost until it's won by making a surge in the second half of the campaign which saw them come through to claim the trophy, while United had to settle for fourth place.

But, by season 1993–94, United had overtaken Liverpool not only in the title stakes, but as drawing cards on television; and there was further aggravation for the Anfield faithful when they read that in a magazine poll United had been voted the world's third-best side in 1993, with Alex Ferguson rated as the best manager in the world.

One Saturday evening when David Mellor, the MP and self-confessed Chelsea fan, was running his BBC radio talk-in programme on soccer, a call from a Liverpool fan living in Essex made his views crystal clear as he scorned United's title success, comparing it disparagingly with the record of clubs such as Liverpool, Everton, Leeds United and Arsenal during the previous quarter of a century; and he demanded to know why United's achievement should merit such fulsome publicity, when others had done considerably better.

You could detect bias against United, and another fervent fan of Liverpool (who had witnessed that comeback from 3–0 down at Anfield) spelled out the feelings of the Anfield supporters when he said: 'If we hadn't come back from the dead to force a draw, the fans would have been walking out in droves – after baying for Graeme Souness's blood!' And when I asked that supporter which team he wanted Liverpool to beat most of all – Everton, Arsenal, Leeds United? – his reply was emphatic: 'You've got to be joking – Manchester United!'

Confirmation that Liverpool – on the domestic scene, at least – had slipped a notch or three came with this assessment from former Sheffield Wednesday manager Trevor Francis, who had played for top clubs at home and abroad: 'I believe the days when Liverpool dominated the game are over. Other clubs like Arsenal, Manchester United and Leeds have improved considerably. Results show that Liverpool are not the force they were.' And, significantly, Francis added: 'Or, perhaps, going to be in the future.'

The chief football correspondent of the *Daily Mail*, Neil Harman, wrote of Manchester United as being 'the sworn enemy at the eastern end of the East Lancs Road', while a former Liverpool idol offered his old club considerable food for thought as he talked about the re-emergence of Manchester United. Kevin Keegan's Newcastle United had hit Liverpool with three goals at St James's Park during season 1993–94, and on the eve of Newcastle's full-house confrontation with Manchester United, he was looking for a victory against Alex Ferguson's men which could put the brake on their charge for the Championship. On the day, however, the Magpies discovered that Manchester United proved to be sterner opposition than Liverpool had been and, when the contest had ended, Keegan had revised his opinion.

'We have just seen the champions of England,' he said. 'The rest of us are merely fighting for the scraps. United have the title sewn up. They are a nightmare to play against. There is only one other place in Europe on offer – everybody else will have to catch the ferry next season.' At the same time, Keegan added a cautionary note for Ferguson's team: 'To convince other people that they are as good as some of the Liverpool teams of the past, they [Manchester United] have got to go on and dominate football like my old club did. But I think they're good enough to do it.'

Well, that season United slipped somewhat for a spell, and Blackburn Rovers became genuine candidates to pip them in their bid for a title repeat, as they kept the race going until the closing stages of the campaign (the Rovers won their duel with Manchester United at Ewood Park). But in the end, Ferguson and his players delivered the title trophy, along with the FA Cup.

Meantime, Liverpool under Roy Evans continued to have their ups and downs as season 1993–94 wound its way towards the close. No one knew better than Evans, indeed, what a mammoth task he had on his hands to get Liverpool back on the rails – which meant harassing Manchester United on all fronts in the fight for trophies. There was also some irony in the fact that as Evans got to grips with the job of succeeding Souness, it was Kenny Dalglish and Kevin Keegan whose teams went closest to catching the men from Old Trafford. Both Blackburn and Newcastle, along with Aston Villa and Chelsea, qualified for European competitions, though Manchester United were the ones who would contest the European Cup once again.

Roy Evans had done some talking about bringing in more players so that Liverpool wouldn't be far away when the honours were handed out in the spring of 1995 and that, as he admitted, involved going into 'the top end of the transfer market.' Evans realised well enough that the 'top end' meant a big-money power game with clubs such as Blackburn, Newcastle, Arsenal, Aston Villa and Liverpool all striving to overhaul cockahoop Manchester United.

If Graeme Souness had splashed out many millions of pounds on players during his reign as Liverpool's manager, Evans joined the ranks of the big spenders when he gambled close on £10 million on centre-backs Phil Babb and John Scales, and his swoop for teenager Mark Kennedy – with the promise of more to come. He recognised that there was no more time to waste if Liverpool were to become serious challengers to Manchester United's current supremacy. Evans steered his club to triumph in the Coca-Cola Cup, so in 1995 Liverpool became the first to qualify for Europe; and even before United's slips began to show (they lost 1–0 at Goodison Park before their 2–0 fall from grace at Anfield, as the title tilted Blackburn's way), it was a former Anfield stalwart, Tommy Smith (one of the heroes of Liverpool's 1977

European Cup triumph), who declared: '*Someone* needs to challenge the new age of Manchester United.' Then, almost disregarding the claims of Blackburn Rovers and Newcastle United, Smith asked: 'What bigger and better club to do that than Liverpool?'.

Almost immediately, Roy Evans answered that question by demonstrating that Liverpool were ready, willing and able to eclipse Manchester United's £7 million acquisition of Andy Cole by making the running, in competition with Everton and Aston Villa, for Nottingham Forest striker, Stan Collymore – and this, despite the £8.5 million price tag. Liverpool it was who landed him, too.

APPENDIX 1

Recent Managers

Bill Shankly	1959–74
Bob Paisley	1974–83
Joe Fagan	1983–85
Kenny Dalglish	1985–91
Graeme Souness	1991–94
Roy Evans	1994–

Honours

LEAGUE CHAMPIONS
Seasons
1900–1
1905–6
1921–22
1922–23
1946–47
1963–64
1965–66
1972–73
1975–76
1976–77
1978–79
1979–80
1981–82
1982–83
1983–84
1985–86
1987–88
1989–90

FA CUP WINNERS
Seasons
1964–65
1973–74
1985–86
1988–89
1991–92

LEAGUE CUP/MILK CUP/ COCA-COLA CUP WINNERS
Seasons
1980–81
1981–82
1982–83
1983–84
1994–95

EUROPEAN CUP WINNERS
Seasons
1976–77
1977–78
1980–81
1983–84

UEFA CUP WINNERS
Seasons
1972–73
1975–76